EXTREME
ADVENTURES

www.**transworldbooks**.co.uk

EXTREME ADVENTURES

A White-Knuckle Journey Through
Britain's Most Challenging Terrain

Andy Torbet

BANTAM PRESS

LONDON • TORONTO • SYDNEY • AUCKLAND • JOHANNESBURG

TRANSWORLD PUBLISHERS
61–63 Uxbridge Road, London W5 5SA
www.transworldbooks.co.uk

Transworld is part of the Penguin Random House group of companies
whose addresses can be found at global.penguinrandomhouse.com

Penguin
Random House
UK

First published in Great Britain in 2015 by Bantam Press
an imprint of Transworld Publishers

A CIP catalogue record for this book
is available from the British Library.

ISBN 9780593071625

Typeset in 11½/16pt Sabon by Falcon Oast Graphic Art Ltd.
Printed and bound by Clays Ltd, Bungay, Suffolk

Penguin Random House is committed to a sustainable
future for our business, our readers and our planet. This book
is made from Forest Stewardship Council® certified paper.

This book is dedicated to Rebecca Biggins . . .
for being generally marvellous.

Contents

Acknowledgements

I'm not sure anyone actually ever reads the acknowledgements section. I never used to but I now realize what an important part of a book it is, so I wanted to include one.

This book did not come unbidden from my imagination. The adventures herein, although all accomplished in the last few years, actually began decades ago, because no one becomes a solo cave-diving explorer over a weekend. There have been people in my life who have made it or me better. The majority, like those I had the honour to serve with in the Forces, do not get a mention here. There will be a time and place for that but it is not now and not here.

In the meantime, there are some others I would like to thank:

First, thank you to everyone mentioned in this book – my partners in crime on the cliffs and waves and in the caves and seas around Britain. And to all those who have joined me on my adventures, to support, record or to share my sufferings.

And thanks to my brother, who has joined me on more failed trips than anyone else and keeps on coming back for more. Although I'm beginning to think one of us is a jinx . . .

Thanks to my agent Luigi for believing I could write and convincing a publisher of the fact. Thanks also to the team at Transworld and especially to Doug for his support and patience (it was the weather's fault, honest) and Andrea and Ailsa for their encouragement and for being so efficient (we love efficiency).

And now a word of thanks to a few people from the past, as they have waited too long and I may not get the chance again:

Thanks to Wilson Moir for introducing me to climbing and being one of those teachers who do even more than is asked of them.

Thanks to my uncle George for showing me the wild places of Scotland. I still treasure our Dunkeld to Blair Atholl trip.

Thanks to Neil Blair and Aberdeen BSAC diving club for adopting a keen, poor and probably very annoying twelve-year-old.

Introduction

This book was never meant to be a list of great achievements by yours truly, although I concede the diving stories will hold their own against most, this being the discipline I am by far the most proficient in. The other chapters, although they involve activities that are advanced, technical or dangerous in nature, are in no way a description of the top end of what's happening in the UK. The elite climbers, cavers and kayakers in the country are doing far greater things than I am. Instead, I wanted to write a testament to the potential for genuine adventure and exploration that lies on our doorstep.

Most of the projects in this book do require a high level of expertise and experience in certain disciplines and these can take years to attain. In terms of investment, some projects, notably the diving one, require some pretty specialist and expensive equipment. But others, like the snorkelling or trekking chapters, employ skills that can be learned in a day and need very little in the way of gear. We have an amazing natural landscape here in the UK. My projects are just examples of what one can do. There is potential there for anyone, anywhere, with any degree of skill to go on an adventure. Time and money are not true obstacles to adventure or exploration.

And by the latter I mean genuine exploration. For example, when I think about a polar expedition, I don't envisage taking a helicopter ride to within 60 kilometres of the South Pole and skiing for a couple of days. This might make you a polar athlete or even a polar adventurer, but I don't see it as doing much that can be considered new and it certainly doesn't result in the collection of new information or in new discoveries about the area. Friends of mine are proper polar explorers and it cheapens their achievements if people use this terminology to describe what is effectively a very expensive skiing holiday. And if you think there is nowhere left to explore in the UK, just read any of the diving chapters here.

Exploration can be a very personal thing. Even while walking on paths that others have trodden before you it is possible to be involved in your own journey of discovery – seeing new landscapes, wildlife and experiencing new emotions. You are exploring your world. If a view or an experience inspires, awes and humbles you, it doesn't matter whether someone else has been there first. Perhaps you can follow in the footsteps of explorers from the past, and the very fact that the first person to stand where you are now did so a hundred or thousands of years ago can actually make the experience more special.

I am often approached by people at outdoor or diving shows and adventure festivals and told how lucky I am and how they'd love to do what I do but 'insert excuse here'. Although I am well aware of how fortunate I am to be able to make a living from my passions, I didn't win this life off a scratch card. Frankly, luck looks a lot like hard work when viewed from the inside. And the most common excuses – lack of time, money or skill – are easily overcome. I've found that hard work can cover for a multitude of shortcomings and I am in no way gifted mentally or physically, nor do I have a natural flair for any particular discipline. I feel the cold, the wet, the heat, the heights, the depths and the dark just as keenly as everyone else. Excuses are abundant and you'll never find yourself in a situation where, if you want to use one, there aren't any available. What we choose to do and how we choose to act is what counts and this is all within our power to influence. In fact, sometimes when injuries are crippling us, time is against us, the weather is beating us back and our kit is failing, our attitude – the mindset we hold as we walk through the world – is the only thing we can control.

And it is all a matter of choice.

CHAPTER 1

Esoteric Climbing

I flinch to the side, blinking furiously as dust and grit falls from the tiny edges that my fingers and ice axe bite into. My left foot slips and my muscles tense to hold me in place as the unstable rock face I cling to shakes. I do not need to look down. I know I am a long way above a grassy ledge covered in shattered, broken rocks that have peeled off this cliff. I have a clear picture of my fate should I fall. Almost 500 feet below that ledge are the crashing waves of the sea. But my mind is not on the view. I need to focus. I need to climb.

The term esoteric is used in climbing circles to mean a form of the sport where you intentionally climb on rock most would normally avoid like the proverbial plague. The rock will be wholly untrustworthy, very loose, fragile and crumbly. No matter how large the handhold or spacious the foothold, no matter how well an anchor sits in a particular crack, nothing can be relied upon. The rock is so unpredictable that even a climb at an easy angle with huge and plentiful holds becomes a minefield. It matters little if you are the greatest climber in the world when the hold you're hanging off breaks. You'll still fall as fast and as hard as any normal human being, and if the anchors you have placed in the rock and woven your safety rope through pull out when you impact on to them then you're going to fall a long, long way. All in all, it sounds like a fairly unpleasant day out.

I, like most climbers, was not too keen on the idea of climbing esoterically. There is enough stress to deal with when you're hanging from tired arms, lactic acid pumping through muscles which are on a rapid decline towards failure, and your last anchor point is ten metres below you, meaning that, if you fall, you're looking at a 20-metre drop, hitting who knows what on the way down. And that's if the anchor holds. For esoteric climbing, you have to make additions to the basic risk analysis – the fact the anchor most likely won't hold because of the soft or brittle rock and that what you're gripping on to is likely to crumble away whenever it feels the urge. It all adds extra, and unnecessary, headaches. However, I was offered the chance to go climbing for the BBC's *Coast* and, as I'd been trying to shoehorn some more adventurous stuff into the series, the chance to go climbing on virgin rock and put up some new routes was not to be missed.

The map of Britain's geology is a psychedelic, multicoloured spread of streaks, slashes and blotches, each shade representing a different species of bedrock. You would assume by now that we'd know what Britain is built on (apart from bacon butties and mugs of tea). But there is a small collection of circles on the Isle of Wight as yet uncoloured – the Needles.

These white fins of rock pierce the sea just off the Isle of Wight and a casual glance reveals that they are chalk. But which of the many types of chalk are they? Although the

British Geological Survey could hazard an educated guess, in order to prove it scientifically a sample was required. And that meant doing a climb. Our research could only produce two established routes on the middle Needle, both climbed by Mick Fowler in 1988 and never repeated. So the plan was for us to use one of his routes to ascend and set up the ropes for the camera team to both climb and descend safely. Then the following day I'd lead a new climbing route, retrieve a sample from the top, abseil back down and deliver it to the scientists waiting in the boat below.

This is where I first met Dave Talbot, who has gone on to become one of my main climbing partners. Dave was an esoteric veteran, which was handy, as chalk is as far from a stable, solid category of rock as one can get without it being classed as gaseous. Any rock that can be pulled off in chunks by hand or dented by a swift kick and which has a tendency to fall down in landslides on a regular basis is not to be trusted.

We filmed Dave giving a quick demo as to the consistency of chalk by pulling great wads of it off and muttering, 'Yeah . . . that's not good', followed by the attempted insertion of an anchor piton (a steel blade with an eyelet in one end – it is hammered into a crack then the rope is clipped to it) that broke the rock around it and fell out: 'Hmm, best thing you can do, the safest way to do this, basically, is not to fall off.'

Off camera we'd been chatting about techniques and he did have some more useful advice: 'Go softly, no big powerful moves, keep the weight distributed as evenly as possible so there's not too much load on any one limb. When you move a hand or foot, do so one at a time and try to keep your weight spread across the other three appendages. Spread the load. And test each hold before you commit to it. Give it a proper pull or kick and expect it to come away. Oh, and when stuff does come off in your hand, throw it well clear of the cliff – I'm at the bottom.'

So, under a phenomenally bright, clear-blue sky and a pulsing October sun, we set off by boat, the film crew in one vessel and myself and Dave in another, towards the iconic Needles. Arguably, the crux move (a climbing term for the hardest section of an ascent) was getting from the landing craft on to the base of the route. A well-timed Hail-Mary leap in six-foot swell on to slick, greasy but sharpened chalk ledges was required . . . I let Dave go first.

The plan then was for me to lead a line that wandered between the worst of the blistered, vertical rubble on the left-hand edge of the south face.

I strike out in the lead and I feel confident. The rock, once past the sea-soaked slipperiness, seems relatively hard and solid. However, this situation is misleading. The wave-battered lower section has been thoroughly cleaned by the pounding sea and most of the loose stuff has been removed. As I move up, every-thing becomes noticeably softer. Anchors that I try to set into cracks slide out when I give them a pull-test, as the increasingly spongy rock deforms around them. It is incredibly loose, and even carefully selected, solid-looking handholds constantly crumble away as I gently pull-test them. I frequently find myself bellowing, '*Below!*' to warn Dave, as cascades of chalk pirouette into the rolling English Channel. And the higher I climb the looser it becomes.

It is a strange experience, climbing on rock this loose. I can't trust any ledge, crack, pinch or crimp, no matter how solid it feels. Every move is tentatively taken and I feel constantly out of kilter and insecure. It creates a very unsettling, confused feeling. My hands and feet, on huge holds, feed back that this is easy and all is well, but my head, knowing the untrustworthiness of the rock, tells a wholly different story. I try not to pull or push too hard on anything, try not to put too much pressure on any hold. I distribute my weight and pad gently upwards. Unlike most other climbs, at no time do I feel entirely in control. There are no solid rests or holds that allow some mental relief. The chalk is also broken every few metres by seams of sharp, shattered flint – not the best geology to drag your safety ropes over. I pull and kick off would-be holds with unerring frequency but, finally, I reach the last move – the crux, the hardest part.

I will have to layback up a thin flake of rock. A layback move allows a climber to ascend a vertical crack when there is something to force their feet against. You insert both hands into the crack, one slightly above the other. You place your feet against something, in a horizontal line with your hands so that your body is near flat, and then push with your legs and pull with your arms. This allows you to lock into position and move one limb up at a time. It's a powerful move and requires a lot of force to be generated against the rock.

The flake is a piece of rock which sits near flush to the face but is detached on a number of sides so that there is a partial gap between the rear of the flake and the main face. Picture a door slightly ajar but with a wall right behind it. And I will have to negotiate it before I can drag myself up the shifting rubble at the top to the finish.

The flake in question – a large dinner-plate-shaped piece of rock about six feet high and wide – looks alarmingly like it is stuck to the cliff by nothing more than encrusting salt. I try to layback without actually putting any force into it. If the flake decides to pop off, I'll be heading seawards, comically clinging to the underside of a large saucer-shaped piece of the Needles.

It is highly likely that my last anchor, as with most I'd put in, would not take the impact of a fall this big, especially as I'd be clinging to a six-foot chalk discus.

I plant both hands in the crack between the flake and the main wall and walk my feet up until they are near level with my hands and my body is horizontal. From here, I walk up hands and feet, legs pushing away and hands pulling in to secure me in place. This puts a tremendous amount of pressure through the rock but the move is impossible unless conducted with force. Paradoxically, I am trying to accomplish it without pulling the piece of rock I am currently clinging to off the wall. I make slow, delicate progress. The top is mere feet away but a sudden fast move could cause the rock to which I am clinging to flick off into the blue. The flake and rock may be solid, it may be here for another hundred years. Or, underneath, it could be gradually loosening its grip on the cliff, tiny landslides of chalk falling unseen behind it. When we assessed it, we were confident that it should hold. We know the odds are stacked in my favour but with esoteric climbing you are always rolling the dice and hoping it doesn't come up snake eyes.

As I shift up, hand-hand-foot-foot and repeat, I finally reach the top. Coming over the lip, I'm faced with rubble and even these last few moves feel insecure as I scramble over the edge.

The view, witnessed by so few, was spectacular. I could see the lighthouse to my right, the helicopter landing pad at eye level, the Needles flowing into Skeleton Ridge and the huge, stunning white-chalk cliffs of the Isle of Wight, all surrounded by a beautiful sparkling sea. I felt triumphant, a real sense of achievement. I felt like a true climber. I don't possess the greatest climbing technique in the world, so the top graded climbs are beyond my abilities. But here I was establishing a new route in truly unique surroundings and battling with the extreme mental aspects of climbing. This was not climbing as a sport; this was climbing as an adventure.

We managed to collect the sample, throwing it into my rucksack, and abseiled back down to the safety of the ledge, which was now being washed by the growing waves. I took the sample out to hold aloft and show the scientists waiting on the main boat, then we threw our climbing kit into the little dinghy as it bumped and slewed in the waves. Two well-timed jumps saw us aboard, too. As we approached and came alongside the larger vessel, the expectant geologists asked to see the sample. I grabbed my rucksack and rummaged to the bottom. I emptied the contents on to the deck and it was then I discovered my mistake. In my triumph and excitement, after holding the sample aloft I had omitted to put it back in my rucksack. We did eventually have the rock sample tested and identified, filling in that blank on the map, but not before turning our dinghy around and returning to the ledge where I had left it.

My first experience of esoteric climbing had not been an entirely pleasant one. I never felt safe or comfortable and was continually on edge. The whole thing was stressful and confusing, regardless of how easy the route was. But most of the projects and expeditions I've done in the past have been exploratory or adventurous – and that's what esoterica offers. My route was one of the strangest, most unsettling climbs I've ever done, but it gave me a sense of achievement and satisfaction I rarely get on standard graded climbs. Esoteric cliffs are among the few areas left in the UK with so much readily accessible unclimbed rock. People simply don't want to go there. If I wanted to experience bold, pioneering climbing, and could deal with the mental challenge of constant danger and the lack of any certainty, esoteric was the way ahead. It had been disturbing and unpredictable to ascend a disintegrating piece of rock – and the most adventure I've had in climbing for years.

I began climbing more often with Dave and kept nagging him to do other new esoteric routes. But Dave was cautious, and justifiably so. When climbing, we place anchors as we ascend, and clip a rope through them, then continue upwards past the anchors. Should we then fall, we'll fall past the anchor, dropping the length of the rope before it goes taut and grabs us. On most climbs, with experience it's possible not only to assess how good each anchor placement is but also, if you're honest with yourself, what your chances are of falling off. Not so on esoteric rock.

It takes experience to be able to make the call whether to forge on or not, to determine when adventure is starting to become potentially self-destructive. You have to have the mentality to appreciate the difference between feebly giving up because you lack courage and sensibly making a clear call to withdraw when the odds are visibly stacked against you. You have to take ego out of the equation. In that respect, it's a lot like cave diving. If you always approach it with the attitude that 'I will not give up no matter what happens' – admirable as this may be in other circumstances – you will eventually die. Maybe not the first time, nor even the tenth, but eventually you will not make it home.

Esoteric climbing is a dangerous proposition regardless of skill, experience and attitude. It is harder to assess or control the risks than with normal climbing, or indeed with cave diving, and you are always taking significantly bigger gambles because you are not in complete control of manipulating the variables in your favour. It doesn't matter how good you are, you're still rolling the dice and at some point that luck will run out. So it can be considered a numbers game and one of the best ways to stack those odds in your favour is not to play too often. But risk does not preclude action and, while bearing in mind all the points made above, I was still interested in doing more esoteric climbing.

Dave and I had spoken about doing the Exmoor traverse, an epic 15-kilometre climbing traverse above the savage seas and tides of the Bristol Channel with only a few, very dodgy options to escape upwards to safety. We decided to recce the environment by climbing a route called the Claw. It's a good hour's walk in from the nearest path along a boulder-scattered rubble shore that only exists at low tide and includes abseiling down cliffs and scrambling over crumbling, grassy scree to reach the bottom. Once there, you are already committed, since the way back is – by this time – underwater and up is the only possible direction of travel.

The climb itself is classed as a multi-pitch route. This means that the route is too long to climb in a single leg. The idea is to climb a section, find a secure place to make a belay and then bring your partner up. He then takes over and climbs up to the next safe belay point and you follow, and so on and so forth until one of you reaches the top. 'Belay' is a common word in climbing, but with slightly different meanings depending on the context. A belayer is someone who holds your safety ropes, being belayed means that person is taking in or paying out rope and a belay is the place where this takes place. So, halfway up a cliff a good belay position consists of places, such as a crack, where you can place secure anchors to fix yourself before belaying up your partner.

When we arrived at what we thought was the right area, we attempted to locate the line the route took. But it was less apparent than we'd hoped. We had found the obvious prominent buttress that ran up the cliff but the start looked different to the description we'd found. Dave struck out initially on what he believed to be the start but soon reached a section that required him to cross an arch made entirely of broken, loose rock and which was suspended above an empty 50-foot drop with nothing but space beneath it for support. Even a herring gull landing on it managed to cause a few rocks to collapse and tumble earthwards, making the arch all the thinner. The gull, very sensibly, took to the air. This section did not match the guide and was guaranteed to disintegrate when Dave put any weight on it. There was no place for anchors, even tenuous ones, and Dave had to withdraw.

Back on the deck, and with low water just past and the tide beginning to make its way in with a speed only the Bristol Channel can produce, we did a quick assessment. Climbs like these on the Exmoor coast are very rarely repeated and clearly it had been some time since anyone had been this way. The first pitch of the route had obviously collapsed, leaving a large pile of rubble and boulders at the bottom of the cliff. This geological detritus was layered with rock that had clearly been there awhile, being weathered and vegetated, and with large deposits that looked fresh enough to have come down yesterday.

Because of the rising sea, we only had one option. Up.

Just to the right of what used to be the first section of the Claw, we picked a vague line. The route was heavily overgrown and, as we couldn't use the buttress, which stuck out of the grass-covered cliff like the bones of an open fracture, we were climbing on what could only be described as a vertical lawn. Patches of stony mud and piles of boulders were islands in the green, promising hand- and footholds, but these proved even harder to climb than the grass and were usually loose enough to pull off the rock face and on to yourself. Luckily, and knowing that we might encounter these sorts of conditions, we had brought an ice axe each. What I had failed to bring was my harness. Its current location – the boot of my car – meant it would probably not do much to arrest a fall during the climb. Fortunately, we had a spare sling with which to fashion one. Unfortunately, the sling was about half an inch wide and, without the usual personal adjustment and padding available on a standard climbing harness, it focused my bodyweight on very sensitive areas of my anatomy. This would make for a pinching, chafing ascent and the sling would act like cheesewire in the event of a fall, threatening to slice my legs off, not to mention other unmentionables. Which was nice.

Dave starts the first pitch and drives his axe into the vertical wall of grass to gain at least one good handhold before trying to grab anything solid. I use the word 'solid' with all due relativity. He then brings his feet up to find any indentations, rocky patches or roots that will provide a modicum of support for his feet. He tries to place an anchor after about 25 metres but how effectual this will be I don't know – the boulder it uses is a little shaky. He passes no good belay spots on the way up and pushes on until he is at the end of our 50-metre ropes. He is forced to improvise a belay as best he can in an imperfect situation.

I climb up to Dave as he pulls in on the rope. I am seconding not leading so am in a much safer position. Supposedly. If I fall, Dave will catch me immediately, but with the untrustworthy anchors I could pull him off and we could both have a 150-foot tumble. I scramble the last few feet, swinging my axe hard into the earth and then pausing to rest. Looking around, I am surrounded on one side by virgin, lush, green-flecked cliffside, splattered with boulders and hard grey outcrops. On the other, the sea stretches out to a hazy horizon, sun shimmering off a mirrored surface. The view is great.

I look up at Dave and smile. 'I'm enjoying this.'

Dave nods. 'It's great out here, isn't it? Right, it's your lead.'

'Roger.'

I clamber past him and he now feeds out the rope as I continue upwards. As I climb, I get into a rhythm: swing my axe into a soft patch, look for a good handhold, find none, grab a clump of grass and try to dig my fingers in, move a foot up to any indentation or grit-covered rock patch to try to gain some friction. I see no likely belay spots and carry on until Dave shouts, 'Forty metres,' referring to the amount of our 50-metre rope that he has paid out.

'Roger,' I reply, mostly to myself.

I cast about and up for somewhere to anchor into but still see nothing ideal. I climb on.

'Forty-five metres.'

'OK,' I shout down. Then I say to myself out loud, 'Hmm, not ideal.'

Just above me is a boulder jutting out from the near-vertical slope with a scrap of miniature scree below it. I throw a sling around it and jam another couple of anchors into some fragile-looking cracks. I sit down and prepare, should he slip, to take as much of Dave's weight as possible on to myself and not transfer it to my anchor. This is the opposite of what I should be doing on a normal climb.

Dave ascends to me with no problems and cracks on once again to near the end of our lines, calling for me to follow. As I top out on to a large vegetated level patch on the cliffside, I can see the area is busily scattered with jagged, angular boulders that look like giant, grey, crooked carnivorous teeth. We have climbed almost 150 metres – 500 feet – and have used only a couple of belays. If we'd fallen from near the end of the rope, we would have dropped, including the stretch of the rope, well over 100 metres. Not falling was a good idea. But so far the climbing has not been technically difficult, just a little unreliable and scarce on anchor placements.

Dave and I chat about where to head next. What looks like the final pitch is mine. The only way out from our current spot is through a choice of two narrow gullies, neither of which look particularly inviting. The left one appears less steep but is soaking wet and heavily overgrown. The right-hand corner is possessed of more exposed rock, which better allows us to assess any anchors, hand- and footholds, and to pick placements – where you hook tiny ledges with the tip of your ice axe – or even the odd crack to torque our axes into. However, it is also significantly steeper and the assessment we make from the base is that it is a very serious undertaking. It is my lead and my call, and I go right, feeling I'll be more comfortable on the mineralized side of life. The ledge at the bottom – with its rockery of large, sharp-angled shattered boulders sticking upright against each other – is pretty much what you'd come up with if asked to design the most imperfect landing spot. I look down at it, up at the route, back down and finally across to Dave.

'Best not fall off then, eh?' I say, trying to sound more confident than I feel.

'Ah, you'll be fine.'

I appreciate the support but I'm not sure he feels any more confident than I do.

I leave the ground feeling psyched by what lies ahead. I am not 100 per cent confident that I have this in me but it's pioneering stuff. I'll be pushing myself and climbing somewhere near the limits of my ability. The sea lies behind me, 500 feet down. I am out in the wilds with no one for miles around (except

Dave, of course), moving across ground that has never been touched by a human before. I feel positive, proud and alive . . . in a good but, to be fair, anxious fashion.

The first few moves are difficult, initially requiring me to use my hand to compensate for my inflexibility, grabbing my foot to pull it up and over a low overhang and get the first foot placement. These first muddy footholds give little purchase, as too much pressure will cause my foot to slip into space. I have to compensate by putting most of my weight on to my hands, and the handholds are no better than the unreliable footholds. A handful of grass in my left hand and a cheeky hook on to a tiny ledge with my axe sees me moving upwards. Using clumps of moss that grow out of the rock to stand on, I make tentative progress. I slip on more than one occasion, still unanchored and effectively free-soloing (climbing without ropes). There are no options to put any anchors in and a fall from here on to those teeth-like rocks below would have a very serious outcome. The near misses not only cause my heart to jump but the repeated injections of fear are also beginning to gnaw at my confidence.

By now I am a long way up and any form of rapid descent will prove catastrophic. I become more and more obsessed with getting in an anchor that will catch me if I slip. I grope around the rock, dismissing a wide crack to my right. The block, which creates the outside of the split, moves significantly when I test its worthiness – any anchor jammed into this crack would simply flex the block outwards when I fell, causing the crack to widen and the anchor to pop out. I try a small crack on my left at eye level. I initially dismiss it in favour of a more secure option but since none is forthcoming I desperately try to find something that will fit. I waste valuable energy hanging, arms locked off and straining to maintain a bent position, trying to keep tension and weight on my axe to hold it on to the crimping ledge, trying to find an anchor that will fit. When I eventually do and give a test tug, the loose rock around the crevice moves and the empty fissure swells. The anchor does not pop out but I know the placement is next to useless. In desperation, I place a camming anchor (a device that uses teethed pieces of metal shaped like Dairylea cheese triangles, which rotate outwards to grip the rock) into the large crack I have previously rejected, knowing full well it is a waste of time, with no practical value – it is little more than an infinitesimally small psychological crutch. The reality is it offers no extra safety and the time it takes to make the placement simply saps more of my strength.

As I move up, the climbing becomes harder and I am just about at the limit of my ability. I am starkly aware of the distance between where I am perched and where my body would stop moving should I plummet, and starkly aware of the utter nonsense that is my anchor placements. I look up, my entire body taut, trying to maintain my position on this wall of unfastening rock and shrubbery, and judge the terrain above me. And so begins an internal monologue:

'OK, that looks like it's getting a lot harder.'

'Are you just saying that because you're scared or do you really think it's beyond you?'

'I reckon it's out of my capability today.'

'You've said that in the past only to breeze up a route when you tried it later on a safety rope.'

'Maybe, but I'm pretty confident the level of ability required to pass this next section is beyond me. Therefore, if I carry on, I will fall. If I fall, I will be dead.'

'Is the failing psychological or are you not a good enough climber? If it's the latter, then the smart move is to turn back now. Pushing on would be suicidally stupid if you genuinely think you cannot physically climb the next section and will fall. If it's the former, stop being a wuss and crack on. If it's the latter, then you'll still have a bloody dangerous down-climb to achieve. Good luck with that. Either way, man the fuck up and make a call – decision time, hombre.'

Contrary to what some people will tell you, I have not got a death wish. I put myself in some potentially dangerous situations, I admit, but I have not succumbed yet. If I wanted to die, I've certainly given myself plenty of opportunities – but I don't. When I was in the Forces, doing operations such as bomb disposal and high-risk searches, I became very good at clinically assessing a threat and identifying all the risks. Once this is done, you can mitigate those risks to an acceptable level.

I take a breath and continue the internal monologue:
 'I do not have the skill right now to climb this next section. If I choose to continue, it is tantamount to jumping from here. There are things worth dying for. This is not one of them.'

This particular inner monologue may not have been quite as erudite and succinct . . . and may have contained expletives and blasphemy.

I backed off. However, even this was no easy task. Down-climbing is more difficult than moving upwards. You can't see where you're going or where you're placing your feet, and the human body is less well designed to make descending movements. If my anchors had been secure, I could have dropped the five or so metres on to them and been lowered the rest of the way. But they were not. The down-climb, therefore, was as stressful as the up phase, as I tried to place my ice axe beneath me then lower on to it, keeping direct force on whichever tiny ledge I'd placed it on to stop it flicking off.

To cap it all, I was now carrying the heavy baggage of failure.

I gave Dave a quick brief on what I'd encountered and my thought processes at the apex of my ascent. He was encouraging and decided to have a go himself. However, this time, he'd take my ice axe, too, as my single one had provided the only real purchase. This meant he'd be able to climb with two effective hands. He climbed upwards, eventually reaching my two pieces of gear, which he quickly yanked out with little effort and laughed. Re-adjusting things, he managed to find some rock which, although not bombproof, at least provided the possibility of safety and, although still a gamble, much improved on my efforts. As I watched from beneath, he continued upwards and began struggling on the section I had deemed too difficult. He was heaving himself up with great effort and was clearly under some degree of stress, as tension-releasing screams and grunts echoed out to sea. He spent a long time on what I thought was the top section, those last few moves I had decided were beyond me. Eventually, after trying to position different gear and testing a range of holds and body positions, he dug one axe deep into a horizontal fissure in the rock and twisted the handle down, jamming the pick in the crack. He then clipped the rope to a hole in the end of the axe, hoping in the event of a fall that the handle would be torqued down more, further securing it into the crack. All I could see was a lunging leap to the left and then he was out of sight. Nothing remained but a few small rocks bouncing down the cliffside towards me. After many minutes, the rope I was holding, which connected me to Dave, had not moved.

Eventually, I shouted up, 'Are you safe?', meaning are you at the top of the climb and secured? Nothing. Again I shouted, 'Are you safe?'

In response I got a sharp, irritated and worryingly strained 'Noooo.'

Clearly, the climb did not end where Dave had vanished from view. Nor had it got any easier.

Time dragged as I waited, standing awkwardly with my necked craned backwards, gazing up the climb.

'Come on, Dave, what's happening?' I muttered to myself.

After what felt like an age, but could have been anything from ten minutes to half an hour, the double ropes that went skyward began to be pulled up. I quickly unfastened the belay device from the ropes so that they could run free, assuming that Dave was pulling up the ropes because he'd found a good belay station and was taking in the slack line between us so that I could start climbing.

It was obvious that I'd struggle to climb this pitch with no axes. Dave had desperately needed both to make this first section. I scrabbled up the first part, initially popping off twice on the first few moves and landing back on the deck as the shock-absorbing climbing rope stretched along its length and grew in size like a piece of rubber. Before a third attempt, I tried dusting as much of the wet mud and soil as I could off the tiny protrusions of rock. I laced my trainers up as tightly as possible to minimize any slippage and tried again. Clawing my way up, standing on ledges slick after two passings, I finally made it to where Dave had left my axe. By this time, I was high enough from the ground that even on a full stretch of the rope I'd probably not hit the ground. Getting the axe back in my hand gave me a feeling of security and confidence, and I struck on to the section where I had previously backed off. Dave admitted later that he'd not have made this next part of the route had he only had one axe but I struggled to see how he'd made progress at all. I was stunned by the physical effort of the climb but more impressed by the fact that Dave had effectively succeeded with no safety rope.

As I perched precariously on a small pedestal of rock it disintegrated and I plunged downwards until the rope took my weight. Twice more I fell before I reached the move where Dave had disappeared left. Oddly, this was beneficial, mentally if not physically. It reinforced the accuracy of my assessment and the decision I had made. I knew now, absolutely, that if I had carried on I would not have had the skill to complete the section of the pitch and I would have fallen.

I looked left and could see a small grassy saddle formed where the bedrock stuck out from the cliff like a horizontal fin. I could see what Dave had done and, balancing on crumbling holds, did the same. I jumped. I threw myself out towards the saddle and landed on my belly, draped over it, with arms hanging either side. I quickly righted myself and walked what felt like a tightrope to the next section of the pitch. It looked fairly straightforward, just a three-metre high grass wall, but, bizarrely, it was slightly overhanging and the loose vegetation offered no hand- or footholds. The only purchase was from the axe, and the drop below, now that we had moved around to the exposed side of the buttress, was a jaw-dropping vertical plummet to the encroaching sea. I now understood why Dave had spent some time here, working out the best way upwards. In the end, I went for simple brute strength – as I later discovered Dave had, too – and just hauled my way up. I was lighter than Dave, as I wasn't carrying the extra burden of my impending death should I make a wrong move.

Once over this it was a straightforward scramble through head-high fern and brambles to where Dave sat with a huge grin. He had been unable to find a belay point to fix to, surrounded as he was by nothing more substantial than ferns and heather, so had just sat down, dug his heels in and wrapped the rope around his back. I thought of my previous falls and winced. The rope would have dug into his back and sides as my bulk fell on to it. He looked at the rope and back at me and shrugged.

'Mate,' I said. 'That, my friend, was a fucking heroic lead.'

With that we spent a final quarter of an hour blundering through the undergrowth back to the coastal path – tired, exhausted and exhilarated. When we stopped in the local pub for a well-earned pint of ale, the conversation turned to our next esoteric outing. We'd take a break, we decided. You don't want to be climbing this style of crag every week. Eventually the odds will catch up with you and, besides, it's psychologically brutal and exhausting.

There were lots of other challenges out there, as I'd discovered when I first set out on the path to becoming a professional explorer and extreme adventurer, and the Three Lakes Challenge had been the start of it all.

CHAPTER 2

The Three Lakes Challenge

I had decided I wanted to turn exploring and adventure into a career after I left the British Army. It was a fairly vague aspiration and one that I had no idea how to attain. In the Army, progression to either a more senior post, the next rank or into a more specialist and elite unit is fairly well organized and has set protocols, routes and standards that one must achieve. Achieving these goals may be hard but defining them is easy. Unfortunately, the path is less clear for someone wanting to make a living exploring the mountains, caves and oceans of the globe. If you want to make a life of exploration and adventure your full-time occupation, I'd advise getting used to the idea of being very poor most of the time.

I've always been of the opinion that hard work can compensate for an awful lot. If you are not blessed with a God-given talent in the field you have chosen to pursue, then you're going to have to work bloody hard. And, to be brutally honest, even if you have an innate gift, if you really want to come out on top then you're still going to have to graft – a lot. The truth of it is, regardless of what your family and friends may say, you are not born special. The world owes you nothing and no one cares as much about your aspirations as you do. You have to take responsibility for your own life. I'm a very pragmatic individual and I'm of the opinion that wishing your dreams will all come true simply does not work, no matter how hard you squeeze those eyes and cross those fingers. Hope is not a methodology for getting what you want. Getting off your backside is.

I soon realized that in this media-conscious age the communication of an adventure to others often means more than the adventure itself, certainly as far as paying the mortgage goes. I decided that there were a number of methods to do this: writing, photography, film-making and talking. Competition in these areas of adventure media is greater today than ever and I decided that writing articles seemed the simplest place to start. Since diving was, of all my skills, the area in which I was most accomplished, I figured that I stood the greatest chance of getting an article published on this subject. As an ex-squaddie with no journalistic qualifications or experience, I could see absolutely no reason why an editor – no doubt assailed on a daily basis by emails from people asking if they could write for his/her magazine – should give me a chance. However, I'm also of the opinion that if you want to get on, then get on. Do it and prove yourself by your commitment. So I decided to come up with an idea that was new, fresh and different to anything anyone else could write for the magazine. I'd then go off and do it, take the photos and write the article. And only then would I knock on the editor's door and hand him the finished product, asking if he'd consider publishing it. Which is exactly what I did.

There is a famous mountain race in the UK called the Three Peaks Challenge, the idea being to race to the top of Ben Nevis (the highest mountain in Scotland), drive to and climb Scafell Pike (the highest mountain in England) before driving to Wales to climb its highest – Snowdon. The full thing, including transit between mountains, is won by completing it in the shortest time, and less than twenty-four hours is the main goal. I thought I'd take a diving-orientated spin on things and came up with the idea of the Three Lakes Challenge. I originally called it the Three Ls Challenge, as Scottish lakes are called lochs and Welsh lakes are called llyns, but it didn't stick and 'lakes' was used to describe all aquatic arenas. It suited the magazine and promotional material better, but went against my Celtic roots and also conflicted with my pedantic approach to grammar and vocabulary. But if it sold as the Three Lakes and not as the Three Ls, then Lakes it was.

The idea was that I'd dive the highest loch in Scotland, lake in England and llyn in Wales in twenty-four hours. This would include the driving required to get to the national parks in which my goals were nestled and the long climbs into the mountains carrying a full set of dive kit.

The first thing I had to do was decide on the venues. After a bit of research, it seemed there is no single answer for which is the highest lake in each country, as there is no standard definition of what a lake is . . . which will always make things tricky. If it dries up in summer or freezes solid in winter, is it a lake? How shallow can a body of water be before it stops being a lake and starts becoming a puddle with an impressive surface area? And what about that surface area? When does a large pond morph into a small lake? So I began a new search for something resembling an official body that could advise me.

Even if they could not give me a black-and-white answer, if we could agree on a set of parameters I could at least answer my critics, who would no doubt crawl forth from the safety of their online aliases on Internet forums. I turned to the Centre for Ecology and Hydrology, which is part of the Natural Environment Research Council. If they couldn't answer the question, no one could.

They couldn't. Apparently even *they* don't have a definition of what a lake is. However, I'm grateful to a very helpful gentleman who took my phone call and spent some time chatting through the various options with me and genuinely tried to help to find a workable and justifiable solution. We decided that depth was a difficult factor due mainly to the fact that the majority of lakes in the UK have never been surveyed, so we'd have to take a view. We reasoned that as long as it was a minimum of one metre deep all year round then that would suffice. Our main criteria would be surface area – the lake must cover, throughout the seasons, one hectare, which is the equivalent of 100 by 100 metres.

Based on this decision, I came up with the following destinations:

- Scotland: Loch Coire an Lochan in the Cairngorms National Park
- England: Red Tarn in the Lake District
- Wales: Ffynnon Lloer in Snowdonia

Now I had my targets, I needed a plan. I looked at driving distances and predicted driving times and had a think about rush hours and when we'd want to be doing which mountains. In the end, it seemed to make sense to start with the largest and work our way down, which coincided nicely with a neat north-to-south route. I decided that mountain safety and the need to share the driving meant I'd be best placed if I roped some poor fool into doing it with me. I required another qualified diver who also had the prerequisite fitness to deal with walking for long periods of time up large hills carrying heavy weight. Any rest periods between these bouts of exercise would involve getting ever more stiff and cramped in a car whilst driving to the next destination. And getting no sleep. I called my friend Monty Halls, who immediately agreed it was an absolutely brilliant idea. I think 'genius' was the word he used.

Monty's immediate endorsement and willingness to get involved should have thrown up a warning signal, as he, like me, is a lover of foolishly punishing and often pointlessly eccentric ventures. The added bonus was that Monty had already made a name for himself in the diving press and had been writing articles for a number of years. He approached one of the editors he was currently working with and pitched the idea. It was agreed it'd be a joint effort, with each of us writing alternating paragraphs, which we knew from the outset would degenerate into textual sparring and belittling of each other. This agreement was good news, as I not only secured an article but was attached to a well-known and much-loved contributor. Things were going to plan.

I decided that in order to get as much bang as possible for my investment of time and cash I should also make a foray into film-making. So I persuaded a camerawoman friend, Lynwen Griffiths, to shoot a bit of film and grab some photos for the article. Lynwen is an adventure camerawoman. She sensibly chose to carry her camera and not a foolish amount of dive kit. Monty (an ex-Royal Marine) and myself (an ex-Paratrooper) had carried a lot of very heavy bergens (Army slang for rucksacks) up a lot of very steep hills during our military careers. However, we'd not done it for a couple of years . . . or in Monty's case about ten. Something as ingrained as this comes back quickly, although maybe not in the twenty-four hours we'd given ourselves. However, rather than taking some time to train to get back to being hills-fit we decided stoic pig-headedness and mutual derision, when one of us fell behind or started whingeing, would get us round. I wanted to kick-start my new career as soon as possible and we could all find the time the following week. We were on.

We drove north from Bristol for what felt like a fortnight and finally reached Aviemore, a small town in the Cairngorms National Park, in the middle of the night. We shared a bunk-room in a hostel and after a hearty breakfast in which we reverted to our ethnic stereotypes – Monty had a full English and I had a bowl of porridge – we were almost ready to go.

I'd checked with the estate whose land we'd be crossing that there was no shooting going on that day. Getting shot really isn't much fun, especially when you've a steel container full of high-pressure gas on your back. The steel cylinders carried five litres of compressed air, which made them rather heavy. We could have got away with three-litre bottles but, amongst the litany of logistics, the procurement of these smaller cylinders was Monty's only job. He turned up with fives.

So, bergens packed, compressed-gas cylinders sticking out the top as though we were on some high-altitude mountaineering trip, we struck out from the car park to conquer the first of our lakes. With the wetsuits, gloves, bootees, masks, hoods, fins and regs (regulators – the hoses and mouthpieces that you attach to your diving bottle to make the gas inside, compressed to over two hundred times atmospheric pressure, breathable without blowing your lungs out of your backside), our bergens weighed about 40 kilograms – half my bodyweight.

'Ah, it'll not make much difference, Torbs. Besides it's all buckshee phys,' Monty reassured me (military jargon meaning that it was just some extra physical training – but this usually takes the form of being beasted until your eyes bleed).

I wasn't convinced by his attempts to placate me and felt that my opinion on the matter would only become stronger the further we trekked and the steeper the slope became.

It was midday. One of the rangers came to ask what we were up to and was most amused, if somewhat perplexed, by what we had planned. He asked where we'd come from.

'Bristol,' said Monty.

'Ah, yes,' he nodded sagely, as if our plan confirmed his opinion of the eccentric and somewhat senseless ways of the city folks who lived 'down south' (i.e. anywhere below Perth). 'Well, it all sounds grand. You have a good time now.'

'Thanks very much,' I said, and a look of confusion crossed his face.

'Oh, where are you from?' he asked.

'Oh, I'm up from Bristol, too . . . but I come from a place only a couple miles east of here.'

'Really? Well, then, what the bloody hell are you doing a silly thing like this for?'

It was November. November is not the best time to be hiking in the British mountains. More specifically, this was Scotland in November and the weather was not ideal. But I'd seen worse.

Loch Coire an Lochan is not just Scotland's highest lake, it is also Britain's highest lake and sneaks in just under a kilometre of altitude at 998 metres above sea level. It nestles in a corrie, a huge bowl-like scoop in the side of a mountain, a natural amphitheatre. Another term for this geographical formation is a cirque, from the French for arena. This particular corrie is on the northern slopes of Braeriach, Britain's third highest mountain. It's 12 kilometres as the crow flies from the nearest place to leave your car and is not an easy place to reach. We were racing the clock, so Monty, six foot two with mile-eating long legs, stepped out and set a swift pace. The fronts of my shins burned as I kept shoulder to shoulder – pride, more than porridge, keeping my pace fast. I must have taken twice as many steps as Monty to get where we were going. We didn't want to burn out early on, so made the call not to tab – which stands for Tactical Advance into Battle and means walking very quickly uphill and running the flats and downhills . . . with lots of weight on. This is what we would have done in the military. For now, we'd just fast-walk it all.

We discussed the three challenges before us as our bodies warmed up and we settled into our stride. We agreed that a 25-kilometre round trip and greater height gain meant this Scottish leg would require the major effort, more than the much shorter legs combined, and that after we'd completed this one we'd have broken the back of the challenge – such naive fools we were. Monty and I had clocked up seven and ten years respectively in the Forces doing exactly this – moving at speed over mountainous terrain carrying knee- and back-demolishing weights. Our bodies would quickly remember what was required and minimal training would have us back on form and mountain-fit. I say 'minimal' when we had actually achieved none. But as we moved through the countryside, our bodies loosened up and we fell into a comfortable pace.

The rough track wound its way southwards through the ancient pine forests of the Rothiemurchus Estate, one of the largest surviving areas of ancient woodlands in Europe, where the average age of the pine trees is one hundred years and some are over three hundred years old. The forest also supports aspen, birch, rowan, cherry, juniper and holly trees, and these in turn are home to rare British wildlife like the capercaillie (the world's largest grouse) and red squirrel. We slowly gained some height and the river valley we were walking along become more pronounced, the slopes on either side of us rising up more steeply and the forest giving way to open mountains covered in thick carpets of heather and moor matgrass. We were forced to cross the Am Beanaidh River twice. But someone had seen fit to build new footbridges, so we managed to keep our feet dry. However, those same feet felt a little bruised and our shoulders were stiff as we finally made Loch Mhic Ghillie Chaoil. This was a waymarker for us and represented the point on the track closest to our goal and therefore the place we'd be forced to leave the path and go off-road.

It's considerably more difficult making progress when the ground is no longer an open track. The ground we were now crossing, as well as being extremely steep, was also soaking wet, boggy and uneven, and the long grass and thick heather made it difficult to assess where to put our feet. We climbed on and Lynwen was disappointed to find that what she'd thought was the summit was simply a flattening out of the ground about halfway up. We took time at this point to have a quick bite and stare at the next section. It was an incredibly steep, wet slope strewn with huge boulders, and moving up with heavy packs was going to be hard work. We gained about 300 metres in height for 800 metres of walking . . . and not long into this last part all four limbs were being used to stabilize and push ourselves upwards. Thighs were burning as we made steady, if not particularly fast, progress upwards and finally staggered over the top. By now we'd passed into the clouds and a thick fog clung all around us. It was soaking through our kit and slowly drenching us.

As we crested the final rise, we saw a small pool of water off to our left.

'Is that it?' asked Monty, disappointed. 'I'm not sure that's dive-able, mate. It looks a bit small . . . even for you.'

Monty had plugged the grid references into his GPS and reckoned the electronic navigation device was pointing at what was, frankly, a rather pathetic-looking puddle.

'I don't think that's it, mate,' I replied and began getting my map and compass out. 'No, mate, it can't be. On the map it's meant to be half a k long and at least 200 metres wide. Besides, I reckon it's over there . . .' I pointed almost directly in front of us ' . . . a couple of hundred metres away.'

We'd stopped for a few moments to work all this out and as we wandered slowly along the last flat few paces we began to cool down. In fact, it was becoming decidedly chilly as the winds swirled around the bowl-like amphitheatre created by the mountain. The wet, grey fog that hung around us didn't help and it gave the landscape a menacing aura. The mist that spread over the surface of the black waters created an eerie ambience, which was threatening and cold. With the weather deteriorating and our bodies quickly cooling down and stiffening up, we did what any sensible chap would do under these circumstances. We got naked.

The thought of stripping off and quickly clambering into our thin wetsuits did not fill us with enthusiasm. We'd chosen thinner wetsuits as they'd be less bulky, less heavy and require fewer rocks to be gathered to allow us to overcome the buoyancy the wetsuits' foam construction created, so that we could sink. However, this also meant we sacrificed warmth. We'd decided a dive would be classed as a minimum of ten minutes to a depth of five metres, or the deepest part of the lake if it wasn't five metres. It would be an unpleasant ten minutes but better that than adding extra kilograms to our already weighty bags.

We slipped into the loch and felt that first rush of freezing water down the backs of our ill-fitting and paper-thin suits. Bracing is not the word. Before we slipped beneath the surface, we gave the 'We're OK' signal to Lynwen on the shore and Monty turned to me.

'We should have brought an SMB,' he said. A Surface Marker Buoy is a float on the surface, which is connected by a line to a diver in order to show the diver's position. 'You know, mate,' he continued, sarcastically, 'so we don't get hit by a boat.'

We grinned and I knew that, like me, despite the cold, the wet, the weight, the trek and the sheer absurdity of it all – or perhaps because of all these glorious gifts – he was really, really enjoying himself.

But Monty had failed to put enough rocks in his pouched belt to weigh him down and kept bobbing to the surface. The loch bed was strewn with the same boulders that littered the sides of the mountain and which had no doubt rolled down to come to rest under the waters in aeons gone by. So he swam down, thrashing as he fought the buoyancy of his wetsuit, and grabbed a large boulder, hugging it to his chest with both arms . . . and bobbed back to the surface again. He swam down again towards the loch bed, now awkwardly holding the huge rock under his left arm, to try to scoop up a second under his right. Finally managing this, and discovering that he was now indeed heavy enough to remain submerged, he bounced along the underwater boulder field, working hard to maintain control of his stones.

In the ten minutes we spent underwater, we saw nothing living. Nothing. It seemed totally lifeless down there, apart from two idiots swimming around. There was not another living thing in this loch. Clearly, the Scottish wildlife possessed more common sense than we did.

But the loch did have one surprise. The water itself. It was the most incredible shade of blue. It seemed to be a frosted but neon azure, brightly lit from some unknown source (certainly not the sun, which was conspicuous by its absence, as is so often the case during a Scottish November). I've returned to this loch since and the colour was not a trick of the light or the onset of hypothermia, as it remained the same stunning hue.

Once back out, we peeled off our wetsuits and clambered around shivering and trying to don our soaking walking gear as the wet fabric stuck to our freezing flesh. The blood started returning to my hands and I suffered from hot-aches, a painful sensation akin to someone scraping the insides of your hand with an industrial cheese grater. Once this subsided, I could finish dressing and before our bodies became hypothermic we threw our bergens on our backs, now made all the heavier since our kit, especially the wetsuits, had absorbed so much water, and marched off. As the water percolated from our sodden equipment and gathered in the bottom of our bergens it slowly trickled through the fabric in a constant flow of cold water, running down our lower backs and legs, ending its journey in our boots.

The walk back down the hill was just as much work as, if not more than, the climb. Our tired legs were not as stable and both Monty and I fell a few times on the steep, uneven ground, the weight on our backs throwing us off our natural balance. We were very tired bunnies when we finally made the track and were both very keen to get some hot fluids and food down us. With this on offer back at the car, we were spurred on and kept moving in the fading light. By the time we returned to the car, it was very dark and almost exactly 1800. It had taken just under six hours of effort to get us there, dive and get back. We felt this was a respectable time, considering the distance, weight and terrain. But, my word, the relief of setting our bergens into the boot of the car was heartfelt. As the pressure of the straps was released from our shoulders, our bodies visibly deflated as the tension drained out. All we wanted was to find a nice pub, sit by an open fire, drink a pint and eat a pie.

What we did was drive to England.

We split the work of travelling into three parts. One driver, one navigator (since we didn't have a satnav and were doing things the old-fashioned way – not a conscious choice to try to make life even harder for ourselves, it was simply that none of us owned one) and one in the back, sleeping. The navigator had a dual function, as they also had to make sure the driver didn't fall asleep and kill us all and, more importantly, someone else. To be honest, this was probably the most dangerous part of the whole enterprise and when others began contacting us about doing the Three Lakes Challenge, the one piece of advice we gave them was to have one or more designated drivers who did not come on the trek but stayed at the car and slept. We may not have had a designated driver but we did have caffeine and service-station flapjacks on our side.

The mistake I made was to end up taking the first shift in the back. Having just completed the first leg of the challenge and with thoughts turning to the next, I found it hard to nod off and got no kip whatsoever. By the time I was slated to drive and then navigate, I was a very tired little boy. On the final stint of the journey, through the dark country lanes of the Lake District, trying to find the start of the path that would lead us to Red Tarn, I kept doing sporadic impressions of a corpse that someone had lashed into the passenger seat as I sat limp and nodding off. I certainly didn't get us lost – perish the thought – but vital minutes were added to our time as, just perhaps, I hadn't chosen quite the best route. Finally, however, we came to the bend in the single-track road where we could dump the car. It wasn't the finest piece of parking but I couldn't imagine there would be much traffic between eleven o'clock at night and two in the morning.

The good news was that being stuck in the sitting position for five hours had nicely stiffened our legs up and we clambered out of the car like people who'd spent some time being broken on the Inquisitor's rack. We heaved our loads up and on to our backs, sure that in defiance of the laws of physics they had somehow increased in weight. We trekked on tired limbs, stumbling as our legs didn't always put in enough effort to make well-balanced strides, and slowly made progress upwards.

We started near the town of Patterdale, just south of

Ullswater, and slogged our way in a near-perfect straight line westwards and ever upwards through the still, moonless night towards Red Tarn. The path is about four kilometres and is well trodden and maintained but it is pretty steep, gaining about 500 metres in height. And by now my knees were on fire. I've had two knee operations, neither of which cured the problem, nor could they have. I have misaligned kneecaps grinding away, leaving me with little cartilage these days. It's been going on for years, including the ten I spent in the Army. But then no one who is a soldier in any foot-borne infantry unit like the Paras or Marines leaves without bad knees, back, hips, shins, ankles or a combination of all of the above. Being a soldier is great; it's just not all that good for your joints.

We realized we had been climbing in the lee of the wind, because by the time we were nearing the top it had really picked up, to the point that we were close to being blown off our feet as we crested the summit plateau. Worse still, it had started snowing – hard. I had expected bad weather in Scotland and we'd got off lightly. Not so here. It merely goes to teach you that the mountains of the UK cannot, and should not, be approached lightly. There are rescues and deaths every year, especially in Scotland, simply because people are naive and ill prepared. They assume that because these mountains are in the UK they can't be that ferocious. Sadly, in certain years, the Cairngorms outstrip the Alps in avalanche deaths. So, here we were, in supposedly quaint and simple old England being battered by what could only be described as an alpine blizzard. These are not the conditions one wants when faced with the prospect of getting naked and, worse, having to climb into a freezing-cold, soaking-wet rubber suit. It was utter purgatory.

As we undressed, we had to stand on our wetsuits not just

to save our poor feet from the sharp stones around the lake edge but also to stop the heavy neoprene suits from kiting off into the darkness. Trying to bend your second arm behind your back, locate and stick it into the armhole of a wetsuit jacket is a mite more difficult when you're shivering, losing patience and the bloody jacket is flapping around as though it's being mauled by a Jack Russell. There was no end of profane mutterings, at least from me. I assume Monty felt as desolate but I could hear nothing over the howling wind. I was cocooned in my own little world of rushing, icy air, uncontrollable shaking and general self-imposed misery.

Suitably dressed up – or, more accurately, unsuitably dressed up, as waters this cold would normally warrant a much warmer suit – we waded with stalwart resignation towards the inevitable. Lynwen lit the edge of the water with her head-torch, but in the blizzard it barely made the surface visible.

Monty turned to me. 'Right, then. Let's not make this any worse than it has to be. Ten minutes and we're out.'

I gave him a maniacal grin, along with the most sarcastic thumbs-up I could manage. 'And not a second more,' I added.

We both stood there, waiting for the other to move. It was a head-shaking moment. What on earth were we doing? Then, with deep breaths and long sighs, we walked out into water we could no longer see. We knew exactly where the surface was, however, because we could feel it creeping up our bodies and leaking into our suits. Its frigid touch rose up our legs and thighs to reach a rather sensitive area, and our voices, had we the inclination to speak, would have risen by a couple of octaves. We stood about waist-deep and with a look and a smile we silently agreed it was time to man-up and dive in.

We both carried small underwater torches and the beams of our lamps showed a pebbled bottom with thin stems of delicate green plants growing from the lake bed. We could have taken this opportunity to go searching for the remains of the Mosquito light aircraft that, on a training exercise in 1940, hit Swirral Edge, which spans the gap between the mountains of Catstye Cam and Helvellyn, and slid down the mountainside, ending up in the lake. However, what we actually did was huddle up together and remain fairly motionless on the bottom with the plan of simply grizzing the long, cold ten minutes (this is another military expression meaning to endure stubbornly or to put up with something unpleasant). My pride was relieved to feel Monty shivering as badly as I was and we kept glancing at his diving computer to check the time. The minutes passed by considerably slower than they should. It felt as though it took approximately a fortnight to reach the ten-minute mark, but when it arrived we locked eyes, gave big, obvious nods and motioned upwards with our thumbs – time to get well and truly out of there.

We stumbled on numb and near-inoperable legs back to shore, almost falling a number of times and finding it difficult to speak through frozen lips. Once back, we began again the deeply unpleasant task of stripping in a blizzard. And this time our naked bodies were soaking to boot. I frantically towelled off as best I could with a piece of cloth little bigger than my hand, which refused to bend to my will and whipped around me. The snow-hail was falling so heavily that I was fighting a losing battle. It made more sense just to get dressed. Even the first few thin, but dry, layers made a difference to how warm I felt and as I finally donned my hat my morale picked up. We did not stop to converse or gripe about the dive but, as before, simply threw our waterlogged bergens on our backs and started moving. The best way to get warm is to move. And in this case it was doubly effective as we were moving back off the exposed mountain top towards the shelter of the mountainside. So why did we not move during the dive? Well, a great deal of exertion can generate heat underwater but we were too tired for that and any movement was likely to be counter-productive. If you don't move in still water, a small layer of water warms up around your body and actually insulates you. Any movement disturbs this. It's basically how a wetsuit does its job: the foam rubber suit holds that layer around you more effectively.

As we descended and the path seemed to swerve slightly to the left, there was a point when the wind noticeably dropped and within a few minutes was becalmed. The snow and hail also ceased – or at least we were sheltered from it – as soon as we got off the high ground. I rewarmed throughout. But my knees were not in the best state and the cold had seeped into my bones. Each downward step proved painful.

The abating winds gave us the chance to talk.

'How was it?' Lynwen asked us.

'Cold,' I said. 'Mostly it was cold.'

'Did you see much?'

Monty made a face. 'Hmm . . . no . . . not really. I did see a little fish. Did you see a little fish?' He turned to me.

'I did see a little fish, yes. He was laughing at us.'

Then Lynwen asked, 'Why did you guys stay under so long?'

Monty and I shared a sideways glance.

'Excuse us?'

'I timed you and you did sixteen minutes,' she said.

'No, we did not,' I said. 'We did ten.'

'No, I timed you from the point you left the surface until you came back up. It was definitely sixteen.'

It turned out there had been a problem with the dive computer and it had paused the timer during our dive. The ten-minute period had seemed much longer for the simple reason that it was . . . by six minutes. Which may not seem a great deal but when you are so cold you can see monkeys, made of brass, swimming around you, holding their groins, six bloody minutes is a long time.

We finally reached the kissing gate at the end of the track and the car – a welcome sight – appeared. We had not managed to do any filming on the mountain as the conditions were too bad but Lynwen, wrapped in all our clothing and an emergency casualty bag, had got a few photos. We decided to do a little piece to camera here at the end. If you ever see the video, my first foray into film production, which is still floating about YouTube, you'll see two very tired boys. We climbed slowly and awkwardly, like a couple of centenarians, into the car and began the final leg. I can honestly say I have no idea what time it was at this point but it was dark, still very dark.

It took about three hours to drive south and then west into the Snowdonia National Park for the final scene of this madcap idea, about which I was having second, third and fourth thoughts. By now it was well after sunrise and I felt more awake, as one always does when it starts to get lighter. In my time in the Forces, sometimes going whole nights and days without sleep, I would struggle in the last hours of darkness but achieve full alertness when the sun began to rise.

By now we had eaten our own weight in flapjacks and chinned enough coffee to induce coronary arrhythmia. Our backs were sore, the muscles of our thighs and shoulders stiff and my kneecaps, grinding as they were against my femurs, were on fire. Apart from that, everything was on course and looking relatively rosy. Actually, it really was looking good. The sun was not only up but out. A near-cloudless day, bright and warm, was a surprise for North Wales in November but clearly we'd accrued some karma points after the English leg and were going to finish on a perfect British day.

This was the shortest leg of the trip and it was also the lowest lake, which is why I thought it clever to finish here when I knew we'd be tired . . . although I admit to underestimating how much under my normal level of mountain-fitness I was. It was only about a 350-metre height gain and a trek of barely two kilometres to our final dive site – Ffynnon Lloer – but it was hard. The llyn's name translates as the Source of the Moon, which has to make it one of the most romantically titled lakes I have ever dived. I was not, however, holding out much hope of finding the birthplace of the lunar rock currently orbiting our planet and I still wonder how it got its name. It's a relatively small lake but sits beautifully in a cwm (a Welsh corrie) between the mountains of Pen yr Ole Wen and Carnedd Dafydd. But most importantly, and as I have already mentioned, it was not far away from where we were able to park the car.

The walk up, although steep – and perhaps not as steep as it felt – followed a thin path that required us to negotiate three high stiles which resembled two ladders leaning against each other to form an inverted 'V' over a six-foot fence. In reality, they may not have been this high but in my memory, and therefore for the purposes of this story, they were. Be thankful I didn't make it 12 feet. But when the amphitheatre of the cwm in which the llyn nestled came into sight, all our efforts were rewarded. With the bright sun and high clouds, the visibility in the Welsh mountains that day was superb. The steep – near-vertical – sides of the cwm rose to ragged-edged ridges, lined like the ruined crenulations of a wrecked fortress, and gave the impression that the little mountain pool was ringed by its own stone citadel.

We dropped our bags by the waterside and checked our watches. It was a little after nine in the morning and we had plenty of time to make it back to the car by noon and within our twenty-four-hour time limit. I can assure you through bitter experience that getting naked is significantly more pleasant on a relatively warm autumn morning than in oppressive darkness and the acoustic onslaught of a frigid night-time storm. It was then that Monty and I, at a fairly leisurely pace, which allowed us the time to appreciate the damage we'd done to muscles and joints over the last day and night, donned our wetsuits for the final time.

Now, it has to be said that as we stood on its bank, basking in the majesty of the surroundings and appreciating the tranquil and benign nature of our final dive site, it occurred to us that the lake didn't look that deep. It's hard to pinpoint exactly what gave us that idea. Perhaps it was that the whole area around the llyn was fairly flat and the banks did not descend steeply to the water's edge. Perhaps it was the fact the edge of the llyn was not well defined and the grass and moss seemed to carry on underwater as if the levels rose and fell easily. Nonetheless, suitably geared up with our cylinders, masks, fins and pockets full of rocks, we optimistically and purposefully waded out into Wales's highest lake. And continued wading . . . all the way to the bank on the far side, without the water ever really getting much past our chests.

However, this was Wales's highest lake and the rules – admittedly made up by me – stated that the dive had to be to five metres or the deepest part of the lake. So we submerged and bimbled about the lake bed in search of a hole. The water, being so shallow, was relatively warm and even in our thin wetsuits the temperature was pleasant. The water was clear and, with the sunlight beaming through and lighting the scene, we could really appreciate our surroundings. The lake bed was carpeted in short-stemmed bright greenery that grew thickly all over the bottom. We spotted some tiny fish, which we could not identify (embarrassing, since between us we possessed degrees in zoology and marine biology), and a collection of tiny freshwater snails. We spent well over our allotted ten minutes in the water, swimming up and down the lake in transects, finally happy to be enjoying a dive – which had more to do with the fact that we weren't freezing than anything else.

We found what we thought was the deepest part of the llyn at around two metres and, realizing that the clock didn't stop until we'd returned to the car, thought we'd best get a shift on. A quick change – faster, easier and more comfortable in the warm, dry, near-windless surroundings – and we were on our way back down. We knew we had plenty of time to make it back to the car but a desire to shave a few minutes off and just to get the whole thing over with before my knee blew out meant we set a good pace down the hill. On shaking legs, we limped back to our vehicle after twenty-three hours and nine minutes.

We raised some money for a Forces charity, had a grand day/night/day out, did something eccentrically British, adventurous and a little bit wonderfully pointless. The challenge has since been taken up by at least twenty teams I know of from the British diving community and many have got in touch beforehand or afterwards. Some have decided to do it over forty-eight hours. Some have chosen to do it carrying only snorkels. Others have done it as a team of six with two members doing each of the three lakes. And some have done it in the same fashion as me and Monty, but faster.

For me, it was also the first step on my adventure and media career, which has led to over a hundred articles, films, TV appearances and talks, and taken me around the world and to this book. And, although not the most extreme undertaking I've ever embarked on (my knees may disagree), it will always be remembered fondly. But I will never do it again.

CHAPTER 3

Exploring the Cave of Skulls

I am alone, blind in the complete darkness. My bare head cracks against the rock ceiling only half an inch above. I lie face down on rough, jagged pebbles, my chest clamped between the stony floor and the limestone roof of this claustrophobic tube. My fingertips tear on the coarse gravel as I try to pull myself forwards. The water level in the passageway has risen and now, as I strain to turn my head, as I try to breathe through the side of my twisted mouth, I cannot get enough air. I am fully submerged in the icy black water. And I am stuck.

The Cave of Skulls, or Uamh nan-Claig Ionn in Gaelic, sounds like a fabled location in deepest, darkest Africa – a deep pit containing ancient treasure and guarded by ingenious traps, or perhaps a lair full of evil goblins from a Tolkien book. But it is, in actual fact, a real place – and it's in Scotland. It lies in the heart of the Appin Mountains on the mid-west coast facing out towards the Inner Hebrides.

It is believed that the name derives not from a mountain of human remains left by a ravenous monster that fed on brave but foolish adventurers but, more prosaically, from animal bones found in the cave. This is not uncommon and bones of animals such as the bear, wolf and elk have been discovered in underground chambers across Britain, sheltered and preserved for hundreds or thousands of years. But the Cave of Skulls is more than just a repository for faunal carcasses, it's also one of Scotland's deepest caves, requiring long abseils down vertical subterranean shafts, interrupted by the necessity to negotiate tight, chest-crushing, serpentine crawls to reach the bottom.

Upon reaching the bottom, most trips to the Cave of Skulls come to an end. But it's at this point that some people have been drawn to a tiny slit in the rock on the cave wall, nicknamed the 'Letterbox' – for very good reason. This opening at ground level is barely 24 inches across and less than eight inches high. The horizontal tunnel that leads on from the Letterbox opening begins semi-submerged and slopes further beneath the water table as it continues deeper into the underground system. It was the Letterbox – more than the long crawls carrying dive kit that preceded it, more than descending the long abseils in total darkness, more than the blind dives through muddy, constricted tunnels – that was to be my nemesis on this project. But passing it was essential, because beyond lay underwater caves that no one had dived since they were first discovered in 1976 and, beyond that, unexplored territory – right here in the UK.

I had planned a trip to investigate a number of sumps – the name given to a section of cave that carries on and disappears underwater. These mountains contain rare areas of Scottish limestone. Scotland is a country built for the most part on hard igneous rock but in a few locations soft limestone can be found. Limestone is perfect for the formation of caves – solution caves to be precise – as the copious amounts of water that fall from the skies in Scotland collect and trickle down through the rock. Exploiting any crack and fault, rainwater has slowly dissolved the limestone over millennia, creating complex cave systems. The Cave of Skulls was one such system and the largest in this mountain range yet to be fully explored – we still have huge potential for new discoveries right here in the UK.

The depths of a Highland winter may seem an ill-advised time to embark on exploring the submerged passages under mountains but I'd chosen to go in during this period for three main reasons:

1. I keep myself constantly busy with work and projects and am forever trying to think up new ideas. I tend to have more ideas for my own projects to fill the gaps between work than I do gaps themselves. So February was the only spare five days I had for the foreseeable future and I decided to seize the opportunity, regardless of the conditions.
2. The winter conditions would be of little significance once I was in the cave system itself. Packed beneath earth and bedrock, caves tend to be a very stable environment and keep the same temperature all year round regardless of what's happening on the surface. Even the water running through the cave from the surface will never freeze, although, as I found out, it can be very, very cold.
3. There are no midges in Scotland during winter. I hate midges. These ravenous, swarming micro-vampires of the insect kingdom are the most aggressive and morale-sapping

organism I have ever come across. Smaller than the head of a pin, they make me react in large swollen lumps where they have bitten me and supped on my blood. These incredibly itchy lumps drive me to despair and last for days. Some people seem to attract midges more than others and some react more strongly. I possess both these attributes. There are literally billions of midges in the Highlands. I grew up in the Highlands. It was not pleasant. There are no midges in winter. So I was going to the Highlands in winter.

Of course, there are disadvantages to planning something like this in the grip of winter. The route up to the cave entrance normally requires a mile-and-a-half walk. Unfortunately, the Highlands of Scotland get the lion's share of snowfall each year and this one was no exception. Small farm tracks and roads don't get gritted or cleared and my Vauxhall Astra was no match for three feet of snow. This meant parking up about two and a half miles away . . . and did I mention it's uphill all the way? You may think a couple of miles uphill should prove no obstacle but bear in mind the amount of kit I was carrying. The 300 feet of climbing rope, two steel diving cylinders, diving equipment, wetsuit gear, climbing harnesses, climbing and caving metalwork and anchors, three cameras, helmet, haul bags, six kilograms of lead weight (to compensate for the buoyancy of my wetsuit during the dives, not just to give myself some extra training) and, most importantly, my lunch. It was heavy. About 64 kilograms. I weigh about 78 kilograms. It felt like I was carrying a fruit machine . . . one that hadn't paid out in some considerable time.

I creaked and groaned under the weight, sweating profusely

despite the sub-zero temperatures. I had decided to try to film this little escapade and, as it happened, managed to convince the BBC's *Adventure Show* to cast an eye over the footage to see if they fancied airing it. My friend Stu Keasley, a professional cameraman – always handy – was accompanying me. He did, to be fair to him, offer to carry some of the kit I was currently losing spinal length under, but I insisted he should just carry his camera gear and nothing else. This was supposed to be a solo attempt at diving the furthest reaches of the Cave of Skulls and I felt a little extra effort was worth it in order to be completely true to that mission.

I admit to possessing a paranoia about credibility and feel the need to live up to any hype generated. You need to be, as an absolute minimum, at least as good as you claim. Therefore, in all things, regardless of who'll know, I am strict with any claims I make. If I was saying on camera and in the written word that I was doing this on my own, then by getting Stu to carry even one torch I would be failing to live up to my declaration – I'd be just another fake. I am capable of compromise in life. It is inevitable, especially in some of the expeditions and operations I've been on. But I tend towards the '100 per cent or don't bother turning up' ideal. And this was one of those times. So the idea was that Stu would film the topside stuff – the approach and kitting up, and perhaps the initial entranceway of the cave. After that, as I descended further and deeper, I'd be on my own.

The problem with filming is that, apart from the extra equipment required, it takes a great deal more time to accomplish the deed. You have to keep stopping in order to set up shots and re-do even simple pieces – like walking past the camera – at least three times to get a variety of different shots for the edit. This meant that a trek that should have taken less than an hour took over two. And it wasn't just the filming and the excessive weight that slowed me down. Trying to find a great big hole in the ground was considerably harder than I'd predicted. Unlike a lot of the caves I've explored, you didn't wander down a subterranean path into a gaping arched hole in the side of a cliff. It was simply a big hole in the ground, a great slash in the hillside. The information I'd been given (which included a ten-figure grid reference but I had no GPS and only a 1:50,000 map) brought me into an area perhaps 200 metres by 200 metres on the side of a thickly wooded hillside, which was evenly layered in a deep duvet of snow. Three very embarrassing hours later, we finally found the entrance. It was surrounded by a small fence and therefore should have stuck out a mile . . . alas, not to me. Once located, and with a healthy dose of self-berating out of the way, I set to examining it. Measuring about seven by three metres, the hole was overarched by a gnarled old oak tree, bearded with hanging lichen and moss.

It was late now, the winter not giving much daylight to play with, and there was no point in attempting to get anywhere today. However, we used the remaining time to find and investigate a much smaller cave further down the hill – the outlet for the underground stream that ran through the Cave of Skulls and whose water filled the submerged tunnels. This underground waterway comes out about half a kilometre down the hill in the resurgence – the name given to a cave where water re-emerges from underground. It is called the Cave of the Black Well.

After a successful dive in the Black Well – a pool and tunnel that sit at the end of a 50-metre horizontal crawl, whose roof and floor rise and fall as its walls flex in and out throughout the journey – I decided to stash most of the equipment, except anything fragile or electronic, at the entrance to the Cave of Skulls. No point in humping all that kit back down simply to make the return journey again under its mass tomorrow.

The next morning was clear, crisp and my breath formed a fog as I exhaled from under my duvet. After unenthusiastically dragging myself from the warmth of my bed into the cold of the little cottage where we were staying, I sorted myself out, drove to the start point and, mustering some energy, set off at a considerably faster pace than the previous day, carrying only a few cameras and without the pauses to film.

Once at our destination, I located and began unpacking what I'd cached here the evening before. As I did so, I noticed a tiny flaw in my plan. After my sojourn in the Cave of the Black Well, my wetsuit had become . . . well, a wet suit. A night out in sub-zero temperatures had left it frozen solid. I unfolded the creaking suit and began to beat it against the frozen earth, trying to break the ice's grip. With it finally showing a semblance of flexibility I put it to one side and cracked on with organizing my gear . . . and there was a lot of it. I placed the smaller ropes and anchors I'd need for the final two abseils and all the dive gear in one bag. The cameras would go in another, so they'd always be locatable and available. The other two ropes – the first to be used on abseils one and two, and the final one on abseil three – were coiled up neatly but kept out of bags. Finally, the two steel diving cylinders were wrapped in layers of snoopy loops to protect them from too much damage (a snoopy loop is like a giant elastic band and is normally created by cutting a cross section about two centimetres wide from car or tractor tyres – they are very,

very useful). I laid out my uniform for the day's merriment – my wetsuit, hood, gloves and bootees, helmet, torches, harnesses and . . . oh, I'd forgotten my lunch after all.

With that morale bruiser on my mind, I now had to face up to the most disagreeable manoeuvre of the day. Dragging on a wet wetsuit is an unpleasant experience that is well known to any diver, surfer, paddler or those who partake in watery pursuits in general. But trying to heave on a frozen wetsuit, in the snow and at minus six, is a whole new line in purgatory, so the trick is to do it without it ever, *ever* actually touching your skin. This incredible feat I did not achieve. As I pulled it on, it felt like my body was clamped in freezing steel and I was forced to bang out press-ups, hill sprints and what we in the Forces used to call 'Bastards' – a combination of a press-up, squat thrust, burpee and star jump. At the height of your leap, you were compelled to scream the aforementioned profanity, directed, albeit only in one's head, at whichever instructor had seen fit to hand out this 'corrective training'.

My body temperature suitably restored, I began the rest of the kitting-up process, eager to get on with it now. I also knew it would be significantly warmer once inside and underground. I threw the two bundles of rope into the opening then lowered the haul bag and two cylinders but kept the cameras strapped to me to protect them on the way down. Stu was kitted up, too, but looking a little anxious. Stu's a very experienced diver but admitted to not being overly enamoured with caves. However, solid bloke that he is, he got on with the job in hand and followed me down the rope.

Once inside, the first problem was obvious. The entrance quickly narrows to 50 feet of tight elliptical tunnel only three feet wide and at times less than a foot high. It's difficult enough moving forward in these conditions if it's just you and the clothes on your back, let alone when you're carrying masses of gear. I left Stu at the entrance and began ferrying each piece of kit through. After five relays, which took over an hour, I was ready for the next section and for Stu to capture a few shots from inside. There was space to stand at the end of the tube – just – and we joked about how much of a pain in the backside the initial stage had been and hoped that was the worst of it. It wasn't. In fact, it got considerably more difficult just a few feet from where we stood.

The tube curled down and around and kept going back in the direction we'd come from, but beneath the section we'd just crawled through. And at the end of this short tunnel was the most frustratingly awkward section of the entire cave. It was not particularly dangerous but I cursed and swore more here than at any other time. I find blasphemy good for the soul.

The passage narrowed considerably then dropped away vertically about 20 feet to another tunnel below. This would normally have been a straightforward abseil. But I was trying to attach the rope to the anchors and to back out through a gap barely big enough to fit me. I'd end up with my feet dangling in mid-air over the vertical drop and my torso stuck fast in the narrow horizontal passage. As I tried to wriggle backwards, my wetsuit kept catching on the tiny sharp pieces of quartz crystals adorning the rocks. Eventually, I realized I'd have to brace my legs against the wall and push myself backwards, propelling my body out into the drop, and hope the anchors held. They did, and swinging out into space came as an enormous relief.

I was through and down. Of course, poor Stu then had to

lower the kit and get himself through, a man who had done limited climbing and even less caving, and it's a credit to him that he persevered. The tunnel we now found ourselves in was large enough to stand in and a few short paces across it found us at another short abseil. This one was easy enough to launch into. At the bottom was a narrow rift, less than shoulder breadth in width but high enough to disappear up beyond our torch beams. The novelty of ferrying gear was rapidly wearing off and I decided to clip the two diving cylinders to either side of my harness, shoulder the haul bag and carry the remaining loose rope and camera kit in my hands. This made squeezing along the close-fitting walls of the rift a bit more difficult than it may otherwise have been, and more swearing ensued.

As my helmeted head rattled off the walls and my shoulders bashed against yet another rocky outcrop, I was losing patience when, suddenly, I stepped out into what felt like a gigantic cathedral. The chamber was shaped like a huge pointed cigar balanced vertically. I was standing on a boulder-strewn ledge two thirds of the way up one of the walls and I could hear the echoing boom of a waterfall off to my right in the darkness. As my gaze tracked up the walls they fell inwards to form the cone-shaped roof. I shuffled to the edge of my precipice and peered over. My torchlight failed to reach the bottom.

I turned to Stu. 'Right then, mate, let's get the big abseil rigged and get cracking. Onward and downwards.'

Stu seemed less than enthusiastic and I could sense he had reservations. I set to work rigging the anchors and tossing the rope off into the darkness to give him time to consider his next move. With that done, I was ready to press on and looked questioningly at Stu.

'What are your thoughts, mate?'

'That's me, man. I'm done. This is getting a bit more serious and I'm not equipped for it. Sorry.'

There was no need to apologize. It can take bottle to put your hand up and say 'You know what? Not today, thanks.' I'd happily go caving again with Stu, or do most other adventurous things, for the simple reason that I now know I can trust him to tell me when things *aren't* OK. There are times when you just have to put your fears to one side and get on with the job in hand. This is nearly always the case in the Armed Forces when your only option is simply to man-up. This wasn't one of them. This was not Stu's project or his thing, and he'd done bloody well to get this far. (I should have mentioned he's a bit claustrophobic . . . potentially important in a cave that appears to be slightly smaller than you.) It was without doubt the right call to make – and it was even more right that he made it himself.

So, with a wave from me and a 'Good luck' from Stu, I headed off into the abyss. At this point, the footage and photos suddenly transition from outstanding to barely discernible. In my defence, I was a busy man down there.

In reality, it came as a relief to be on my own. There is often great comfort to be had in company, especially when you are doing something you are unsure of or which is at the extremes of your capabilities. However, when doing something technical and potentially dangerous, it is easier just to look after oneself than to have someone else to look after, too. Down there, I was confident in my abilities to deal on my own with what was to come and therefore felt shackled by having to think about someone else. I have done many diving, climbing, mountaineering and caving projects solo. They are less fun and require more mental fortitude but I have come to realize that I am often more comfortable relying on myself, as at least then I am confident about what is achievable and am not carrying the extra responsibility of someone else's safety.

I didn't want to lower my kit down the side of the cliff face, as I wasn't sure what the bottom looked like nor did I like the idea of it smashing off 80 feet of rock on its pendulous way down. Instead, I strapped it all to me and swung out off the ledge. The height of the ledge compared to the anchor necessitated a bit of a drop on to the rope and, with all the extra weight, it required a moment of internal meditation as I tried to bolster my courage before I stepped out. As I dropped on to the rope, the harness went tight and the weight pulled on the strapping, cutting into my chest and across my kidneys. Another one of those now commonplace expletives resonated around the chamber. I abseiled as fast as I could but the weight on the rope was making progress staccato and with each bounce the shock was driven into my kidneys. With relief, I made ground fall – and found myself ankle-deep in a gravel pool at the bottom of a huge waterfall. I'd now used the two large loose ropes so only had the two diving cylinders, haul bag and camera bag left to carry. I ditched the kit in one corner while I searched the perimeter for the entrance I was looking for – the entrance to the House of Cards.

The House of Cards is so named because of the card-shaped slabs of rock that are lodged precariously along its length. It's another narrow rift, less than eight inches wide but potentially 30 feet high. Over the millennia, giant playing card-like slabs of limestone have peeled off the upper walls and tumbled downwards. None, however, have made the cave floor. They have become lodged against the walls and against each other at jaunty angles, perilously balanced and, in some cases, wobbling. In order to pass through the House of Cards, you must get on your belly and, as tentatively as possible, crawl beneath this fragile structure.

I was intensely aware of the tonnes of poorly balanced rock above my head as I crawled through the freezing waters of the small stream that led away from the plunge pool at the bottom of the last abseil and continued its way deeper into the cave. As I reached the end of this constricted passage, I had to duck under a slab of rock, approximately diamond shaped, with the two pointed corners at the sides jammed against the rock. This allows it to pivot and swing if you knock the bottom point, and, as it's pretty much the lowest spot in the tunnel, your head can do little else. As it swung back and forth above me, my only thoughts were to keep moving and try not to spend too much time dwelling on the possible consequences.

I successfully passed the House of Cards and stood up, the chamber now allowing me to stretch. That last section had been the most physiologically uncomfortable so far, and the, albeit unlikely, potential of setting off a natural booby trap above my head had made it pretty fraught psychologically, too. However, I had only managed to drag the camera bag through, so three more trips back and forth under the 'Cards' were required before I could move on. By then, the novelty of the relay had well and truly worn off.

The final two sections that needed to be overcome in order to reach the bottom were relatively straightforward. A short abseil down a waterfall into a waist-deep pool – this time lowering my remaining kit first – and a second abseil through a crack in the cave floor. This second one was a bit more problematic than I'd first thought, as the cave at this point is shaped like an hourglass that has been stretched sideways. I fixed my final rope and stood above the narrowing crack, feet placed either side, with the rope disappearing into it. I could make out that after the constriction the walls flared out again into a much bigger chamber and I'd only have to pass through a few feet of tight rock.

I lowered the last of my kit down, which was now just my diving kit and cameras, and pondered the best way forward. I decided I'd give myself a little slack on the abseil rope and jump. Momentum and gravity would drag me through the constricted part and I'd be left dangling on the rope on the other side, still well above the ground and now in plenty of space. Foolproof.

Apparently not.

Years of running up and down hills carrying huge bergens and countless mountaineering trips doing much the same but in brighter-coloured clothing have left me with larger thighs and backside than your normal caver. The dedicated caver tends to be a wiry, svelte chap built like an Ethiopian marathon runner and capable of contorting through the smallest of gaps. Which is why, mid descent, I got my arse stuck. I wriggled and bounced up and down and, with my wetsuit tearing on the rock, eventually felt myself slip away.

Years of Army training and assault courses, as well as even more years of rock climbing, have left me with a larger chest and shoulders than your normal caver. Which is why, on this next phase of my descent, I got my chest stuck. As I frantically kicked my legs and began to move downwards, it occurred to me that my nose is probably bigger than the average caver's, too. I just managed to flick my head to the side as the abrasive rock face flew past it.

I slid down the final few feet of rope to the cave floor and had a chance to examine my surroundings. I was in the final chamber on the map. There were a number of unobtrusive plaques placed on ledges, testament to cavers who had reached this point in previous years. And this is where the normal caving stops. The passages beyond this disappear under water and diving equipment is required. As far as I was aware, no one had visited these submerged tunnels since they were first explored by Alan Jeffreys in 1976. But there was a final obstacle between me and sump one – the Letterbox.

I spent long minutes searching for any sign of an opening, dismissing a tiny slit at the bottom of one wall and moving on. Having checked the chamber a third time and found nothing else, however, I finally realized that the insignificant crack, barely large enough for me to get my head through, was in fact the way ahead. I lay on my belly and shone a torch inside. The slit was no more than six inches high at the entrance. It was also filled with water and I could see the roof dipping lower and lower further inside. I thought I could make out the end of the tunnel, where it opened into a larger chamber, but by this point the water was less than an inch from the ceiling and I had no idea how far below the waterline the floor lay – would I even be able to get through? It was clear that in the decades since Jeffreys' adventure debris had been washed down this cave and into the Letterbox. The floor of the horizontal crack was covered in small rocks and rough gravel. I began digging it out in order to give myself a fighting chance of getting through. After a few minutes, I decided to crawl inside and see how much more work needed doing.

I didn't get very far before the floor raced up to meet the roof and I couldn't squeeze any further forward. I withdrew and began digging out more geological overspill before crawling back inside. After several unsuccessful attempts, I checked my watch and realized I was close to my cut-off time. I'd left instructions at the top that should I not return within the allotted time then it could be assumed that something had gone wrong and the emergency services should be called. I had been underground for almost eight hours and was dangerously close to that phone call. It was then that I realized I'd failed. Carrying too much kit, requiring too many relays, the filming and photos, the time spent trying to dig a way through the Letterbox – it had left me insufficient time to make even the first sump.

I turned my torch off and for a few minutes just sat in the dark thoroughly dejected, feeling wearier than I had done at any other time on the trip. I was tired and the thought of now having to drag all the kit back through those passageways and heave my way back up the ropes I'd left dangling down the underground cliff faces meant I was not a cheery fellow. However, in these circumstances, motivating oneself is actually very easy. You simply don't have any other options. Whether I could really be bothered to climb back out was immaterial. I couldn't simply give up and go home. I had to *not* give up in order to go home. So, after a quick word with myself about my attitude, I gave my head a good shake, packed up my kit and started the long drag back to the surface and the failing daylight.

We had obtained some good footage. Well, Stu had obtained some good footage. And I handed it in to the BBC. They were happy, despite my complete failure to achieve what I'd set out to do. They said it would still make an interesting short film and they'd transmit around May.

However, saying I would do something and then not doing

it did not sit well with me. I tend to keep ideas close to my chest until I am about to begin a project or have successfully completed it. I've heard a lot of people over the years expound on the great achievements that they will be making one day, only to watch them do nothing more than continually try to impress people with their claims of future plans. So it was time to put up or shut up. I called the BBC and asked for an extension. If I guaranteed them a conclusion, how long could they give me? They said they could push back the transmission date but would have to have the final footage and story by 28 June. I would have one day off in that period and decided to go for it.

Second time around, I'd take an alpinist approach – fast and very light. So I cut my ropes down to the exact lengths required, deciding to climb down and up the first two abseils so I could take three ropes rather than five. This also meant cutting back on the metal anchoring equipment I'd need. I decided to take two diving cylinders again, as it's essential in cave diving to have surplus, but they'd be three litres rather than seven. I'd also take just one small camera, a GoPro Hero cam, which could take HD video and semi-decent photos and is less than half the size of my fist. I managed to fit all this into my one haul bag. There would be no equipment relays this time.

I left my home in Bristol on the Thursday night and drove nine hours through the night to Appin. This time my plan was to finish the project in a day and be back in Bristol by breakfast on Saturday. After arriving in Appin, I parked up as close to the cave as possible. This time, without the snow, I could cut the walking distance by a mile or so. It was three in the morning and I decided not to set off before six, so managed to grab a few hours of sleep. This was not as uncomfortable as it sounds, as I had a cut-down narrow mattress, duvet and pillow laid out down one side in the back of the car.

At six, the alarm on my watch signalled it was time to go. I quickly dressed, ate a breakfast of oats and protein powder and drank as much water as I could stomach. Grabbing my comparably featherweight bergen, I headed briskly towards the cave entrance. On arriving and realizing that the place was festooned with a voracious and biblical plague of midges, I roped down into the hole and in the entrance rapidly got changed into my wetsuit. I still wasn't quick or sheltered enough for some of them. So, somewhat down on blood volume, I entered the Cave of Skulls once again.

This time I knew what to expect. I did not have to waste time trying to work out the way ahead. I knew exactly where and how to rig each abseil, was only making one trip through each section and was not stopping to film or photograph anything. Which all meant I flew through the cave system and was at the Letterbox within an hour.

I can see the Letterbox in the light shaft thrown by the torches mounted on my helmet, the rough floor at its entrance still showing the scouring signs of my previous trip. I know what is required of me and I set to work digging out the gravel and rocks. I dig further and further in, clearing the debris behind me like some giant turtle creating a nest in the sand, sweeping out armfuls of sediment. I come out for a breather and clean the debris from the entrance to give me more space upon which to heap more deposits. I crawl back inside, my straining and grunting seeming louder in the confined space. I can see, as I twist my head sideways and strain my eyes into the corners, that the chamber ahead narrows and the roof descends closer and closer to the immoveable waterline.

I inch further inside and am now forced to remove my helmet in order to give my head more clearance against the ceiling. I am forced to crane my head to one side and press my cheek against the cave roof and twist my lips upwards in order to get a breath of air. With my helmet on, I can't manage this, as the bulky brim prevents me from getting the side of my face far enough out of the water – and I'd rather bang my head than drown. I retreat once more and try to stretch out my twisted limbs and strained neck before returning to clear more of the debris. And repeat. And repeat.

Eventually, after continuous bouts of crawling in, clearing an area and withdrawing whenever I take a mouthful of water, banging my head and painfully twisting my neck, I think I have done enough. I tie a loop around my ankle and attach it to the haul bag. This way I can crawl through then pull the bag after me. I slowly slither my way in, taking breaths from the side of my mouth, cheek pressed against the cold rock ceiling. I plunge my face back into the icy waters so that I can crawl a few more inches forward. As I near the end, through the tiny gap between the ceiling and the water level, I can see the tunnel opening up into something less torturous. I decide one last big push will have me through the last few feet.

I set my feet against the walls and brace my hands. With one last big intake of air, I duck my head into the frigid black water and push. I slide forwards. And then stop. I can feel my back being compressed by the rock ceiling and my chest being pushed hard against the gravel floor. I can feel the movement in the stones on my chest and decide I've just not put enough effort in. I brace myself again and thrust forwards. I move slightly but am now well and truly wedged. I am underwater, alone and in complete darkness between, quite literally, a rock and a hard place.

Time passes differently in these situations. What happens next probably occurs in less than two seconds but I recall the following thoughts did not come fast and furious but unhurried and relaxed. It felt as though I had time to consider each one.

'Hmm . . . This is not ideal . . . Man, this water is cold. It's really stinging my eardrums . . . Can I move backwards? . . . Nope, not really . . . Man, my eardrums are really sore . . . Right, I need to do something here . . . Aha . . . Of course, I know what to do . . .'

The problem is that my chest is lodged. And it occurs to me where my mistake has been. The normal human reaction when one is about to put one's head underwater is to take a deep breath. You do this before a significant physical effort like lifting a heavy weight or trying to push yourself through a hole smaller, as it turns out, than you. I have just experienced both scenarios so have truly filled my lungs. I have found the solution to my situation and try it. I breathe out. As I vent my lungs of precious air into the icy waters I feel the bubbles gush up the sides of my face. I can sense my chest deflating and reducing in size. As the pressure from the floor and ceiling reduce, I give another heave forward, powered by the motivation to live, and break through.

With the top half of my body clear of the Letterbox, I take a moment to gather my thoughts, which go along the lines of, 'Well, that was *lots* of bloody fun!' I then pull my backside through – no simple task but significantly less stressful with my head in open space and above water. After pulling through my dive kit, I am left with a short, easy crawl on hands and knees to the first sump.

I don't believe anyone has dived it since Alan Jeffreys in 1976 and his guideline was still evident, disappearing deep into the thick silty mud that had built up over the intervening time. This was a relatively short sump and I tied my guideline off above Alan's, checked and clipped on my diving cylinder and slithered into the grey-brown water. Visibility was non-existent and the border between the watery mud floor and the muddy waters above was not readily apparent. The passage is very low and it was difficult even to crawl and impossible to swim with the roof pressing on my back. However, there was no epic squeeze like the Letterbox and, after about ten feet, I resurfaced into the next section of dry cave.

It was a little awkward exiting the sump, as it's an uphill belly-slide. Once there, I continued on hands and knees to another lower tunnel. Alan had apparently had enough water on his trip to lie on his back and float along, which allowed him to keep his mouth within the small airspace between the roof and the waterline. There was much less water during my attempt, so I had the physically more demanding task of leopard-crawling along on my front. But then at least I wasn't under constant threat of drowning.

The topography of the cave then changes dramatically and a six-foot-high narrow rift runs through the rock. Sidestepping along it I came to a small pool – sump two. I donned my diving gear – no easy feat in an area you can't bend down or turn around in – and pushed head first into the unexplored waters. I needn't have bothered. If I said I got in past my knees, I'd be exaggerating. But the tunnel quickly contracted around me and I could not get any further. I pulled my glove off and extended my hand further into the tube, feeling around to see if I could detect some clue to another way onwards or even a final end to the system. But the cave continued, only inches wide, out beyond my reach.

There is always the potential in a cave to have missed some tiny crevice in a dark corner that leads to new chambers, and there is even more chance of this happening underwater, where our field of vision is so restricted. However, I could find no feasible way to advance. I had been the first person to lay eyes on sump two in thirty-five years and explore its limits. I realized then that I was using near-identical kit to Alan and reflected on how little diving and climbing technology had changed in the intervening decades.

I had finally done what I set out to do, what I had said I would do. I did not feel triumphant or elated or smug but sat there alone in the dark by this unassuming little pool of black water in one of the most isolated places in the country. I felt only a moment of quiet satisfaction and peace.

Of course, I still had to get back out . . .

Having spoken subsequently to Alan Jeffreys and Ivan Young from the Grampian Speleological Group, it seems that a few years ago a stream at the entrance passages had to be diverted to make rescue attempts easier. Less water flushing through the cave may explain why so much gravel and silt debris had built up at sump one and the Letterbox. Who knows, but if the stream manages to re-assert itself to its original course it may wash away some debris and reveal a way on for a game caver and diver in another thirty-five years' time.

Any takers?

CHAPTER 4

Walking the Longest Line – Part I

Most of the pursuits I indulge in require at least a degree of technical skill, although these skills could be gained by anyone who is willing to put the effort in. But in this book I wanted to include one thing free of this constraint, one thing which, although physically demanding, is not technically difficult. It's as simple as it gets and if anyone wants to do something similar it's a matter of will rather than gaining huge amounts of training and experience. In this one instance, it's all about attitude over technique. It's something that involves nothing more complicated than walking.

It occurred to me that if I wanted to make the point that there are still wild, uninhabited places in the UK reachable by the simplest form of transport, then the best idea would be to answer the following question: in the UK, how far can you walk in a straight line without crossing a road?

And so the idea of Longest Line was born.

I'll be explicit in my definition. A road is any passageway wide enough to be navigable by a car and classed as motorway,

A road, B road or indeed C, D or U (I'll wager most people were unaware it went past B), paved by tarmac, asphalt or any such material. A rough track used by a tractor or off-road four-wheel drive and not marked on a map or on the Ordnance Survey map as a 'path or track' or 'bridleway' does not count. Besides, some of these can appear and disappear overnight and never make it on to an Ordnance Survey map, so I'd struggle to plan and didn't fancy driving to Scotland and trekking for days only to be scuppered because the local ghillie had driven over the hillside in his quad bike last week leaving a new temporary track.

After poring over Ordnance Survey maps for hours, armed with a wooden ruler circa 1986, I surprised myself by discovering the Longest Line was not where I suspected it to be. I initially thought it would be in Knoydart, a peninsula in Scotland with no roads and the most unreachable pub in the country. Or surely it would be in Cape Wrath, that storm-beaten, dark rock fortress on the furthest north-west corner of our isle, facing off with the fierce North Atlantic. But no. Then it had to be in the East Cairngorms, my home patch. I was hoping this would be it, as there would be plenty of personal history to tie in with the story and a chance to reminisce along the journey. But, no, it wasn't there either. It was across a range of mountains that doesn't get much press and most readers will never have heard of, let alone be able to pronounce – the Monadhliath Mountains.

The name is pronounced Mon-ach Lee (the 'ch' is the guttural sound made when a Scotsman pronounces the word lo*ch*) and translates from Gaelic as the Grey Moor Mountains. The description is quite apt. The range covers an area in the Central Highland Mountains, lying north of Ben Nevis in the west and the major mountains of the Grampians in the east. The range is bordered by Loch Ness to the north-west and the River Spey to the south-east. It is not the highest mountain range in the country, with the highest peak being Creag Meagaidh at 1,128 metres, but it contains nine mountains above the magic 914.4 metres (3,000 feet) and therefore classed as Munros.

In 1891, Sir Hugh Munro produced the first list of all peaks in Britain over 3,000 feet and so gave the collective its name. There are now officially 282 Munros. I'd be spending much of my time above 700 metres and the highest point on the journey would be around 865 metres, when I would skirt north of the top of a mountain called Gairbeinn. The area is often divided into the Monadhliath region to the north-east and the Loch Laggan region in the south-west. However, I've always known it all as the Monadhliaths, so I'll be sticking with that.

Between these steep mountains are many flat areas, both on the high grounds between peaks and in the valleys. These moorlands gather water and hold on to it, so a scan of the maps showed plenty of streams and rivers and large patches of what looked like tiny blue plants. It's a nightmare to cross these seemingly innocuous patches, as the blue sprigs denote areas of bog.

The Line itself ran from the edge of the main A95 road immediately north of the village of Carrbridge directly on a bearing of 241° to another main road, the A82, a few miles north of Spean Bridge. It would cross streams, rivers, bogs, forests, plateaus, valleys, mountain slopes, mountain peaks, craggy buttresses, scree slopes and cliffs. Fortunately, my path – through genuine luck rather than clever planning on my part – avoided the many lochs and lochans (small lochs) that were scattered across the area. I did not fancy having to swim across the frigid black waters of an upland Scottish loch. In fact, it may well have been suicide without some kind of thermal protection like a wetsuit, and using one would have meant humping around significantly more weight than I'd like.

Armed with my ruler, I worked out that the total distance of the Longest Line was 78.8 kilometres. That's exactly 50 miles. Far enough, but not too far – the perfect adventure for someone with finite time. Cue my older brother Jamie. He still serves in the British Army, although currently on attachment with the French Forces, and so his time off is limited. We were keen to do something together, so he took a week off work and caught the train over to Blighty to be my wingman. This meant we'd be making the crossing in winter, allowing me to make the point that the UK is an adventure playground twelve months of the year, with some of the best activities only available in winter. The plan was to drive up to Spean Bridge from Bristol on a Saturday, dump the car near the finish line, sort our kit out and get a lift round to Carrbridge, the start line.

We got dropped off just outside the village at about 2200 hours. It was an opaque, frosty night and the wind, although not fierce, was bitterly cold. But it wasn't raining . . . everything is better when it's not raining. Our plan was to walk only a couple of kilometres into the woods near Sluggan Bridge and camp for the night. I set the bearing on my compass and off we went. We initially went slightly off-piste but by no more than 100 metres or so in order to cross a farmer's field using the public right of way so as to not disturb any stock and, if I'm honest, make use of the small bridge that crossed the first stream rather than having to either strip or get our boots wet within five minutes of the start line. We entered the forest and the cue to set up camp was the first spit of rain. We managed to get into our beds before the heavens opened and prayed it would be gone by morning. Tabbing in the rain is not so bad but setting up and breaking camp even in light showers is a pain. It's much easier to cook and pack and unpack when it's dry outside and you must, at all costs, keep your sleeping bag dry.

On this trip, we'd decided to try to travel reasonably light. We'd predicted the journey would take three days. We knew the ground would be difficult and daylight limited as we navigated our way as close to the Line as possible. We also had to plan for deep snow, especially on the higher ground and given the sub-zero temperatures. So we had a lightweight tent between us, sleeping bags and mats (never underestimate the value of a good sleeping mat – it can keep you warmer and provide a good night's sleep, which makes it well worth the extra weight). We had plenty of food, a cooker and fuel to keep us in hot drinks and hot food for the seventy-two hours of our ordeal. Because it was winter we carried crampons for the upper hills where snow was abundant and plenty of warm and waterproof clothing. (Crampons are those metal spikes that mountaineers wear on their boots in winter to climb snow and ice.) Our bergens were not overly heavy and by the end we had used everything we had taken, proving our kit choices had been on the money.

The next morning, we struck camp and set off just after dawn in the inevitable rain. It had been raining hard the last few days up in the Highlands and that was a cause for concern. The combination of a deluge and a slight increase in the winter temperatures meant a thaw was setting in. This meant that as the snow melted on the higher areas and the deluge continued there would be a lot, an awful lot, of water coming down the mountains. How this would affect our path we didn't know but I suspected there could be even more blue on the ground than on the maps. We stuck as close to the Line as possible whilst picking our way through the close rows of pine trees and using wider gaps in the forest to box around areas of crowded growth until we finally fell out of the trees on to the banks of the River Dulnain.

The river level was right up and the black waters swept past us. The prospect of stripping off and crossing this did not fill me with glee. It was clearly very cold indeed. But, more importantly, the strength of the river, bolstered by the heavy rain and thawing snow, was such that any crossing would have seen us swept off our feet. River crossing may seem a fairly straightforward affair to the inexperienced but any outdoor professional knows that they are one of the most dangerous things in the wilds and, unfortunately, they often claim more lives than any other activity over the course of a year. This is especially true for school groups, although in recent years, because of past incidents, river crossings are treated very seriously, which has led to a reduction in the number of deaths. Any good mountain leader will tell you the best way ahead is to avoid them in the planning stage – find an alternative route. If in doubt, I would allow myself to go off-Line to a better crossing point up- or downstream rather than to drown . . . which I think was fair. But on this occasion no such melodrama was necessary, as I could see an obvious way over the water obstacle: the magnificent Sluggan Bridge. This steeply curved single-arch stone bridge was constructed in the 1830s after a previous one, built in the 1760s, had washed away in conditions not unlike what we were now facing. An original bridge had been part of General Wade's road, built in the 1720s and 30s to help move troops north and try to tame the unruly Highlands.

It was a thing of beauty and my brother was extremely impressed, especially since the old track that ran over it saw little traffic except the odd walker in the tourist season. It was a bizarre sight, this old, handcrafted, picturesque bridge sitting in the middle of the quiet wilderness. We appreciated the chance to keep our feet dry and navigated our way through the forest and back on to the Line. We took another slight detour, only about 150 metres off course, a kilometre further on in order to take another bridge back over the same river. And now we left the tracks and occasional farmhouses behind us and began the long march over the wild land. We hand-railed the north bank of the raging river – using it as a visual reference to follow in the same direction – for another five kilometres before it turned south and left us.

The terrain became easier as we rose in altitude and came out of the trees. It is slow going moving through a thick forest and it's harder to navigate across long distances. Now out in the open we could see the far horizons . . . and they all went up. We hopped, skipped and jumped a number of little streams and made our way up the rough ground of Carn Caol, our first major hill. The plan was to aim for a saddle, the lower area between two peaks, which nestled between Carn Caol and another mountain.

I was yomping along, head down and feeling a bit hot, bothered and generally rained on when a flash of white caught my eye. My head jerked up and I saw a small pale meteor race over the surface of the heather. I'd never before seen a winter hare in the wild in all my time on the Scottish mountains. I've seen plenty with their common grey-brown colours on show but never their winter ermine coats. Hares turn white in the winter because they live up in the snowbound areas and use this as a method of camouflage against predators. Of course, if the snow starts to melt before the winter is over and your coat has changed back, then you stand out like a gleaming bright-white thing on dark-brown hillside. We stood watching him as he bounded away, backside bobbing furiously, chuffed that we'd seen a wild sight few people get the chance to witness, and it made for a credible excuse to stop walking for a minute.

'Shame *we* can't move that fast . . . in fact he's probably just showing off, laughing at us. Come on!' Jamie quipped. And we walked a little further.

Within the next ten minutes we saw six more white hares racing up the same line of the slope.

'I reckon we take the same line to the saddle, mate,' I said. 'They must know what they're doing, better than us.' I couldn't help but think about the line from *Alice in Wonderland* – 'Follow the White Rabbit'.

We soon reached what was left of the snow line at about 600 metres altitude and trudged onwards. Snow can be a blessing to walk on when it's firm. But when it's soft – for example, when there has been a thaw and heavy rain – then your feet sink knee-deep into the slush and walking becomes painfully slow and temper-frayingly frustrating. The other problem is that it can lie across gaps; it doesn't fill them in, just creates a fragile roof over holes and ditches which makes them look as flat and seamless as the surrounding ground. You have to listen for the trickle of streams to detect these water-filled ditches under the snow and some can be up to thigh-deep.

We both fell in a couple, which, although it meant a flurry of profanities and general throwing of teddies out of the pram by the individual caught in the trap and peals of laughter from the other fellow, did not cause any major injuries. People have damaged ankles, knees and even broken legs by stepping on to a snow bridge. Jamie's knee was cause for concern in any case, as he'd severely damaged it the previous year and it was far from fully fit. We both carried walking poles, which helped bear the load of the bergens, helped to stabilize us on these numerous falls and took the pressure off our knees on the uphills and especially the downhills.

As we finally crested the summit, having been lured onwards by a series of inevitable false summits (an illusion created by the steep hillside hiding the peak from view and making it look as though the top of the particular stretch of slope you're on is the summit), an expanse of high moorland plateau rolled out before us, covered in patches of white snow and brown earth. This was where the majority of our tumbles through the snow bridges occurred, from short stumbles to Bruce Lee-esque splits, of which neither of us were naturally capable.

The wind and rain had picked up and we had to keep moving to stay warm. We'd been going almost five hours and had only made about 15 kilometres of progress. This was not a bad rate considering the quality of the ground we'd covered but the late winter dawn start meant it was already the afternoon and we needed to stop for something to eat. This plateau would not do, as the biting wind would soon chill us if we failed to generate body heat through movement. I checked the map and confirmed there was a re-entrant no more than a kilometre ahead (a re-entrant is a small valley that runs down the side of the hill). We could try to shelter there, although my hopes were not high.

When we eventually reached it, the sides were much steeper than I expected and we had to sidestep our way down to the bottom, where a small trickling stream was meant to run. However, it was not a small trickling stream but a swollen flowing torrent of water that covered most of the valley floor, swamping the heather and grass that grew there. We huddled to one side of the bank and Jamie quickly flashed up our stove to get some water on the boil. It's very important, and often instinctively overlooked in cold and wet conditions, to keep drinking fluids, especially hot ones. We downed a pint of cup-a-soup each along with a flapjack and a Peperami. Not the most scientifically advanced sports nutrition but it contains carbs, sugars, protein, fats and salt, and it tastes good. Food as a mechanism for morale should not be overlooked either. Besides, with all the camping kit we were carrying, packing energy powders and gels to save grams of weight wouldn't have mattered much and fatty foods contain the most energy per gram. So the most efficient food to carry is, theoretically, lard.

I was starting to feel the cold even having had my soup and wanted to start moving again before my muscles started to shake even more. It is one of the disadvantages of not carrying too much body fat. All else being equal, if you sit an athletic person and an overweight person in a fridge overnight and tell them not to move, the latter has a far greater chance of surviving. However, I've always found staying warm is a matter of eating and drinking the right things, wearing the right kit, planning correctly and, more than anything, keeping moving. So off we went.

We had to walk downhill, along the side of the re-entrant, to find a place narrow enough for us to leap across the 'stream'. We soon found ourselves at the confluence of three of these streams and, with some difficulty and time wasted trying to figure out the narrowest and safest place to attempt a crossing, finally made it to the far bank. But this only led us to another, much larger, river, the one all the previous streams flowed into. And we needed to be on the other side.

These waters were named Allt Mor on the map. 'Allt' means burn or stream and 'Mor' means big or great. So, yes, it was named Big Stream but in reality this was a white-water river . . . and it looked really pissed off with someone. The peaty-brown liquid frothed as it rocketed past us down the hillside, thundering abuse as it went. We walked up and down looking for a point where the banks were close enough to jump across. We could have risked wading it but there was an exceptionally good chance that one of us, if not both, would be knocked off our feet and swept away. If either of us got injured then the other would have to make a solo journey to get help, which might take a day or more from the remote location in which we now found ourselves.

As too often happens in life, we wasted a great deal of time procrastinating and planning possible solutions and alternatives rather than just getting the hell on with it. We searched the banks again and decided backtracking was our only realistic option, demoralizing as it sounded. We had cut back no more than a minute when we spotted what looked like an old railway sleeper in the undergrowth. What the hell a long lump of wood from a rail track was doing there, I'd no idea. Things like this are often used to lay over ditches or streams to allow off-road vehicles to cross, but it was all alone and no vehicle, not even a fully off-road one, could have reached this point. Our plan was to lay it over the river and simply walk across the maelstrom.

We tied a piece of cord to the end so we could lower it down and, should it not be long enough, retrieve it. We pulled the heavy lump of wood on to our shoulders, handling it gingerly so that none of the protruding nails caught us. We both commented on how little we wanted holes in our waterproofs in this weather. It's funny looking back now that this seemed a more pressing priority than avoiding stab wounds and tetanus. But, then again, one should always be most concerned with the crocodile nearest one's canoe.

We hoisted the thick plank vertically into the air and wedged the end as close to the edge of the water as possible before I braced it with my foot. Jamie then began to let out the cord and lower it, like a drawbridge, over the rapids.

The end was at least a foot short of the opposite bank and, as it slipped towards the water, it was caught by the powerful flow and pulled in, the water attempting to sweep it off downstream. Jamie held tight, the thin cord wrapped around his hands and digging in through his gloves. We managed to haul it back in against the current but, clearly, this strategy was not going to work. Still determined not to have to backtrack or trek miles upstream to box around it, we walked along the riverbank one more time to investigate it with new eyes. Was there any way we could get across with our 'assault bridge'?

I jogged up the side of the bank, then stopped. I cocked my head backwards to look again at a rock I'd just passed. It was an almost perfect pyramid, with its point protruding a good two feet out of the waves rushing around it. I looked up to find Jamie staring at the same rock. He looked up at me. The rock was out in the middle of the river and the distance to it would be close to the full length of the sleeper. It was still a long jump to the other side but we'd have a few feet of extra height from the top of our rock, which would give a bit more horizontal distance to the leap. Nothing was said. We just ran back and picked up the sleeper, carrying it in silence.

There was no way we'd make it with our heavy bergens on, so the first job was to lob them over.

'Right, mate,' said my brother. 'You've been on the bench presses and pies lately, so you get to throw them over.'

With that, he began shuffling the plank out towards the rock.

'What are you doing, mate?' I asked. 'I'm not throwing them from the end of the sleeper.'

'Why not? It's closer.'

'Because it's a five-inch wide, slime-covered, wet gangplank balancing on the point of a pyramid . . . I'll end up in the river and about ten miles downstream by the time what's left of my body gets caught in an old tree!'

'Do you reckon you can make it from here?'

'Better bloody that than trying it from out there!'

In any circumstances, the twisting and jumping motion required to propel the 20-kilogram sacks over the river would throw me off balance. Now combine that with being stood on a crumbling bit of wet wood, see-sawing on a rock and I'd be white-water rafting *sans* raft. So, from the safety of the bank, and with a mighty effort – channelling the spirit of the Highland Games' hammer throwers, if none of their skill or power – I hefted my bergen into the air. It hung there, then arced down, landing safely on the other side. It was then I realized my camera was in the top pouch. Too late now.

I picked up Jamie's sack and with a similar effort, but perhaps less care, I let his fly. It probably travelled further but because I'd thrown it so that its trajectory was at more of an angle over the churning river than directly across, it was heading for the water. I had that sinking feeling as an image of me sprinting over the near-vertical riverbank, trying to catch the bag as it barrelled downhill, came to mind. Time paused. Then it landed on its end on the very edge of the bank and bounced . . . away from the water. It came to rest safely, with just the odd, particularly enthusiastic wave breaking rank and washing over a strap.

Done. Well, apart from us.

The person who ventured out first would have the benefit of the other being able to secure the landward end of the sleeper with his foot. That said, we had no idea how stable and secure it would be on the rock point nor if the rotten ends were robust enough to take our weight. So going first or second both had their pros and cons.

'OK, I'll go first,' I volunteered. This whole trip was, after all, my fault.

What I remember most about this incident is the laughter. At the ridiculousness of our makeshift bridge, at each other, at the fact that suddenly we felt, in a very tiny way, like Indiana Jones. I edged out towards the end and stood there, balancing. The far end of the sleeper rocked on its insecure footing and I tried to work out how best to launch myself without the thing tipping me off. After due consideration and a lot of fannying about, I decided to employ the 'Fuck It' method. I stopped thinking and just jumped, expecting my foot to slip or the end to crumble as I tried to power off it. But, no, I made it with room to spare.

Jamie was up next. He sidled out with a massive grin on his face. Now our walk was getting adventurous, more interesting, we were both filled with energy.

'Bloody hell, mate,' he proclaimed. 'It's a lot further than I thought. It didn't look that bad from back there.'

'You've got the extra height, mate, just push off. Even if you can just get a toe to the bank, I'll grab you and haul you in.'

He shook his head. 'I don't reckon I'm going to be able to make this, mate,' he said, then smiled and jumped.

A moment later we both stood on the far bank, laughing and shaking our heads, perfectly dry and feeling an overwhelming sense of achievement. It was a tiny victory, a fairly insignificant adventure compared to most. But at that point in time and in that place we were heroes. We'd conquered the river of doom and the bridge of death. We even stopped to take a photo to record the moment, as the camera had survived the impact.

So, with our feet dry and our motivation renewed, we struck out once more. After slogging uphill, avoiding hidden ditches, wading through snow and trying to negotiate yet more waterways that did not, in width or ferocity, resemble the spidery-thin blue lines suggested by the map, we eventually came to a major obstacle. Not a stream or tributary but an actual river, which is also how it appeared on the map. Needless to say, if the streams had become rivers due to days and days of torrential rain and thaw melt the river had become . . . well, a bigger, faster, wider river. This one was over 20 metres wide, deep and flowing fast and powerful. Fording it was out of the question and, for obvious reasons, jumping it wasn't really an option either. Even our lucky railway sleeper wouldn't have been much use.

By now we had lost a great deal of time finding ways around the various water obstacles along our route. We were nowhere near as far on as we'd planned and dusk had arrived. We set our tent up, got some food on and pored over the map.

Of course, the problem was I had only taken those maps that I required to complete the Line, not wanting to carry extra material. Travelling south-west would force us to cross this river eventually, without any obvious crossing point, and throw another river of similar size in our way. Going north was possible but the drawback was that after about fifteen minutes of tabbing we'd be off the edge of the map. There could be a bridge sixteen minutes' walk away . . . or we could punch north all the way to bloody Inverness before we caught sight of anything that would help us. The weather was also deteriorating severely.

If we could get across this river, and the next and the next, bearing in mind that the waterways got more numerous as our journey continued, it would take us longer than planned. At our current pace, it'd be more like five or six days rather than three and neither of us had that time. I was also concerned about getting across a major river, then, as we tired and the waters rose, finding ourselves not only unable to get across the next one but also being unable to get back across the previous one, effectively trapping ourselves in the wilderness. So we made the call.

This can often be the hardest part of any expedition or adventure project and it's a call I've made many times in the past. Was it the right call to make in this situation? Was it the right call all those other times? I'm still here, which is a major endorsement of decisions I have made, considering some of the situations I, or Her Majesty's Armed Forces, have

Left: The greenery and questionable nature of the rock makes this look a bit like a shot from *Gardeners' Question Time*, but in fact it's a long way up on Pitch 4 of our new route on Exmoor. On unstable ground and with no anchors in, this was tough climbing.

Below: On the route we named Brittle Bone Coast – the Needles on the Isle of Wight. I had to move cautiously off from the safety of the ledge and try not to cut my ropes on the first seam of shattered flint.

Bottom: The rock was getting even more brittle as I approached the top ... but the view was spectacular.

On top of the world. Well, on top of the middle Needle with Skeleton Ridge and the Isle of Wight in the background.

Above: Monty and me psyching ourselves up against the cold as we prepare to dive the icy waters of Britain's highest lake, Loch Coire an Lochan in the East Highlands, in wetsuits that are too thin for the job.

Below: Not your normal hillwalking clobber... Gearing up for the last time ahead of diving Wales's highest lake, Ffynnon Lloer in Snowdonia.

Above left: Carrying 62kg of kit uphill to the entrance of the Cave of Skulls in Scotland's Appin Mountains.

Above right: And this is what 62kg of kit looks like. Admiring everything I took on my first attempt at the Cave of Skulls.

Right: Squeezing back through the Letterbox, having successfully dived Sump 2 of the Cave of Skulls – at the second attempt.

Above: Approaching the top of the dark, damp but beautifully relaxing climb of the King's Chimney, part of the Cuillin Ridge on the Isle of Skye. It's classified as a VDiff climb but looks worse than it is.

Below: A well-earned sit-down at the halfway point of the Cuillin Ridge and a chance to enjoy one of the most magnificent views in Britain.

Above: A quick way to start a snorkel. A high-entry leap into the Linn of Dee in the Cairngorm National Park.

Above: Sound advice for the unwary at High Force Waterfall in Teesdale in the Pennines.

Below: When freediving it is essential to stay as relaxed as possible. Chilling out on the bridge of the HMS *Scylla*, submerged off the Plymouth coast.

Admiring the view above and beneath the waterline. Snorkelling the River Etive in the Highland mountains as part of my Britain by Snorkel project.

seen fit to put myself in. I am very, very far from perfect. But I am still alive. So we made the call to head home.

Our best bet was to turn north and follow the river. I knew that the nearest main road was to our north, so we'd find ourselves in civilization eventually. Of course, we could have just walked back the way we came but we believed north was a shorter journey with fewer river crossings. Besides, the idea of retracing the last 25 kilometres would have been enough to make us fill our pockets with the granite rocks strewn around and launch ourselves into the very waters we'd been striving to defeat.

The next morning, after four hours of walking and, eventually, a bridge crossing (by now my brother and I were becoming connoisseurs of a good bridge), we found ourselves on the one thing I had set out to avoid – a road. Following this road for another hour or two brought us to a sign that read: 'Tomatin 5 miles'.

I knew where we were. I had been to Tomatin years before . . . it's home to one of the highest whisky distilleries in the country.

We lay on the ground outside the village shop, resting our heads on our bergens, waiting for a pick-up.

'Sorry, mate,' I said to Jamie. 'You've come all the way from Paris for nothing.'

'Not at all, mate. We don't get to spend much time together any more. We've had a few good days of driving and walking to catch up. It's been great being out in the hills again.'

He was right. The journey, the experience, is as important as the destination, the goal. And by the same token I had enjoyed myself and even if an adventure does not go to plan, if the final goal is not achieved, as long as it was still an adventure then it was something worth pursuing.

And he was also wrong. Here is the complicated truth about how I feel. As much as I agree that an adventure should be about the journey as well as the destination, that a trip – if not successful but still enjoyable, useful or productive in some way – is just as worthwhile, I'm afraid I also think that it's better to take part and win than just take part. If you're taking part without trying your damndest to win, why did you show up in the first place? I know myself well enough to know that for me the journey is as important as the destination, but without arriving at the destination the whole journey seems hollow . . . and I'm not a man to get knocked down and stay down.

I wearily lifted my head from my makeshift pillow and turned, squinting one eye against the bright winter sunlight, to look at Jamie.

'I'm not done with this yet. Not by a long way,' I told him.

'Hmm,' he mused, sarcastically. 'About 80 bloody kilometres, to be exact.'

CHAPTER 5

Along the Cuillin Ridge

The Cuillins are a clan of high, barren, jagged-peaked mountains in the south-western area of the Isle of Skye. The entire group is actually, more accurately, two collections of mountains. The Red Cuillins, which lie to the east of the area, are lower, more rounded, less severe in nature and less bereft of vegetation and water. However, it was their more imposing and threatening brother I was interested in – the big, brooding, quick-tempered and unpredictable sibling – the Black Cuillins.

From the most southerly peak to the tip of the most northern mountain is a distance of approximately only 13 kilometres. Along this seemingly short and innocuous route there are twelve Munros – twelve Scottish mountains over 3,000 feet in height. If one determines to journey from the first to the last, whether starting from the north or south, you will earn one of the most sought-after ticks in British mountaineering for completing the United Kingdom's answer to the Alps – the Cuillin Ridge.

The Cuillin Ridge is the collection of those twelve jagged

mountain peaks strung out in a line that gently curls around like the tail of a waking dragon. Like the nodules on the dragon's spine, these peaks rise and fall in rigid triangular lines. And what a beast it is. The dark gabbro rock, created from crystallized magma erupting from the earth, is coarsely grained, sharp and shattered, and tears at exposed skin. This dark rock creates a shadowy cloak over the mountain and gives the range its name.

The Ridge is no mere hillwalking experience; it is not a gentle, undulating ramble along some high hills. From start to finish you must navigate your way through true mountain terrain, along a ridge line where the best route is often along the crest of the Ridge itself – a thin, pointed apex with the world falling steeply away to your left and right. As you move along this narrow edge with precipitous drops on either side, you also have to negotiate vertical descents using technical rope work and abseils. And you face equally vertical ascents up graded rock-climbing routes on crumbling, polished and often damp, slippery rock. You can bypass some of these arduous ascents and descents in places but this not only requires long, circuitous rerouting to box around them but also means you have not actually completed the genuine Ridge traverse. You will have missed out the hardest, most challenging and most rewarding sections, and of course the best views and the most spectacular terrain are found at the most extreme points of the route.

This is not an easy route and most of its length involves scrambling on all four limbs, not trekking. All this plus the fact that during the 13 kilometres of horizontal travelling you will rise and fall over 4,000 metres. Four kilometres up and four down. That is almost equivalent to climbing Mont Blanc by the standard route and returning home – twice. People often do each mountain separately or link two or three peaks together in a section, returning again and again to tick off more peaks. In fact, the twelve Munro peaks are essential ascents for those diehard Munro-Baggers, the dedicated hill-walkers who try to climb all 282. Some people, having completed the list, go on to climb the whole lot again and even repeat it a third or fourth time.

To complete even a single peak on the Cuillin Ridge requires a great deal of uphill effort, as, unlike many of the British mountains, you start at sea level. For most of the single-summit trips, scrambling techniques are required and sometimes basic safety rope work is employed. However, technical rock climbing and rope descents are only really required on the traverse to move between the peaks and overcome the steep gorges, gullies, cliffs, chasms and rock crevasses that obstruct your progress.

The most common way to link the entire Ridge in one journey is with a partner and over two days. This journey is considered by many to be one of the greatest challenges in British mountaineering. Those undertaking the Ridge will normally work in roped pairs to overcome a number of dangerous vertical descents using ropes and abseiling techniques to gain the bottom of rock crevasses between mountains, called slots. Once inside these slots they will then have to climb out, often in big mountain boots and in wet, slippery conditions, in order to carry on their quest. As it takes two long hard days to complete the Ridge, they will also be carrying a lot of equipment. On top of the ropes, harnesses, helmets and climbing metal-work they will also bring what's called a bivi-kit. This is the minimum equipment needed to spend a planned night out on the Ridge, sheltering from whatever elements assault these lofty stopovers. At the very least, climbers will carry food, fuel, a cooker, sleeping bag, sleeping mat and some kind of shelter.

There is an alternative, although less tempting, way to attack the Ridge – true alpinism. This means fast and light . . . very light. A decision to go light is not for everyone. Using this method, you ditch weight in order to move faster across the ground and attempt to complete the Ridge in a single day, exposing yourself to fewer potential issues such as an unexpected deterioration in weather or a forced overnight bivi. You strip your equipment back to the bare essentials and the goal is to move from the southern peak to the northern in less than ten hours. You don't even have to carry any real food. This is the method I chose.

I would also save time by attempting the crossing solo. It meant I would move faster – or at least spend less time not moving. I would rest when I needed to (not when someone else needed to) but also, crucially, it meant that time would not be wasted in a second person completing the dangerous vertical descents and ascents. And of course this lack of partner meant there would be little point in taking any climbing kit, as I'd have no one to hold my ropes for me as I struggled up the sheer cliff faces. This meant all rock-climbing sections would be soloed – climbed on my own without safety ropes, leaving no room for error. I toyed with the idea of taking a rope to use to abseil into those sections where a vertical descent barred my way. A rope would also be handy if things got bad and I had to make a quick exit off the side of the Ridge in a place where there was no easy escape route down. I decided not to take the rope.

Any decision taken in the mountains, or in this case before entering the mountains, has consequences even if everything goes well. As a climbing instructor, mountain guide and a soldier who has spent a great deal of time out on the hills, I've an appreciation of my true capabilities and limits. I have done a great deal of solo climbing in the past and was confident this route was within the limits of my ability. Solo climbing may seem a reckless and needlessly dangerous thing to do but actually it needn't be, or at least not as much as it may seem on first inspection. Without a rope dragging behind you, the weight of carrying extra gear or the constant need to stop, hanging off tired arms, to place protective anchors, the climb is physically easier. Therefore, although the consequence of any fall is greater, you're more agile on the rock and the chances of a fall are reduced. And if you do trip over, you're more likely to catch yourself or recover than if you are wearing a heavy backpack. This is assuming you can control the mental pressure that comes with having absolutely no room for error.

The other factor in soloing is how you do it. When I climb with a rope, I am bolder, take more risks and will push myself to my limits. When soloing, I maintain complete control, constantly making sure I am well within the bounds of my physical and technical skills so that I have enough in reserve should things not work out as I predict. I'll also do my homework more rigorously, reading any information about the route and doing a thorough assessment of it on the day with the mark one eyeball (a military expression simply meaning 'your eyes').

So I chose to solo the climbs and down-climb the possible abseils, completing the route with the minimum of gear. There are, as with many things in adventurous sports or undertakings, pros and cons for different plans and more than one right answer. If you have the knowledge, experience and common sense to assess these and understand the drawbacks of any decisions you make, then you're halfway to avoiding problems in the first place.

The Cuillins are a maritime mountain range, as, along their entire length, they are never more than a few kilometres from the sea. This, coupled with the extremes of wind and rain normally experienced in the north-west of Scotland and especially in the Hebridean Islands, means that they get more than their fair share of inclement weather and thick, vista-thieving mist. Poor weather can make the traverse not only longer and more difficult, as route finding is harder in the reduced visibility and movement becomes slower over the wet rock and in high winds, but also downright dangerous. At the summits of the mountains, winds can get above 100 miles an hour. As I was planning a summer traverse, I wanted warm, dry, windless weather and watched the meteorological forecast until, in the middle of July 2013, a long, settled period of high pressure sat over the UK and even the Isle of Skye was dry.

I would carry the following equipment:

- buff – to wear as a hat initially as I climbed in the chilly darkness and on any rest breaks I took. It could also be refashioned into a headband to keep the sweat from my eyes in homage to the 1980s.
- sunglasses – it was summer. We've all been sunburned. If that is what it does to your skin, imagine what it does to your eyeballs.
- T-shirt – because no one wants to see a naked man running across a mountain . . . especially one with my pale-blue Highland complexion.

- thin, super-lightweight windcheater jacket – for the early-morning journey to the start of the Ridge, the late-evening return journey from the finish and for any points where the wind picked up, rain started falling or I wasn't moving fast enough to stay warm without it.
- shorts – it was forecast to be a warm day, so I wore a pair of rugged, pocketed trekking shorts to allow a bit more freedom and cooling.
- approach shoes – these are tough trainers with stiffened soles made of the same sticking rubber used in rock-climbing shoes. They are a mix between mountain trainers and climbing shoes and were perfect for a fast summer crossing of the Ridge, where trekking, scrambling and climbing would all be involved. I also put on some cushioned running socks.
- water carrier – I had three litres of water held in what is effectively a tough plastic sack, with shoulder straps so that I could wear it on my back, and a tube which came over my shoulder to act like a giant straw, allowing me to drink on the move. To this I bungeed:
  1. a small roll of zinc-oxide tape, which is great for sticking over hot spots on your feet to avoid them developing into blisters, taping up cuts and scratches, torn nails and even injured limbs like a sprained ankle. It also works as a temporary clothing repair;
  2. a GoPro mini-camera with a mini-tripod (about four inches long) and a small, light, short collapsible pole;
  3. two protein bars and two flapjacks (because you can't go on the mountains without a flapjack);
  4. a mini head-torch . . . always carry a head-torch;

5. a super-lightweight titanium lock knife. Because, like a head-torch, I always carry a knife;
6. a map – essential for finding your way along the Ridge and off it should things go wrong. It's hard to make decisions if you don't have the necessary information. Also, they don't break down or run out of battery;
7. my iPhone – surprisingly, you can get a signal at numerous places along the Ridge, handy in an emergency. It also had a PDF of the route guide on there for my reference.

You may have spotted the lack of a compass on the list. I did not carry a compass because the gabbro rock is magnetic and therefore throws compass bearings off by enough to cause confusion and possibly accidents. Besides, my watch had a good compass on it if I really needed one.

I set off from Bristol for the 600-mile journey north, which would have taken significantly less time had not a German in a huge campervan been doing 20 miles per hour up the A82 where it skirts the bank of Loch Lomond. There are no opportunities to pass for about 20 miles. Finally, after twelve hours and at about eight o'clock at night I crossed the Skye Bridge and made my way along the east coast of the island before cutting inland and turning south, following the road as it drew three sides of a square to avoid the impassable feature of the Cuillins. I was going to start my journey in the south and work my way north, so I parked near the southern end of Glen Brittle and prepared for the day ahead. The weather was incredibly warm and clear and, since I was going to spend the night in my car – or at least the first part of it – I had to construct screens for the windows, using fine muslin and duct tape, so that I could roll them down to let the air circulate but keep the midges out. They were so bad that I cooked using my little gas stove inside the car and only left it to take a speedy pee, the idea being to get out, go and get back in before the midges got me. With my clothes and kit all prepped and laid out, I settled down to get some sleep. It didn't come easy. I was full of anticipation about the following day, and the long summer's evening meant that it was still light well past my intended bedtime, so I got little shut-eye before my alarm sounded at thirty minutes past midnight.

Why, you may legitimately ask, did I choose to rise at such an ungodly hour? In mountaineering, early starts are pretty standard on big mountain days to give you the most daylight to get the job done or in case things don't go to plan and your trip is extended. Sometimes the job is so big that you expect to be coming off in the dark and plan for it, but life's always easier in daylight. I wanted to get the fairly non-technical trek up to the first summit done in darkness, while I was still mentally and physically fresh, so I could make use of first light to start the traverse. I expected it to start getting light by four and not to get dark until after ten at night, so I had a good eighteen hours to complete the route. The other, not insignificant, factor was those bloody midges. The midges tend not to be too bad when the temperature falls, so the dead of night can be a relatively good time to be out. You will also not find them above a certain altitude on the Ridge. But they do love to come out at dawn. So I intended to be well up on the mountains and above that critical altitude before the sun rose and they came out to swarm over me and send me into hypovolaemic shock.

The approach route is a gentle warm-up and I was well on my way by half past two. The early-morning darkness was warm and fresh and, apart from a wrong turning on a path less than five minutes after I started, things were going well. Realizing that dehydration would be a problem on the Ridge, as there is no water source along its length, I took the opportunity to drink as much as I could on the walk from the car. As the pre-dawn light spilled out over the landscape, I passed a little lochan and took the opportunity to refill my water supply from a beautiful cascade, plunging my face into the waters before I set off again for the first summit.

The scramble up to the Ridge was over huge, broken, angular boulders and it was now, employing my hands to move upwards, that I got my first tactile sensation of what gabbro is all about. Gabbro forms when molten magma is trapped beneath the surface of the earth and solidifies as it cools into crystalline rock. And the gabbro here resulted from the volcanic eruptions that formed the Cuillins around the same time the North Atlantic was being born. As well as its anti-compass magnetic qualities it is also an incredibly hard rock, similar to basalt or granite, but it has very large, coarse, sharp grains and crystals, which makes it rough with incredibly good friction. Friction is the friend of the climber, as it helps you to stick foot placements and grip the handholds. However, rock as sharp, rough and coarse as this, although giving phenomenal friction, is so harsh that it begins to shave off skin and make micro-cuts on your fingertips as you climb. Slipping can also cut slashes in the soles of your shoes and falling down on to it is not to be recommended. It's fantastic stuff to climb . . . just not for very long, or at least not until your palms have toughened up. The full-time mountain guides working in Skye must have hands like rhino hide.

I was excited to get up on to the Ridge but held myself back

from sprinting off, as this was an endurance event and knack-
ering myself before sunrise would be a schoolboy error. By
four in the morning, I was at my start point, the peak of the
most southerly mountain in the range – Gars Bheinn. First
light, appearing well before sunrise, spilled out over the range
and I began to appreciate the vastness of the landscape
spreading out on either side of me in shades of iron and indigo.

Now, you'd think of all the timings from the day I would
know my start time and end time with some precision. But,
I'm afraid, perhaps due to excitement or nerves, I forgot to
note the exact time I set off. Off to my right, sea fog hung over
the Loch Brittle bay and everything on the lower ground was
carpeted in white clouds. This soft, flat, white flooring only
served to accentuate the dark and angular Ridge, which
speared up through the mists behind me. I turned and gazed
north, realizing how lucky I had been with the weather. I could
see the entire length of the serpent snake out in front of me
and could even see what I believed to be the final peak set
boldly in the distance. It must be an extremely rare thing to be
able to see the whole of the Cuillin Ridge at one time and I had
been spoiled on my first visit. It was a spectacular sight, hard
to reconcile with its location in the UK, as it seemed more in
keeping with some lost world in South America. It was inspirational. But it looked a very long way across some very serious
ground.

The first section of the traverse is fairly straightforward and
I only had to refer to the guide on my phone for a couple of
tips and hints on the best path to take at certain locations. I
took it steady and let myself warm up to the movement and
flow. I was travelling across the ground faster now that I was
used to the terrain and the light was up but still had to be

careful not to twist a knee or ankle. After summiting the second peak, Sgùrr nan Eag, I scrambled on towards the first of the major obstacles on the route and, by reputation, the hardest and most dangerous I'd face – the TD Gap.

The Thearlaich Dubh Gap is an intimidating slot – a slash in the Ridge that looks as though someone has cut a neat square slice out of the mountain. As you stand on its southern edge, it is not that far across to the northern side and the path on to the next peaks and the highest summit on the range. However, there is no way across the Gap but to descend into it, walk the few metres across the gully floor and climb the facing wall. Of all the graded climbs, this is reputed to be the hardest, although opinions differ on its actual grade, as conditions (whether it is wet and slimy, the wind is buffeting around you, or your fingers are cold), tiredness or the amount of kit you're carrying can affect how hard the climb is and how hard it feels. For climbers used to climbing on crags next to a car park, there's also the extra psychological pressure of being so high and remote.

I got on my hands and knees and peered down the near wall, which I'd have to descend. It was very steep, even over-hanging in sections, and, although the myriad of shattered cracks across its face seemed to promise plenty of hand- and footholds, it looked difficult. It was about seven or eight metres to the floor of the Gap and a hard landing was a promise if any slips occurred. I scouted left and right along the edge to see if there were any easier lines. On the left-hand side, the ground looked gentler but I could see the lower section this way was much looser. I decided to climb down this seemingly easier ground, making sure I could escape back up if necessary. This would give me a chance to get closer to the looser stuff and better assess it. As I reached the halfway point, facing into the rock, I leaned back, extending my arms on two good hand-holds, and craned my neck to look down over my left shoulder.

The stuff beneath me was definitely a bit chossy – poor-quality rock unsuitable for rock climbing as it crumbles under pressure – but it was held together by grass and vegetation that looked as though it had been there a while and which should hold everything together if I was delicate. I chose each hand- and foothold carefully, making sure the others were secure enough before trying the next. I made it down and tra-versed into the centre of the Gap over some horrendously loose rock, but by now I was on a crumbling ledge and it was very easy climbing.

I stood at the bottom of the Gap and inspected the route upwards. Although the sun was up, this space in the mountain was in complete shade and sheltered from any gentle breeze. It was still damp from the night's dew. I made the first few moves to inspect the line and, although wet deep inside any cracks, most of the superficial rock was dry enough. I decided that, as long as I was aware of any deep holds or those in shadow, I would be fine. I actually climbed about half the route leaving behind my camera set up to take a shot every few seconds in order to get some photos of my 'ascent' then had to down-climb to retrieve it and start the route again.

I'm not great at remembering how climbs went or how exactly I did them. Even immediately after I've topped out on a climb and someone asks me how I overcame a particular section or whether I used my right or left foot on that little edge, I'm never very sure. Things always look different from the bottom or the top of a climb to when you're in the moment, scrabbling for the hold or gear placement that will delay that heart-stopping moment when you jolt from stationary into freefall. I do remember that the route was not as difficult as I had anticipated and I never felt out of control or unsafe.

There was, however, one section that was a little damp. I found myself standing before a rounded crack, wide enough for a whole body to sit in sideways. The hand- and footholds were wet and smooth. I felt reticent about trusting them and decided the safer bet would be a full body jam. As its name suggests, this technique requires you to stuff your body into the crack and move upwards. In this instance I went in sideways, leading with my left hip. As I braced my backside against the left-hand wall, I heard a pop and the beginnings of a cracking sound. I realized I had not transferred my iPhone from my left buttock pocket . . . I also felt my foot slip. It didn't ping off, only moved a little. However, it was enough to give me some serious pause for thought. And that thought was: 'Upon reflection, I would rather have a broken iPhone than plummet to my death, which, in all fairness, would also probably do the iPhone even less good.'

So I forced my back and bum hard against the rock, with my feet and hand on the opposite wall, and shifted up. I felt more than heard the phone crack. I shifted up again and grabbed a left handhold above my head before twisting out of the cleft and swinging around and up to face the cliff. I finished the climb off with some straightforward moves. Topping out, I felt great. I had overcome what, according to the various guides and trip reports I'd read, had promised to be the hardest section. I hadn't really struggled on it. It was a nice confidence booster and I wasn't dead. So far so good. Frankly, my iPhone didn't bother me too much. When I took it out of my pocket, I saw the screen was a cracked mess and nearly unreadable. By the time I'd taken a few more photos, it had died due to some battery damage. This left me in a bit of a predicament because my route guide was on the phone and I hadn't printed out a hard copy. Fortunately, though, I'd had the foresight to bring a paper map. There is something very reassuring about a map.

Navigation along the Ridge was very simple in the clear, bright conditions in which I found myself. The heat created a soft haze and made the distant peaks seem almost slightly out of focus. I was able to see the next peak along my journey, so I always knew in which general direction I should head, though the best path to take to get there was not always obvious. I was looking for the fastest, easiest and safest route onwards and this was sometimes unclear. If I made an incorrect choice when there were potential avenues on the left and right, it could mean wasting time having to turn back if I came across a sheer drop. When the course was not apparent, I also had to take extra care, as naively moving ahead with joyful abandon and little appreciation of my surroundings was likely to have me pitching over a cliff to my doom – not that I want to be dramatic or anything. So micro-navigation on the Ridge was very important in staying safe and not wasting too much time. Even wasting time can be dangerous – it can lead to problems as you are expending valuable energy, water and increasing your chances of being be-nighted on the rock.

To reach each of the summits, I decided that the simplest method was best. I stayed on the apex of the Ridge, rather than moving along on a side slope just off the top, and used the Ridge like a visual navigation handrail. This kept things straightforward, since as long as there was no higher ground anywhere but in front of me I had to be on the Ridge. It allowed me the best – that is, the highest – position to see as much of the ground as possible in order to assess what was coming up and to make a decision on any route changes. It meant that I did a bit more technical scrambling or low-grade climbing than was strictly necessary but it was all simple and enjoyable and I prefer to do a bit of engaging climbing to break up the steep treks.

I left the TD Gap behind me and, pausing only to take a photo of myself with the rest of the Ridge casting out before me, made my way towards my next peak and another major landmark – Sgùrr Alasdair. Alasdair is the highest point on the Ridge, at 993 metres above sea level, and lies just east of the main Ridge line. As I scampered up the rocky slope, the sun lit the dew droplets still clinging to the surface of the stone. These looked like frozen beads of water or semi-orbs of glass stuck to the rock. The air was so still I was sure they were solid, but it also seemed too warm for them to be ice. I extended my finger and touched one, convinced it would be unyielding. But as my finger glanced its surface it collapsed and trickled away in a tiny tear. I climbed the last few steps and marvelled at how beautiful it was to be up here on this spot and on this day. You have moments when everything seems stressless, where the air seems cleaner and fresher and easily flows into the lungs. When things feel settled, right and there is a sense of peace. This was one of those moments. But these are often finite spells within greater, harder and more stressful tasks and I had to keep moving. With one final 360-degree spin to appreciate the vastness of the view, I set off down the jagged slope towards the King's Chimney.

The King's Chimney is graded as 'VDiff', an abbreviation of Very Difficult, which sounds a lot worse than it actually is. A VDiff is in reality a lower-grade climb and, contrary to its name, not very difficult at all for an experienced climber. The British Grading System has been around for a long time and started back in the days when enterprising folk would take to the cliffs and crags of Britain in nowt but a thick three-piece tweed suit and a pair of leather hobnailed boots. If they were feeling particularly cautious, they might have extended their arsenal to include a bit of old hemp rope tied around their waists. Under these conditions, I imagine this climb would have been bloody difficult indeed. By today's standards, however, I expected a nice, easy climb to present itself.

However, when I reached the foot of the short section of steep ground that leads up to the ledge where the climb begins in earnest, I felt unsettled. This area was in shadow and felt very cold after the sun-soaked Ridge line. The black rock was still wet and slick with dew that had had no chance to evaporate. A few loose rocks peeled off under my grip as I scrambled to the start ledge feeling less than 100 per cent at ease. I pulled my jacket on, did a full mountain warm-up (gave my arms a quick shake) and set off.

I needn't have been so concerned. The climb is more of a narrow V-shaped corner than a chimney and allows you to use the walls on both your left and right rather than just the one in front of you. This not only gives you more options for holds but also makes climbing more comfortable and feels more stable. Higher up, the rock was much drier than the stuff below and was solid all around. There was a multitude of fine hand- and footholds all the way up, big and reassuring. And, in fact, within moments of starting, the climb had changed in character to feel light and warm, and I paused near the top to extend my tiny camera out on a collapsible monopod to capture the moment. It proved to be one of the most relaxing and enjoyable parts of the entire day and I felt re-energized with enthusiasm to get to the next climb, the most famous of all – the Inaccessible Pinnacle, or the Inn-Pin, as it's known.

As I crossed An Stac, another of the Ridge's peaks, I thought I could make out its distinct but confusing shape on the mountainside of Sgùrr Dearg. The Inn-Pin is the peak of Sgùrr Dearg but it takes a second glance from the right angle for this to become obvious. Just below the mountain's 'summit', the Pinnacle sticks out like a shark's steeply angled dorsal fin. The top of the fin is higher than what would normally be considered the mountain's top and therefore the Inaccessible Pinnacle is the true summit of this mountain. It's a unique shape and something I have never seen before in Britain.

The normal way to tackle the Inn-Pin is by climbing the south-western side at a climbing grade of Moderate, which is the lowest grade for a climbing route in the UK, then to abseil down the more vertical north-eastern face, graded VDiff if one was to climb it. However, as I had no ropes, abseiling was not an option. Down-climbing is harder than climbing up, so the sensible thing would have been to continue north, flanking the Inn-Pin, then turn back on myself and the harder northern section, down-climbing the easier southern part. However, since I was moving south to north this didn't seem quite right to me. It felt right to be moving ever forwards rather than taking easier but more contrived options. So I set off up the narrow fin's more gradual edge and made short work of the summit of what is reputed to be the hardest Munro to bag. It has this reputation because although all the other 281 mountains over 3,000 feet are challenging treks, this is the only one that requires the ascent of a graded rock climb to reach the top. Sir Hugh Thomas Munro himself did not manage to summit the Inn-Pin in his lifetime.

I took a few breaths to once again enjoy the view and look out over the peaks and ridges yet to come. The morning haze was lifting and I could now very clearly see the final summit and all those in between . . . it still looked an awfully long way away and it was difficult to imagine that I could cover the ground in the allotted time. But then I swung around and looked back. I could also see those first peaks that I'd already climbed and realized that, although I was only about a third of the way through, I was making good time and feeling reasonably fresh. Or so I thought.

I clambered off the peak to reach the anchor points that people normally use to abseil down and began my down-climbing descent. I made a lax foot placement – not taking the time to spot and feel it was correct before putting my weight on it – and slipped. Fortunately, when climbing without ropes I am super careful and will always ensure I've at least two good holds before committing entirely to the next. So when my foot slid off I took the weight on my hands and caught myself. It was only about 40 metres to the ground but it would not have been a soft landing and, since I had seen no sign of another living soul since I started the Ridge, it could have been a long time before what was left of me was discovered. Clearly, I was a little more physically and mentally tired than I had thought. I would need to police any further mental complacency or physical laziness.

I continued the climb down until the last six feet, where I couldn't quite work out where to go. I'd obviously gone a bit off-piste, as the final moves seemed a little harder than they should have been for such an easy climb. Under normal circumstances, I'd simply have jumped but the uneven ground was just begging for a twisted ankle and getting down even with only a simple ankle injury can be a major logistical challenge from such a high, steep and remote location. I eventually made it, forced by necessity to make an awkward move. But I was down and making progress ever northwards.

Descending from An Stac took me onwards to cross more peaks with easy treks and scrambles to their summits, passing features such as the Three Teeth, the Wart and the Three Tops of Mhadaidh. None of this proved technically challenging, although I confess to taking the wrong route off one particular peak. I'm certain it was the wrong route, as it twice required me to hang from my fingertips to minimize the length of drop I had to make on to lower ledges. I'm convinced this manoeuvre would have been mentioned in the many guides I'd read before attempting the Ridge.

As I was descending the Three Tops of Mhadaidh, I was feeling the effects of the heat, the effects of my rationed water supply and the effects of nine summits on my legs (and especially my poor knees). But morale was lifted as I gazed upon the Bealach na Glaic Moire. This pass between two of the mountains is, unlike the rest of the Ridge, carpeted with grass. The growth was limited to the small area of level ground but it looked like an alpine meadow. This may be a slight exaggeration, as it was actually more of a dry bog covered in stubby sprigs of green growth than a flower-filled alpine Shangri-La, but it did have sheep. I found this both surprising and surreal given the last few hours of nothing but vertically sided, razor-sharp ridges of hard climbing and huge vistas that did not contain another living animal. The sheep seemed fairly nonplussed and happy to be munching on the limited greenery. As

I jogged past, I appreciated the shock-absorbing capacity of the spongy grass compared to what I had encountered up until then. It was also a delight to be moving on the flat rather than up or down. It didn't last.

The next section to overcome was the traverse of Bidein Druim nan Ramh, which is described thus in the guide I had on my mobile: 'involves some of the most complex route finding of the Ridge . . .' Nice . . . especially as I no longer had access to the notes and diagrams that described how to negotiate this traverse, what with me crushing my telecommunication device between a rock and my left arse cheek.

It actually went reasonably well but it was apparent when I reached this section that pausing often to scout and consider my route choice would be time well spent. I descended into a very steep-sided ravine and became momentarily uncertain if this was the correct path to take until I noticed scratch marks on the rocks made by crampon teeth when mountaineers had passed this way on a winter traverse of the Ridge.

In the middle section, however, I almost became unstuck. I began to descend and was forced to drop down on to some large flat ledges. After doing this for the third time, I realized the final drop had no more ledges and was sheer for about 20 or 30 feet. The wall was slightly overhanging and blank of any features, so climbing down was out of the question. I would have to retrace my steps. When I'd dropped down on to the ledges before, a height of no more than ten feet, I had hung from my arms and dropped that last three feet or so. Climbing back up would not be so easy. I had visions of having to be rescued at great financial expense to the mountain-rescue team and even greater expense to my self-esteem. I had been rather too fixated on pushing on and hadn't really considered the potential cost of my commitment.

I had to make a couple of jumping, awkward and very vulnerable short climbs to get back out of my predicament, followed by an upward crawl on hands, knees and belly along a ledge that was barely a foot wide, which sloped upwards to reach the top. Then I had to look for, find and descend the path I should have taken in the first place. I spotted some abseil anchors and realized that this was definitely the way down. It didn't even require any climbing but was accomplished by a controlled bum-slide down a smooth rock ramp, which was fun but left the backside of my shorts shredded. This was not the first nor the last time my backside has been used as a tool in my climbing arsenal.

Despite the errors, I was on the home straight with just three more peaks to summit. The first, Bruach na Frithe, was fairly straightforward and from its top I could see the final big challenge – the Basteir Tooth. This pinnacle has to be negotiated to reach Am Basteir, the penultimate peak. But before starting the route you need to traverse out over a long drop, so the feeling of exposure and vulnerability is heightened and leads to more psychological pressure. Of course, the other problem was that I was now very hot, weary, on the last few mouthfuls of my rationed water and dehydrated. I felt pretty weak and unenthusiastic as I traversed out to start the climb.

As I made the first move, a piece of rock pulled out and sailed over my head into the drop below me. Not a great start, especially as I was not feeling very comfortable. The Basteir Tooth is only grade VDiff or Severe (one grade higher than VDiff) but it felt like the most difficult route on the Ridge. I considered turning back and using an alternative route to the top on at least three occasions but I was too tired and just wanted to get up there and rest. On awkward, shaky limbs, I finally made it over the final moves of the climb. I felt that, even though I had made it without plummeting to my death, the call to turn back might still have been the right one.

I sat for a minute. I took off and shook my water bag to assess its levels and had my last piece of food. I could have done with a snooze. I had about three or four mouthfuls of water left, so I took two, slung the bag on to my back, picked myself up and carried on towards Am Bastier's summit. This final challenge turned out to be simple and only required a short, easy climb up a cool, shaded chimney (which was a little damp but by that point this was welcome). At the bottom of the chimney, one of the Skye mountain guides had taken a client up and they were just abseiling back down. As he sorted out his ropes and gear, he asked where I'd come from today. I explained I had started at Gars Bheinn.

'What, this morning? On your own?'

'Em . . . well . . . yes,' I answered, wondering if he'd disapprove.

After a quick chat, his final words as we parted were, 'Aye, goodbye and . . . well . . . bloody good effort on today.'

The professional mountain guides working on Skye spend most days in these mountains, summer and winter. It's always nice to get an approving nod from someone whose opinion is really worth something.

With that, I disappeared up the chimney and the last few steps to the top.

I summited the final peak after seven hours and fifty-six minutes. It was by no means a record time but it was respect-able for a first attempt and my first time ever on the Cuillins

. . . and without my reference guide, although I did have the perfect weather conditions on my side.

I took the very last gulp of water and inhaled my surroundings. The Cuillin Ridge, on a day like this, when you can see the full length of this impressive collection of stark and intimidating but wordlessly beautiful mountains, has to be one of the greatest natural spectacles in the UK. They look impressive and otherworldly from the road but the best place to appreciate them is up amongst their jagged peaks and lofty slopes. Sometimes it's better to gaze within a view than to gaze upon it. I can only imagine how much like other great ranges of the world they must look on a clear day in winter when blanketed in snow and ice, and a winter traverse is now firmly on my to-do list.

However, I have to admit to not feeling completely elated as I stood on my final peak. I knew that I still had to walk back to my car.

CHAPTER 6

Britain by Snorkel

This idea arose from giving talks to the general public rather than the outdoor, adventure and diving communities. These were people who were perhaps new to adventure sports and looking for ways to take that first step, especially school and youth groups like my local Scouts. I realized, as I stood before them full of my own importance, waxing lyrically about my last great adventure ('Here I am diving the deepest part of this complex, unexplored cave system using a mixture of helium, nitrogen and oxygen gas in my closed-circuit re-breather diving apparatus . . .'), that my hopeful attempt to inspire them to take up the adventure and exploration baton might be falling short. The gap between the complete beginner and, in this example, technical cave diving was so big that, inspired or not, they were no more able to take that first step. It's a bit like encouraging someone to get interested in astronomy by asking them to listen to Neil Armstrong talk about his big day. Well, perhaps not quite that grand. I'd be a downright idiot to compare my latest jaunt to being the first man on the moon but you get where I'm coming from.

I want people to get out there and enjoy the outdoors. Not only because I want to inspire the next Shackleton but, more importantly, because Britain is a phenomenal place to be out in the wilds. I want to show people that anyone can have an adventure regardless of age, money, skill and degree of free time. I want to show that exploration is just as possible for a twelve-year-old on a Saturday morning as it is for a fully qualified international mountain guide with three months spare and a ticket to northern China. So 'Britain by Snorkel' was born.

I spent most of the summer of 2011 driving the length and breadth of the country. It's surprising how well you can transform a Hyundai Santa Fe into a one-man campervan. In total, I spent eighty days living in my wagon. With the back seats down and flat, I slotted in a cut-down mattress with a pillow and duvet (no need to rough it). I installed a caravan leisure battery and tucked it behind the driver's seat, wiring it to the alternator. This charged the battery as I drove and allowed me to power my laptop and cameras and a small in-car fridge. I cooked on a camping stove and generally treated the car like a luxurious metal tent. It was great: there was no need to put it up or take it down, it was waterproof, wouldn't blow away in even the strongest winds and everything was nice and organized in the various shelves, storage holes and gloveboxes around the place (I'm a bit of an admin fanatic, especially when it comes to kit and trips). And I snorkelled. I was in and out of the water at least twice a day so managed to maintain a reasonable standard of cleanliness in a rustic kind of way. I had some biodegradable eco-soap I could use if I wanted to turn my latest dive site into an al fresco spa. In addition, I'd occasionally hit a gym or climbing wall just to keep my fitness up and have a decent shower. I went from Cape Wrath to Cornwall, from Swanage to Staffa. I snorkelled rivers, lochs, gorges, waterfalls, mountain pools, shipwrecks, aircraft, caves and piers. I snorkelled offshore islands, high-altitude lakes, low-altitude lakes, with seals and sharks, around lighthouses, from boats, from kayaks and even from my bike.

During subsequent talks, I was keen to call it snorkelling and not freediving, which is more difficult and has more technical connotations. However, some of the outings were fairly advanced, including breath-hold dives of over two and a half minutes and other dives inside caves and shipwrecks 70 feet down. But I wanted to show that anyone can pick up some basic kit and go snorkelling, to give the whole project a feeling of accessibility rather than it being for the elite, and to convey that just about anyone can not only have an adventure but also carry out real and genuine exploration.

We have over 20,000 miles of coastline in the UK (depending on how you choose to measure it), about 12,000 miles of river and between 10,000 and 12,000 lakes, lochs and llyns, depending on your definition and who you ask. Only a tiny fraction of the underwater landscape of all this has ever been observed by the human eye and yet the vast majority is explorable with the humble snorkel. However, not all of it is easily navigable. For my own snorkelling quest, I wanted to push myself and investigate some more adventurous locations, hopefully showcasing some level of progression within the sport and what can be achieved with more advanced techniques. But I would still use the same basic kit, and sites would still be reasonably accessible and on home soil.

Some of these projects were quite 'extreme' but some of the best were also among the easiest. The UK's only snorkel trail, at Kimmeridge Bay in Dorset, is a great place to start, especially for young children, and the pier in Swanage was potentially my favourite site of all, so good we snorkelled it twice during the day and then again at night.

Most people think of the sea when they think about diving but in fact Britain has a spectacular diversity of freshwater sites, too. I snorkelled half a dozen different rivers on this project and can thoroughly recommend certain stretches of the rivers Orchy, Etive and Dart. But since this is a book about the less sedate side of life, let me begin by taking you to the River Dee.

The River Dee is the river of my youth. It has the highest origin of any river in the UK. From its birth in the Pools of Dee high in the Cairngorm Mountains it flows through Royal Deeside, past Balmoral Castle and at Aberdeen discharges into the North Sea. It was just down the mountainside from the Pools that I chose to snorkel, a point at which the river is at its most exciting and effervescent – the Linn of Dee. The Linn, which is a deep, steep-sided gorge in the Scottish Highlands, is situated deep in the Cairngorms National Park but is crossed by an old road bridge, opened in 1857 by Queen Victoria, so is accessible to all. The gorge is where the River Dee plunges down a white-water cascade, spins through boiling pools with names like 'the Washing Machine', then flows over rapids before running out into a flatter, wider river, which is more in keeping with its nature over the rest of its journey to Aberdeen. The lethality of jumping into the Linn is rather dependent on how much rain has fallen recently: the more rain the more water, the more water the more impressive the spectacle but the greater the forces involved and therefore the more dangerous the proposition of trying to 'ride' it. I should remind you this is the Scottish Highlands – lack of precipitation has never really been a major issue this far north.

People do scuba-dive it when the power of the water is judged safe but snorkelling it was a more intimidating proposition. This was because I wasn't sure what the water was doing. Any unpredictable down currents or stopper waves, which could pull me down and hold me under for minutes at a time, would not prove a major concern if I had over an hour's worth of air in a scuba cylinder strapped to my back. But if I had only the air in my lungs, and with panic sapping my ability to hold my breath, there would be only moments to attempt an escape. Luckily, the first time I visited the site I was with some people from an Aberdeen dive club who dived the Linn frequently. They judged conditions to be reasonably safe and jumped in for a scuba recce first. The Linn is only a few hundred metres in length, so dives tend to consist of jumping in at the top plunge pool – the Washing Machine – then riding the roller coaster along the river bed, about six or seven metres below the surface, to the shallow water where the river exits the gorge and spreads out. Of course, for your second go on the ride you've got to trudge back up the riverbank in full dive kit, which can suck the fun out of it somewhat.

Ahead of my snorkel, the Washing Machine looked a little frisky and the dark, cinder-brown water was churning up from beneath, writhing like a swollen serpent. As long as I stayed clear of the area directly at the foot of the waterfall, I'd be thrown out and down the river rather than held beneath the falls. So, clad in neoprene and bedecked with mask, snorkel and fins, I leapt into the erupting pool.

I plunge and find the water to be remarkably light and clear, like swimming in peaty whisky, many a man's dream. I feel myself drawn to the outflow of the pool immediately. I speed up as I reach the narrowing where the water flows out of the pool through a deep cut in the wall of this tiny amphitheatre. I see the sculpted walls of the submerged gorge fly past. The flow of the river keeps me from bashing into anything but, even though the underwater visibility is good, I am moving at such speed I feel the same discomfort as I would running blindfolded across a field – even one I know to be empty of obstacles. I am confident all will be well but nevertheless find I have to convince myself of the fact. I feel a drop as the river plunges down an underwater step. It performs like a submerged waterfall. The downward pull is sudden but no more than a metre or so and lasts only seconds. I manage to surface for another breath and spot one of the side pools created by millennia of eddies wearing away the rock. The water within them is still; they are like lay-bys on a busy road. I find it hard to break from the river's current and take a breather in the calm waters.

I dive down and, without the water's movement forcing me onwards, have time to linger on the bottom. This pool is about seven metres deep and I look up at the walls, eroded and carved by the flow of the river. The form reminds me of the rocks of the Sinai desert, scoured and sculpted by the dry winds and blown sands. Perfectly round, smooth bowls have been worn out of the river bed by tiny pebbles spinning in the water over the years like a perpetual pestle and mortar. As I float, motionless and quiet, I see a brown trout off to my left and then an eel. The river appears clean, healthy and full of life. After catching my breath on the surface, I strike back into the current and am immediately swept onwards, diving into the water to fly along the river bed. Drifting with the current, at this speed and this free from the clutter of kit, it is more like flying than diving.

I got the opportunity to return to the Linn of Dee to film a piece for a series on snorkelling in Scotland that I did for the BBC. It had been raining heavily for the previous week and the rain had dragged down silt and soil off the mountains, so the visibility was not as impressive. However, the surface was far more lively than before and the Washing Machine looked more deserving of the name than ever. The high waters churned and rolled in the rock cauldron and it was far too dangerous to enter there; I had to enter at the next pool down. I was filmed doing three runs. We thought we might only require one but I was moving at such speed the camera couldn't keep up. By the third, I'd managed to crack my shin and knee on an underwater ledge and the water levels were increasing along with the ferocity and drag of the currents. We were forced to call it a day. It was a salient reminder that the outdoor environment is not a constant thing and that external factors like weather can completely change the aspect and degree of risk. What is safe on one day can be suicide on another.

Not all white water comes in the form of rapids and I also swam in the plunge pool of High Force in Teesdale, by volume the largest waterfall in Britain. I am trying to avoid the phrase 'Don't try this at home' because, quite frankly, I do want you to try this at home if you have the appropriate skills and experience for the more advanced activities. Otherwise, I'm afraid you'll simply be a footnote in the next run of *The Annual Diving Incident Report* under the heading 'Fatalities'. However, if you can't or shouldn't do something today but want to, then with a bit of effort you can and should do it tomorrow. What's unsafe for one skill level may be perfectly reasonable for another. I say all this here because as I approached the viewpoint by the bottom of High Force I was greeted with a sign at the end of the path, which read: 'WARNING – It is dangerous to enter the water at any time.'

I have no problem with signs like these. They are not erected by the Fun Police to spoil our activities but to save the lives of those stupid enough to think they are more capable than they are. Most people wouldn't dream of swimming in this pool; the sign is not there for them. Strong and experienced wild swimmers and freedivers would look at the current conditions critically and then assess their skill level and take a view as to whether they should enter and what is appropriate and safe. The sign is not there for them either. The sign is there for the people who don't think, either about themselves or about the nature of the environment they are about to enter. As long as you are honest with yourself about your ability, understand the current conditions and apply a little common sense, you will be fine. On that basis, I went for it.

I enter the pool and the water is heavily tinted red-brown, like rusting iron. The bottom is level and the smooth rock is cracked like a badly maintained pavement. The water is remarkably still, which seems incongruous alongside the waterfall. I can see some little caves on the far side split by thin walls and natural pillars and decide to have a closer look. Although I'm swimming across the pool, keeping the falls to my right, I begin at the bottom corner and move diagonally to the far bank. As I swim, I can feel a slight current as I get closer and closer to the waterfall. Halfway across and I am in the middle of the pool. There is now a definite current created by the falls, which is pushing me off to the left, but what is more surprising is the wind. The plunging waters summon an airstream generating from the bottom of the falls that degrades very quickly as you move away from the point of origin. On the bank where I started, the air was perfectly still, now the waters around me are choppy and I feel the cold wind buffeting around my face, even with a hood and mask on. What adds to the intimidating feeling of human insignificance in comparison to an unstoppable force of nature is the noise. Like the wind, like the current, the noise has become tremendous, so much louder than on the shore.

I make it across to the caves but the physical impact on the senses of my closeness to the falls is daunting. I can shelter inside the shallow caves, which in reality are more like mere recesses in the high gorge wall. I feel like a climber taking brief respite from a fierce deluge. I try to swim upriver, in the direction of the falls, to the next cave, only a few metres away. But now I'm having to cling to the rock, finding the best grip on the wet, scoured-smooth stone, and drag myself forward. After ducking into the final cave, I can rest awhile and look upon the face of High Force. It is both menacing and inspiring to be this close to such raw strength. 'Force' is a term used across the north of England to mean a waterfall, usually one of significant size, and it is more than justified here. (I should add that this was July and fairly average in terms of rainfall for the time of year – I can only imagine what it would look and feel like after a wet winter month.)

Still clinging to the rock, I decide that I want to see if I can dive under the waterfall itself and re-emerge on the inside of it, behind the curtain. I hope there is a gap between the wall of water and the rock behind. I am aware I'm not absolutely certain what the water is doing in terms of its sub-surface movement, flow and power, so will investigate cautiously. I release my grip and launch out from the depression in which I've been taking sanctuary. I'm wearing my long, powerful freediving fins and am in reasonable shape but as I force my way forward it feels as though I am tied to the shore by a bungee cord. I throw my arms into the mix, attempting a fin-assisted front crawl. I can hear my panting breath amplified within the snorkel. I can feel the wind whipping the snorkel and the heavy droplets of spray that rain down on my hood like a high-tempo drumbeat. I pop my head up to see how close I am now and find I have barely moved. With an exasperated whimper, I flip on to my back and start kicking. It is much easier to swim hard with fins on when you're on your back. I struggle on but am tiring; this is like doing the 1,500 metres at 100 metres pace.

I am near the edge of the white-water zone, where the plunging falls create a bubbling ring. This is as close as I will ever get. The wind is ferocious now and the roaring bellow of High Force is near deafening, even with my wetsuit hood to muffle some of the sound. With the noise, the wind, the waves and the current, the awesome spectacle is truly intimidating and I can feel my pulse being raised by more than just the extreme physical effort of trying to stay in this location. I quickly dive under and am immediately aware of moving without being under control. I push downwards and am now in total darkness, the feeling of uncoordinated movement is even worse and I'm no longer sure of my location or orientation. I am struggling to hold my breath, having already begun gasping for air, and mentally anxious under the sensory onslaught of proximity to the falls. I am not happy with the situation and quickly surface to find myself bobbing near my original start point on the far bank. As the current ebbs away, I am left in waters that are once again serene and composed. Even in this short distance, the noise reduces and the wind dies away, and the falls merely look impressive rather than overwhelming and frightening. It's amazing what 100 feet or so can do for your perspective on the world.

However, it is not only fast rivers and spewing waterfalls that offer a challenging freshwater venue for the adventurous snorkeller. Because of its lightweight nature, snorkelling lends itself better than scuba diving to reaching those more inaccessible wild places on foot-borne underwater exploration. Nowhere is this better illustrated than in the British mountains, where lofty pools form in rough, craggy ground and are fed by copious, if not continuous, rain and snow melt.

High Chief among these dive sites is Loch Coire an Lochan – the highest lake in Britain. It sits at 998 metres above sea level, just below the dappled summit of Braeriach, the third highest mountain in the UK, in the Eastern Cairngorms. I'd first visited it as part of the Three Lakes Challenge. My plan this time was to mountain bike 12 kilometres along the valley track before trekking three kilometres over rough, boggy, boulder-strewn and very steep slopes to reach my watery goal. I figured it'd be considerably easier without the diving kit this time. But not in this particular instance. Oh no. Instead of a pleasant hike, I had torrential and horizontal rain. The 12-kilometre cycle with cold legs proved more difficult than I expected and the extra weight on my back kept me off balance as I attempted to hurtle along uneven, rocky paths. At one point I was forced to throw myself left into a bog as I lost control, the other option being a near-vertical descent down a cliff on my right. Then came the time to ditch the bike in the heather and start the long climb.

It was a bit of a slog. Thinking I'd make a fell run of it, I'd worn mountain trainers. Not the best footwear to deal with the calf-high heather. I soon found my bare ankles bleeding from a thousand tiny lashes. The slope steepened and became strewn with large, slick-wet boulders as I climbed ever onwards.

I crest the top of the rise and can make out the beginnings of a crater ahead of me. The ground starts dipping away, falling at a gentle gradient. I've been here once before and I know that if I follow it downhill I'll find the loch. It's barely a 200-metre hop amongst the boulders to reach my final destination. The wind whips in gusts around the little bowl of the coire, driving the rain near horizontally into my face. I wipe the water from my eyes and survey the snorkelling site. Bearing in mind it's July, I am still not surprised that at this altitude and on a north-facing aspect there are large patches of snow on the upper slopes of Braeriach and surrounding the waterline of my loch. This does not bode well for the potential pleasantness of my upcoming swim.

I stand for a long moment, the icy winds lashing my exposed face, hands and bare legs. I am not feeling particularly keen on the idea of stripping off what little protection I have. My shoulders drop and I consider for a second the fact that no one is here, no one would know if I don't actually do it. I can make the whole thing up . . . but in that case I needn't have bothered leaving the car. Bizarrely, this is the first time such a thought has occurred to me, and I quickly realize it would be a slippery slope. One little white lie, one tiny exaggeration of events – not exactly a lie, you tell yourself, just an extension of the truth – quickly grows bigger and bigger. Soon you are nothing but a Walter Mitty, a pathetic fake. It's the death of moral courage and personal pride. One must always be watchful for even the slightest signs of surrender to anything short of the absolute.

I shake my head, unhappy but resigned to my fate, and, questioning what the bloody hell I'm doing, peel off my clothes, exposing my pasty-white Scottish skin to the elements so it can begin its rapid discolouration to pale-blue. Climbing into the wetsuit is like ripping off a plaster. I stand there in nothing but my birthday suit and, rather than rush to get the wetsuit on – as would seem sensible – I pause in resigned anticipation of how miserable it will feel. I know that the faster I get on with it the

faster I can be moving again and generating some heat.
Specifically, I can be moving towards my car, its heaters and my
duvet. I even had the foresight to make a flask of cocoa before I
left. Prior preparation prevents piss-poor performance and all
that. So I begin to pull the suit on and it rakes and squeals up
over my skin. There is a lot of 'C'mon!' and 'Yeah, I love it!' and
various other manly and encouraging bellows and roarings as I
dress. Finally, I stand there bedecked in my freediving kit almost
a kilometre above the sea – the absurdity of my current predicament is not lost on me; in fact, I am now keenly aware of it.

'Right then, Torbet, you flaming idiot – get in, get out, then get
off this bloody mountain.'

And with that, and after a few photos to commemorate (i.e.
prove) the event, I wade into the waters. The downpour has
caused a rain-haze over the loch and I can barely make out the
ghostly line of the far bank. The waters are choppy, driven by the
blustering wind, and are an inky-black, reflecting the dark mountain skies. It looks cold. I wade out and feel the chill as the water
seeps through the wetsuit and runs into my boots.

The water was once again the most magnificent bright crystal
blue, bordering on neon. The photos I took show the stunning
shade. It reminded me just how diverse the colour of our
waters can be in Britain. From whisky-golden, charred-red/
brown to pale-indigo, emerald-green and a spectrum of hues
in between. Perhaps I did not pick the best conditions, nor was
the pay-off particularly high, but the sheer challenge, the
adventure, of snorkelling what is arguably the hardest dive site
to reach in the country was still a grand mini-adventure.

But it's not just these lofty snorkelling sites that prove an
attraction. There are wrecks to dive, too. On my first visit to
Red Tarn, England's highest lake, we didn't have time to search

for the remains of the Mosquito aircraft that sank there in 1940. During a training flight, it crashed into Striding Edge, the famous ridge which crests and falls from the summit of Helvellyn in the Lake District, then slid down the side of the mountain before sinking into the lake. When we'd reached Red Tarn as part of the Three Lakes Challenge, I had been tired, cold and it was the middle of the night, so I'd seen nothing of this underwater world. This time, after a short, sharp hike up the hill from the car park, I donned my wetsuit and snorkel kit and struck out for the far side. This was where I'd been told the remains of the old Mosquito lay. Apparently, it was located at a depth of between six and sixteen metres, depending on who was answering the question. However, they could all be right, as after a number of unsuccessful investigations into the cold mountain water I finally found pieces strewn from about fourteen metres up to about eight. Pieces of fuselage, fuel tanks and some struts were scattered about the sloping lake bed. The waters were an incredibly vibrant green and seemed to glow with a milky emerald radiance, like a ghost from an abandoned nuclear plant. It struck me, as I surfaced in the gigantic grey-green amphitheatre of Striding Edge, that the first plane I had ever dived was with a snorkel . . . in a lake . . . on a mountain.

No snorkelling of the British Isles is complete without a swim in Loch Ness. This is the largest single collection of freshwater in the UK. You could empty every lake in England and Wales into it and still not fill it. At its deepest point, it is nearly 800 feet straight down. I arrived there on an overcast, wet afternoon not untypical of a Scottish summer and couldn't really muster the energy for the third dive of the day. I decided to have a relaxed evening, taking a drive around the loch and finding a shady place to park up for the night. When the sun did finally rise the following morning, the weather had only deteriorated and I sheltered under the door of my boot to get dressed in my wetsuit. Having parked near the shore, I crossed a field to a jetty in Urquhart Bay, named after the vast but now ruined castle that sits on the banks of Loch Ness and features in so many photographs. I didn't use the jetty but slithered down the wet grassy banks into the cold, forbidding waters.

I'm not a man to let my imagination or primeval instincts run away with me but as I swam the mile or so out into the centre of the water it was hard not to let paranoia overtake me. Why swim out there at all? Well, the visibility is very poor in Loch Ness due to the dark, peat-stained waters. It's like the strongest tea ever brewed. So there wasn't much to see and I thought it might make a nice story if I went 'monster hunting' with my snorkel. However, in the middle of this vast ebony water, with hundreds of feet more of even blacker water beneath me, I felt very, very exposed and vulnerable. I threw my legs in the air and, head first, swam down into the depth. After only a few metres, I was in a void of absolute darkness and, because it was daytime, had not brought a torch. And there I hung, for maybe only a minute, staring into nothing, devoid of light. But I could feel the depths below me and felt a very long way from shore. Those tales from my childhood about monsters of the deep or of kelpies (which, if you're Scottish, are magic spirits that inhabit watery areas and often take the form of black horses or bulls) came flooding back. And then, of course, there was Nessie, often thought of as a kelpie. And in the old stories, Nessie and the kelpies are not always benevolent spirits and have often dragged unsuspecting people, including children, to their watery graves in the dark abyss. The fairy stories I grew up with were less Disney and far more Grimm.

So, as I hung in the Stygian gloom, I said to myself, 'Bugger this, I'm going home.'

I swam back to shore at a considerably less leisurely pace than on the way out.

So let us move now to the British coast. I wanted to go shipwreck hunting. I've covered the search for unknown and undived shipwrecks deep under the ocean in a later chapter but this time I was looking at what could be achieved with just a snorkel. By their very nature, ships tend to get wrecked on parts of the British Isles known as high-energy zones. That is to say they experience a lot of waves and wind action, i.e. they get battered a lot by the sea. Usually, the shallower the water the greater the sea's destructive force. Therefore many of the shipwrecks that are reachable by riding a snorkel down are in a fairly poor state, with perhaps an intact boiler to be found and a debris field of metal bulkhead plates. Generally, the site resembles the wrapping paper on a living room floor on 25 December . . . unless your entire family is made up of those people, like my gran, who remove the wrapping paper carefully so it can be used again next year. There are some great examples of these storm-torn wreckages of our maritime history within the reach of even the novice snorkeller. Freediving is the best way to open up the possibilities and even allow you to penetrate inside these wrecks on a single breath – but it's not advisable if you're inexperienced, in which case you need to use scuba gear. After two World Wars and a long history of folk working the waters around our island nation, we have these sites in abundance.

My first wreck of the project was the HMS *Port Napier*, which lies in the Kyle of Lochalsh between Skye and the mainland. The Second World War minelayer caught fire and sank in 1940 and now lies on its (right-hand) side. Incidentally, the word starboard comes from the old term 'steer-board', where the wooden plank used as a rudder would jut out to one side. Not wanting to smash it against the wall of the harbour, sailors would bring their ship into port with the opposite side next to the port wall, hence port side. Every day should be a school day.

The wreck of the *Port Napier* is a perfect snorkel because in all but the highest tides its upper parts break the surface. Even beginners, if they can get a boat out to it, can swim amongst the full 150 metres of its intact length. However, the real interest lies deeper.

I breathe up on the surface. This is a method used in freediving to extend the length of the dive. It consists of calming the mind and body, trying to reduce the heartbeat, taking long slow breaths, filling the lungs first from the stomach, then the chest, before inhaling one final lungful. This is the simplest of the freediving exercises that can be done in preparation and, with regular practice, can allow anyone to hold their breath for minutes at a time. Of course, lying still and holding your breath is not the same as doing it under the physical stress of swimming underwater nor with the extra mental stress of being many tens of metres underwater inside the bowels of a shipwreck. I can hold my breath for over four and a half minutes lying still but I'd never normally spend even half that time finning around underwater.

EXTREME ADVENTURES

I duck-dive down, a technique where, whilst lying prone on the surface, I thrust the top half of my body vertically down, bending at the waist, then pick my legs up vertically, too, so that my whole body points downwards, head first, and my legs are above the water. The weight of my legs pushes me into the water and drives me down. I have weighted myself with lead around my waist to compensate for the buoyancy of my wetsuit, so that after about eight metres – reachable after my duck-dive with only a few long, slow, efficient fin kicks – my wetsuit is compressed enough that I become negatively buoyant.

As a diver descends, the increase in pressure squeezes the air from the foam rubber suit they're wearing and it becomes less buoyant when the uplift from the suit equals the sinking drag of the lead weights. Then they are neutrally buoyant and should float. Above this depth the suit will exert more upward lift and if the diver does nothing they will move upwards to the surface. Below this depth the suit is compressed too much and does not provide enough lift and the diver will sink. So I plan on being neutral at around eight metres, which means I only have to swim down to this depth and after that can relax and passively sink the rest of the way. Of course, it also means I will have to swim back up to eight metres in order to start floating and get a free ride up to the surface.

For now, I am sinking. Sinking is good on the way down, as it uses less energy, which means a longer breath-hold dive.

I pass through a hole in the hold and enter the inside of the ship. The world goes black as I swim into an enclosed space and my eyes adjust to the low light. I can see light coming from somewhere ahead and swim on through the ship. I see a green window up ahead, where the light travelling through the sea creates a green glow through any opening, and I make for it. Squeezing through a small, kelp-covered opening I pass into the final dark room and see bars across my 'window'. I am still confident about getting out, even if I have to swim back the way

I came. I have enough breath left in my lungs to make it. Fortunately, the window, the space between the bars, is huge and the bars themselves are the old girders that extend across the deck. Because the ship now lies on its side, the deck has become this wall in front of me. The girders are at least two feet apart and I can easy slip through them.

I have been under for over two minutes now and I am about 16 metres below the surface. I twist as I exit the ship and begin to ascend, looking back at it in the shafts of sunlight that spear the water. I pause to inspect the old wooden decking, preserved and intact, although thankfully it has rotted away in places to create the hole, the window, through which I've just swum. I break the surface after over two and a half minutes underwater and the first lungful of fresh air is a rush. I make sure to take a few shallow breaths before sucking up a fulfilling, chest-inflating inhalation. It feels good to breathe. Freediving gives you a new appreciation for one of the simplest but most essential biological mechanisms, which we usually take for granted.

The ship is huge, with more holds, broken masts prone across the seabed and even torpedo tubes capable of fitting a man inside. I take another breath and descend back into this submerged piece of history.

Wrecks are great to dive. There is something endlessly fascinating about swimming around a sunken ship, which is so out of place under the sea, regardless of how mundane its back story. I think it harkens back to adventure tales from our youth. And of course, for those more interested in wildlife than hulks of man-made metal scrap, they are also abundant artificial reefs often containing more biomass and diversity than any neighbouring shoal.

But some wrecks make even more challenging venues to explore. The HMS *Scylla* is a Royal Navy frigate that was deliberately sunk in order to create an artificial reef and is observed and maintained by the Plymouth Marine Aquarium. It has attracted an abundance of wildlife over the years and the bulkheads have become thickly encrusted with marine growths, soft corals and kelp. This metamorphosis from steel warship to marine jungle has also attracted the critters found along and under our shores, from crabs and lobsters to a vast diversity of fishes. (Yes, the plural of fish in this instance is fishes. An example should make it clearer: one salmon is a fish, three salmon is a group of fish. But three salmon, three trout and three bass is a group of fishes – that is, the plural of fish, if the group is made from more than one species, is fishes.)

This wreck attracts divers from all over the UK not only because of the vast abundance and assortment of nature but also because the wreck is completely intact. Its sinking was carefully done to retain the integrity of the vessel, so it makes a fantastic playground where you can explore the inner parts of the ship.

Penetrating a shipwreck can be potentially hazardous; the greatest risk comes from losing one's way. Unfortunately, people have died in shipwrecks and one of the most common causes is silt. Entry into, through and around a corridor or room inside these metallic labyrinths can be a straightforward affair when visibility is good and a diver can see the shape of the surrounding environment. But a loss of control in an enclosed space where every surface is coated in deep, fine sediment can be disastrous. The silt quickly spreads like an omni-directional avalanche around the diver, instantly blinding and disorientating them. It may take hours, or even days, for the sediment to settle back down. However, a diver's gas supply will not last this long. If they cannot find the exit and get back to the surface, the panic rises, the breathing rate sky-rockets and they will quickly use that gas supply up. At that point, I'm afraid there is only one outcome. Much like cave diving, divers can lay line to follow in a case of a silt-out, or they can ensure they are correctly orientated and aware of their situation and the layout of the wreck, but all this takes experience. The *Scylla* is a safer wreck than most, as before it was scuttled, and knowing that it would become a diver attraction, the doors and windows were all removed to make access and, more importantly, egress much easier. As well as this, any cable, chains, ropes or other entanglement hazards were removed. However, as proven by the fatalities inside ship-wrecks including the HMS *Scylla*, diving into a complicated network of steel passageways and cabins, where a direct exit into the clear water is not always obvious or possible, is to be done with due care. With this in mind, it was my intention to freedive through the wreck on a single breath.

The conditions on the day we'd chosen to dive the wreck were far from ideal. I was joined by Dan Bolt, a gifted under-water photographer who, diving with only a snorkel, has captured some amazing images and won numerous competi-tions. We'd done a lot of freediving together by that point and were happy that this was within our capabilities. The problem was that the winds were higher than expected and the surface was choppy and confused. This may not seem like a huge problem but it takes effort in these conditions to keep your position in the water and to keep your head clear enough to converse and breathe. This means that when you resurface you never get a chance to relax and properly catch your breath from the previous dive and therefore freediving becomes much harder. However, these were the conditions we had, so, rather than abandoning the whole show, we thought we'd have a bash.

We planned on doing a couple of warm-up dives, just to the top of the wreck, to get a feel for the depth, underwater visibility and conditions, and to ease ourselves into the environment. We lay face down on the surface and breathed up. The main component of a pre-freedive routine is relaxing. There are all manner of yogic, meditative breathing techniques that help at the highest levels and when attempting big single dives. On days like this, where I'm out in the stormy English Channel doing twenty-plus dives on the trot, I keep the prep basic and just relax as much as possible between dives in order to recover quickly and get my breathing under control. Of course, it was more difficult that day in the wash, waves and slop. I breathed up, filled my lungs, bent at the waist, kicked my legs high and straight and plunged downwards. At around the eight-metre mark, I stopped kicking my fins and began to drift downwards. Sinking. Out of the bright-blue haze of the sea I began to see shadows, then the shape of a ship began to form beneath me.

I glanced across and spotted Dan on my right and slightly beneath me making for the roof of the bridge of the ship. I joined him there and we could tell from each other's body language, without signalling, that we were both well. The ship has changed dramatically in the time since its initial sinking and, although it has retained the same shape and form, every square inch is now covered in marine growth – algae, kelp, anemones, sponges, corals and a myriad of static beasties. Swimming and crawling through all this were pollack, wrasse, crabs and conger eels. I swung my gaze back to Dan and only caught a glimpse of his heels as he slithered through the bridge window and into the frigate's control room. This hadn't been part of the plan but we were both clearly feeling relaxed and I followed him in.

The inside of the bridge was clearer of life, especially kelp, and therefore it was much more obvious that we were in a man-made room. There were numerous windows, all with the glass removed, and even an opening in the ceiling, so we had choices about where to make an easy, fast exit. The walls were brown and orange with rust, not surprising in this salt-water environment, but over this, in patches, was a layer of red and orange sponges and the white of the dead man's fingers soft corals. What surprised me was the distinctness of the pale-blue floor covering, a kind of dimpled-rubber, non-slip matting.

Still feeling fresh but approaching the minute-and-a-half mark, we decided to head back to daylight and fresh air but we took a circuitous route through the passageway that ran from the back of the bridge. This corridor hit a T-junction. No light was visible. No exit was obvious. Swimming into the darkness, I judged how easily I could spin around in the narrow labyrinth in order to retrace my steps if I found my way ahead blocked or too confusing. I moved forwards slowly, as I could not see well enough to be sure of what was ahead of me and did not want to waste air by smacking my forehead against a steel bulkhead. Forward, right, forward and still in blackness – but my eyes could now make out a grey light coming from ahead. As I swam on, it changed from dark-grey to a lighter shade and I finally turned a left-hand corner and saw the blue-green lighted window, framed by metal blackness, and kicked out. I glided towards it, arched my back and kicked upwards. In freediving, everything needs to be relaxed. Impatiently kicking or panicking does not help you. You'll be more comfortable taking a slow, steady ride to the surface than a fast and frantic one, even if the latter has you topside sooner. The light increased and seemed dazzling when we surfaced, a little over two minutes after plunging down. I turned to Dan, spat out my snorkel and smiled.

The greatest pleasure from this snorkelling project was that it gave me an excuse to visit corners of the country I would normally never see. Not only the vast diversity of underwater environments but spectacular and beautiful panoramas and natural phenomena that most inhabitants of the British nation don't even know about, let alone visit. Although I've only given a few of the more extreme examples in this chapter, my 'Britain by Snorkel' adventure – spread over eighty days and 140 dives in 132 different locations – sums up the philosophy of *Extreme Adventures* better than any other challenge. Namely, that Britain is a vastly more varied place, in possession of epic landscapes, with a greater potential for adventure and genuine exploration than we appreciate. And with the right tools and skills we can achieve an enormous amount without ever leaving home.

CHAPTER 7

Inside the Blowhole – An Experiment in White-Water Diving

I had the idea after freediving in the Linn of Dee – the steep-sided, narrow gorge that the River Dee surges through in spectacular fashion, and with even greater gusto after rainfall, which, in the Cairngorms, is no rare event. I'd likened the experience to white-water diving and thought I might have invented a new sport.

Diving is not an activity normally associated with adrenalin. Even the extreme forms – cave diving or deep-mixed-gas diving (using special mixtures of helium, nitrogen and oxygen to make cocktails of gases that are safe to breathe at depth) – although extremely serious and potentially very hazardous, come packaged with a continuous low-level mental pressure and a long-term anxiety as opposed to the sprinting surge of excitement one would get whilst kayaking over a waterfall. So I decided to look into the sorts of environments where I could put my new sport to the test. I considered waterfalls and rapids, overflows and seabed anomalies, but for the inaugural outing I decided on a blowhole.

There are two types of blowhole: the biological and the geological. The former is the opening through which marine mammals like whales and dolphins respire. A geological blowhole is where the wave action of the sea has worn away a horizontal tunnel in a cliff. Eventually, because of natural weaknesses in the rock, it begins to erode the roof of the tunnel at the very back, eventually exploiting any flaws to break out into the cliff top above. What it leaves you with is, in essence, an 'L'-shaped tunnel inside the sea cliff with the horizontal tunnel underwater and open to the sea and the vertical shaft rising upwards through the rock and opening up on the ground at the top of the cliff. In calm conditions, these formations simply allow the water to move slowly through the lower tunnel, with the level rising and falling slightly inside the vertical shaft. However, when storms hit, their character changes completely and they begin to earn their name.

I visited various blowholes around the UK. Some had tunnels that were never fully submerged, so you could kayak through them. Some were so small that swimming into them would have been possible but the opening at the top of the vertical shaft was so diminutive that I'd simply have got stuck and struggled to return along my entry route. I did, however, find one that fitted the bill.

Just outside Abercastle, on the western coast of Pembrokeshire in Wales, is a blowhole that suited me perfectly. I first went to visit it with my friend Fin, an aptly named Irishman who as well as being a diver is also a ninja-surfer and an ocean yacht-master, so knows a thing or two about waves and water. We chose a calm day and an early start had us down the M4 and all the way to Pembroke for low tide. The blowhole is on a little 'island' cut off from the mainland at high water but accessible by a causeway that is uncovered as the tide lowers. Fin had dived it years before and on this serene day we managed to find the entrance on the seabed at a depth of only about eight metres from the surface. It was great to have the opportunity to recce the dive site on such a benign day when the waters were calm and still. I could get an appreciation for the dimensions and try to spot any specific hazards and landmarks that I wouldn't be able to see when the storms hit.

It's billed as a fairly easy dive, so I was surprised that within a few metres the light is extinguished and you find yourself in total darkness. It was unexpected that on such a short stretch of tunnel, one with openings at either end, and on such a sunny day, there was an area of total darkness. And neither of us had brought a torch. We swam on, using the seabed and walls of this narrow fissure to guide ourselves by touch until we eventually reached an illuminated area after finning about 15 metres inside. On looking up, I could see a circle of light above me and we surfaced inside a beautiful cave with walls that went near vertically up to a large oculus and the blue of a clear sky beyond. I noted from my position, floating at the waterline, that it would be an impossible climb out even in these calm conditions, as the walls were not only smoothed by the repetitive actions of the sea but slippery wet and slightly overhung all the way around. With this better understanding of the cave, we submerged, swam back through the tunnel and, exiting through a green window at the end, returned to the Irish Sea and to shore.

*

I then spent some considerable time waiting for the right weather in order to make an attempt in true blowhole conditions. It's ironic that most of my projects in the last few years have been unavoidably delayed because of the record-breakingly atrocious weather we've been experiencing. For this project, in order to dive through a 'blowhole' as opposed to a 'hole', I needed a big swell and high winds. I needed an Atlantic storm. So I waited.

I kept an eye on various Internet weather-forecast sites but the most important is magicseaweed.com. This is primarily a surfers' website and gives details on waves. It was waves pounding against the cliff that I'd need to create the blowhole effect. With some advice from Fin, I monitored wave height and period – the length of time between each wave. It is this latter data which is more telling about the size of a wave and how much power it will have. It also gave me an indication of the window I'd have between the biggest sets of waves to get from the cliff top and into the sea.

The plan was to set up two ropes on top of the sea cliff. The first would drape over the edge of the cliff and drop directly into the water above the seabed where the entrance to the blowhole was located. I would then get kitted up, abseil down the side of the cliff – trying to time it so that I minimized the battering I'd inevitably take from the incoming surge – hit the water, unclip from the rope and descend towards the relative safety of the seabed. Once on the bottom, I'd orientate myself in the pummelling surf, find the entrance and make my way in.

I was under no illusions that swimming through an active blowhole would be straightforward. The motion inside would be incredibly strong and the sea would constantly rush in and out, dragging me inwards then hauling me back out again. But if I could ride the inward push and hang on to the rocks and boulders on the sea floor while the current dragged back out, I should be able to make progress. Then, when I finally made it into the vertical shaft I could surface, in what would no doubt be a storm of white water, grab the second rope I had dropped into the blowhole, and ascend the rope whilst at the same time being thrust upwards by the next 'blow'. Simple. But nothing is ever that simple.

As I waited for the weather to deteriorate, I researched previous examples of blowhole diving around the world. I could not find – and still have not managed to find – one example of anyone trying to scuba-dive through an active blowhole. I also decided to make a short film on the endeavour using the search for the animals that live in the blowhole under these extreme conditions as, if I'm being honest, the excuse for carrying out the stunt. But there is a valid point to make here on the nature of the wildlife inside the blowhole. Many animals use the blowhole as a refuge, even in the stormiest seas when the system becomes a tumultuous maelstrom. Creatures like velvet swimming crabs, shore crabs and northern prawns all seek sanctuary inside, since their predators simply cannot enter the blowhole when the water movement is so fierce. Ironically, this seemingly boiling cauldron is in fact, for these animals, the safest place on the coastline.

Eventually, the charts showed conditions that would be suitable and I mustered my team. It was a cold winter's day on the wild west coast of Wales when we arrived, with winds of over 60 miles an hour and waves of up to 22 feet. I watched from the opposite side of the bay as the waves struck the point from which I'd be abseiling and their frothy plumes raced high up the cliff face, almost breaching the top. I realized that even the abseil was a robust proposal. I began to organize my equipment as we waited for the tide to drop low enough to walk the equipment over to the island. Although the water temperature was likely to be a chilly eight or nine degrees Celsius, conditions in which I'd normally wear an insulated drysuit, I decided to wear a wetsuit. It would be more robust than a drysuit, as the seven millimetres of foam rubber the suit offers would give some degree of protection against the pummelling I was likely to take. The sacrifice was that a drysuit, with the correct amount of fleecy layers underneath, is significantly warmer. On top of this, I'd sourced a set of motocross body armour to further protect against the bangs and scrapes as I was tossed around inside the blowhole. And, to cap it all off, I wanted to wear a helmet for very obvious reasons. Being knocked out or even dazed for a few seconds is not life threatening on the surface but could prove fatal underwater in these conditions.

I had initially opted for a motocross helmet, too. It was possible to fit my mask on inside it and the mouthpiece from my scuba cylinders also fitted underneath. It would protect me from blows to all sides, including frontal strikes to the face. I had already tested all my equipment out in a swimming pool to see what, if any, tweaks and alterations were necessary. But I ride motorbikes and therefore should really have known during this kit test what would happen next.

Motorbike helmets provide protection with a thick layer of compressible foam between the outer shell and the inside. Foam floats. In fact, it is very buoyant indeed, as I discovered when I stepped off the edge of the swimming pool. I hit the water and, as the weight of the kit around my body dragged me under, I was left hanging from my chinstrap, choking and dancing the Tyburn jig as the helmet remained robustly floating on the surface. A kit rethink was in order. In the end, I wore my cave-diving helmet, which is really just an old canoeing helmet with a couple of bungees on either side to hold torches, and I screwed a cricket face guard to the front to stop me losing teeth should I face plant into an underwater obstacle.

I also decided to side-mount my scuba cylinders rather than have them on my back. I intended to wear two bottles, which was unnecessary at this shallow depth but allowed me a back-up should one malfunction. I was unsure of just how powerful or turbulent the water inside the blowhole would be, so had no idea how long it would take me to remove myself from a situation should something go wrong – and I'd rather have too much breathing gas than not enough. Having the tops of the cylinders held against my chest and under my arms also meant that I could protect the valves, as a serious blow to them could cause a catastrophic loss of gas and failure of the system – not great when you're trapped underwater with no idea which way is up, let alone out. The side-slung system also positioned my centre of balance in a more manageable place for manoeuvring on a rope compared to back-mounted cylinders. This would be key during the abseil-descent and climbing-ascent phases of the operation.

On top of all this diving equipment, I also had the two ropes and the climbing equipment that would allow me to set up the ropes and descend and ascend in one piece. Although friends had come to help, I always prefer to go through all my equipment myself. If you've checked it yourself, you've no one else to blame when it all goes horribly wrong. If you're in a bad place and you desperately need a piece of emergency equipment to work, you want to be 100 per cent certain it will, and you need to know where to find it. Psychologically, 99 per cent confidence might as well be zero.

We sat and waited for the tide to lower and uncover the causeway but it was taking much longer than I'd predicted. In the UK, we get two high tides and two low tides roughly every twenty-four hours. So that gap between a high and a low is about six hours. For some reason, I had assumed the causeway would become uncovered about halfway through this drop and become covered again halfway back up the rise in tide, thereby allowing me a six-hour window, three hours either side of low tide. I'm not sure why I made this assumption but it was wrong. The causeway finally broke the surface about an hour and a half before low tide but was still being swept by breakers coming in off the sea. By the time it was open to foot passengers, we'd have barely a two-hour window to do the dive and get back. We rushed to make multiple journeys to carry over the equipment and I began searching for suitable anchor points for my ropes. The wind at the top of the cliff was incredible and just standing up became a battle, forcing me to move around on all fours. I kept monitoring my watch, aware my window was closing. I managed to find some strong and reliable places to affix my ropes so I could run them over the cliff and down into the blowhole. And so, in order to feed in the rope, I looked down the blowhole.

I'm sure there are many expressive, even poetic ways to describe what I saw, which would convey the raw energy produced by the blowhole, but what crossed my mind was: 'It's like a giant, violent toilet on a permanent flush.' Water spun and boiled at the bottom of the shaft, fierce and explosive. The level would suddenly drop away before crashing 30 feet upwards and spraying out. The noise was an intimidating roar, a thrashing of white water, and I looked back up into the faces of Fin and my cameraman Dan. Dan just laughed and shook his head, saying, 'You wouldn't catch me going down there.'

Fin was taking it a bit more seriously and did not look happy. 'I don't know about this, mate.'

I was unusually silent for a while. 'Hmm,' I finally conceded. 'This may be a borderline call.'

I had not seen the blowhole under these conditions and was not expecting how much the intimidating noise, the power and the feel of being out on the edge in such high winds and big seas all around would affect me. I looked at my watch and we had an hour to go. Both Dan and Fin thought we were short on time and I already felt rushed. I walked over to the very edge of the cliff and stood buffeted by the wind and seaspray, playing it out in my mind.

'This is what I do. This is my job now, the career and life I'm trying to carve for myself. I've made commitments, wasted the time of my friends on this. I'm speaking at the Dive Show in a couple of months and have already told them this would be part of the talk. This is my niche, this is why the sponsors invest, people read the articles, listen to the talks – they want to hear about extraordinary things. I need to get this done . . . But not today.'

I have always taken calculated risks but this time I had miscalculated a number of factors. There are things worth risking your life for. This was not one of them.

I turned and walked back to the group.

'I messed up. We're out of time. Get the kit back to the cars. I'll make sure I'm happy with the ropes and the kit I need for next time and note where everything goes. If I crack on now,

I'll have to rush it. I don't have the time and if I tried, I'd make a mistake. I'm sorry.'

Of course, no one seemed bothered. We filmed some more topside footage and they all affirmed it was a good call and that they'd still enjoyed the day out and were well up for coming again. Which was all great to hear but did little to alleviate the weight of failure I felt. However, I did not and do not regret the decision; you should never try to second-guess a decision you made out in the thick of it from the comfort and safety of a cosy armchair.

So I returned home and continued watching the weather, waiting for the right conditions.

I had committed to a speaking engagement at the Dive Show in London in February and had told the organizers that my talks would consist of some UK-based diving adventures. This being one of them. Of course, I had thought the idea of getting storms in winter a pretty safe assumption but time ticked on and the seas around Abercastle remained relatively calm. Eventually, I saw a window five days before the show.

There was very little about my plan that I could amend – it was, after all, pretty simple. My equipment, too, I assessed as still being up to the job. But now I had a better appreciation of what lay in store and had wound my mind around it, focusing on what I needed to do and what would be required of me. Even though little had changed, I felt far more prepared. There is an age-old military saying that goes like this: 'Time spent in recce is seldom wasted'. And although I had scouted out the blowhole under benign conditions it was not until I had seen it in all its power and glory that I had truly understood the task.

I knew I somehow had to increase the amount of time I could spend getting equipment to the island and setting up. For this, I had a new plan. So, before the causeway was uncovered, Fin and I donned drysuits – a thick rubber suit that, as its name suggests, is sealed at the neck and wrists and keeps the wearer dry. We loaded everything into two huge 160-litre drybags, tied them to us by short leashes and swam out through the surging surf. By the time we reached the shallows, we were in hysterics. Having fought our way through some six- to eight-foot waves while trying to surf on the back of our giant, inflatable, sausage-like bags, we were then hit by the same waves, which caught the huge sacks and dragged us and them back, dumping us painlessly if unceremoniously back in the sea. Eventually, wet, snotty, a little battered and still laughing, we hauled ourselves out. After stripping off our drysuits to reveal normal climbing clothing underneath, we scampered up the steep side of the island and began unpacking.

Now I knew the exact layout and conditions I set to work quickly and efficiently. The lines were secured and run out to their drop points, my dive kit was sorted through, assembled and laid out ready to don. By this time, the causeway was clear and Dan had made it across with the camera kit and my friend Raz, who had come along to direct. I have learned that self-directing films is easy enough when the subject is straightforward but when I am attempting things of a technical, difficult and dangerous nature I usually work up the story and style with someone like Raz and then hand the responsibility over to them on the day. This allows me to focus on the important part of the day: i.e. not getting too dead.

I checked the conditions nearer the edge. The weather report for the day had said there would be winds gusting up to

65 miles an hour and waves up to 28 feet. The conditions seemed, if anything, slightly less serious than last time but I think, in retrospect, this was due to my greater degree of mental preparedness. However, they were by no means gentle and I was still struck by how intimidating the waters looked.

I asked Fin for his opinion on what the waves were doing. He turned to me: 'I've been watching the sets, trying to time the periods between each set of big waves. Normally, I'd expect about three big waves to come one after the other with about eighteen between them. Then maybe a minute or more before the next set of three.'

'And?' I asked.

'These don't seem to be following much of a pattern . . . Basically, I've no idea what they're doing.'

And therein lay the problem with this little venture. What I do is often perceived from the outside as foolhardy or down-right suicidal and more than once I've been accused of having a death wish. In fact, the opposite is true, which I think is evident from the fact that I put myself into these situations and don't die. I must be making a great deal of effort to keep myself alive. I take risks. I'd be a fool to try to convince anyone that many of the activities I undertake don't carry some element of danger, but I spend a lot of time making sure that it is mini-mized. Cave diving is always a good example to use. It is seen as a hyper-dangerous pursuit but, if conducted with the right training, kit, plan and attitude, can be very safe. I have com-pleted hundreds of dives and returned in one piece. In fact, a flooded cave is actually a very benign, controllable environ-ment if you know what you are doing. The real danger in cave diving is psychological. The idea is to assess the risk, to ensure you have identified every factor and its consequence accurately. Once you understand all the things that could go wrong, all the worst-case scenarios, you then adjust your plan or equipment to cope with this in order to allow yourself a very good chance of survival.

In this example of cave diving, one of the potential problems could be that my diving cylinder has a catastrophic failure – so I carry a spare. If my torch goes out, I am blind – so I carry two spares. If I get lost, I have a line that will lead me back to the entrance even in total darkness. If I get tangled in my line, I carry two cutting tools. Having cut my line, how do I get out? I carry a compass and map my way in and follow this until I pick up the line again on the far side of the cut. The entire plan is not based around exploring the cave. That mission is actually the second priority. The plan is based around making it out alive no matter what. *That's* the main goal. I undertake these projects with a full, critical understanding of what can go wrong and what to do about it. But the problem with *this* project was that I really had no idea what I was facing and therefore no idea what to do about mitigating the unassessable hazards. I felt a little out of control. It happens, especially when climbing a difficult route and more so when climbing on esoteric cliffs, but it was unusual for me to feel so vulnerable and lost on a diving project. I could hit the water and find that it was easy to swim through, clip the rope, climb up and the whole thing be a complete anticlimax, unworthy of retelling. Or I could hit the water and never be seen again. I was nervous.

I hesitantly began kitting up, double-checking every item. I also decided to make a few adjustments to the design of my gear. I removed one of my diving cylinders. This left me with no redundancy should the single one I now had become damaged. I'd never normally consider diving without some form of redundant gas supply but I realized the extra weight and bulk of a second cylinder would be a serious obstacle in the final stage because the water was now completely draining from the bottom of the blowhole. As the sea surged outwards, it dragged the water away to reveal the bottom of the seabed at the foot of the vertical shaft. I had hoped I could surface in the water, be buffeted but cushioned by it, ride it until I could clip on to the rope and begin my semi-controlled ascent. Whereas now I would be dumped heavily on the rocky, uneven sea floor to try to balance as I attempted to attach myself to the rope and was hit by the next incoming barrage.

I also decided to remove the cricket face guard from my helmet. As I had put it on, I'd realized something that hadn't struck me before. I'm not sure why I'd missed this, as it was now very obvious. My regulator – the mouthpiece that is con-nected to my gas cylinder by a hose – only just fitted inside the face guard and was forced tight against my front teeth. I gave it a solid tap and nearly knocked them out. I made the decision to remove the guard based on the fact that it could do much more harm than good, directing any force from a frontal rock strike directly through my two front teeth. Even a glancing blow could easily see me whistling a different tune. It was also more comfortable without it and feeling as relaxed and free to move as possible was becoming increasingly important. So it was that eventually I was dressed up and ready to go.

I stand at the edge of the cliffs attached to the rope by my abseil device and look over my right shoulder to see the ground beneath my neoprene-booted feet fall away into the churning sea. I look up and meet the gaze of my friends. They look worried. I close my eyes, feeling my mind taking charge of my body. I actively subdue my anxieties now. The decision has been made. Worrying about what-ifs is now counter-productive. I am either ready or not; there is no in between.

I find a moment of peace, of calm and clarity, and hold it. I open my eyes, smile behind the mask and give one nod to the group – it translates as, 'I'm good, I'm ready, I'm off . . . and I'll be coming back.' Now I am in my own world. No one else matters and I can afford to be guiltlessly selfish in caring about nothing except me. I smile inwardly to myself.

'Time to go to work.'

This is not said with bravado or to bolster failing confidence. It is to reaffirm that I must walk the walk. I used to say the same thing before walking out alone on bomb-disposal tasks. I have always craved credibility and to be, at the very least, what I claim to be. So if I am going to stand in front of a crowd at an international dive show, billed as 'a real-life underwater action man, the diving daredevil', I'd better bloody well live up to the hype. Humility extenuates great deeds.

So, with that in mind, I swing out over the edge and begin to descend the rope. I notice a small ledge disappearing a few feet under water before popping back into terrestrial existence and aim for it. Swinging down on to it, I brace myself as the surge sweeps up to my waist and ebbs away as quickly. As I unscrew the abseil device from my harness, a huge wave hits the cliffs. I am suddenly picked up and find myself moving rapidly back up the way I've just come. The world through my mask has suddenly become a window of moving black slab and foaming white bubbles. My thick neoprene rubber hood dampens the noise and I can at least hear my own thoughts. By the time the confusion settles, I am metres from the face, out on a slack rope. I start to feed the rope through. I do not want to be left swinging back into the cliff if the water level I am currently occupying drops away beyond the extent of my line.

The water starts receding and I furiously pull the rope through to its end so I can be free of it. I fall back down as the water level is sucked back out and away, and manage to free myself from the rope. I kick away from the rock face and find that, with a bit of effort, I can hold a rough position while I bob up and down in the 30-foot waves. It's a chance to take stock. I look up. I can make out the faces of my friends, peering apprehensively down. They shout and gesticulate but I can hear nothing over the thrashings of the boiling waters so I raise my right arm and give a thumbs-up. It's all going according to plan . . . ish. I take a minute to watch from sea level what the hell is actually going on. I can see the crack in the rock wall that leads down into the submerged coast and widens to become the entrance to the cave. I rehearse my plan, simple as it is, in my head.

As my head breaks the surface of the water, my world becomes one of uniform colour and texture, as if someone has thrown a mouldy hessian sack over my face. I can see no more than a foot in front and my entire vision is filled with a turbid brown-green cloud with only the occasional passing piece of seaweed, shrapnel from the seabed, to give any sense of form or perspective. Diving in waters with zero visibility is like being in a white-out; it is not like being in complete darkness. In darkness, your eyes don't try to search to find anything to focus on. But here, as in white-outs, there is enough light, enough colour to fool your eyes into attempting to see outlines, shapes, changes in texture, which only succeeds in inducing confusion, disorientation and often feelings of vertigo. So I hold my hand up against my mask, moving it no more than half an arm's length away to get an idea of the extent of my visibility range.

I descend quickly to the seabed, a mere eight metres below me, and settle down. I grab a rock, a fixed position in the maelstrom, but not for long. I am flipped over and flung away. I see a rock hurtling towards my face and the visibility allows me a fraction of a second – enough time to appreciate my fate but not enough time to avoid it – before I face plant into the boulder. I do manage to throw my chin down and present the lip of my helmet. Rather that than the glass of my mask. I get away with an easy bang to the head. Thank God I binned the face guard or I'd be at least two teeth down by now.

Dentally intact and mentally alert, I realize I have absolutely no idea where I am. I know I'm on the seabed and in the area of the blowhole entrance but, with the aqua-waltzer I've spent the last few moments riding, I no longer possess the slightest clue about how far and in which direction the cave lies.

I slowly surface, although, in the spinning waves, it's faster than I safely should. I reorientate. I am nowhere near where I thought I was. I'm now on the far side of the little bay and over 100 feet from my target. Again, I look up at my ever-vigilant companions and offer another, if somewhat less energetic, thumbs-up. I am already tiring as I strike out towards the crack, deciding that I will touch the wall above the undersea entrance and descend, maintaining this contact if I can. When I feel the wall open up, I'll push inside . . . A flawless plan.

But as I descend I encounter another problem. I begin to force my way in and I can feel the water around me being sucked inwards. I am suddenly unsure of what happens if I want to bail out. Once I begin, do I have any options or will I have to ride the flow, hoping to make the blowhole and my exit rope? This is not a good feeling. I have always said that hope is not a method-ology or an action. It is an abandonment of control . . . but sometimes it is the first option on a list of one. I push into the entrance, keeping both hands against the side wall to give myself the illusion of context, so I can feel up from down. By maintaining contact, I can also try to judge how fast I am moving, blinded as I am by the murk of my surroundings and now the blackness of the cave. I realize my progress is slowing and I kick harder, trying to grip the walls and, if not make progress, at least stop myself from moving backwards in the out-flush. But I can feel the wall slipping past my fingers, rushing away in front of me. I am being pulled backwards with ever-increasing ferocity. I am flung to the surface and feel like I am being swept downstream in a set of rapids. Once again I find myself at the opposite side of the bay, gasping, breathing hard through my regulator and sweating inside my wetsuit, despite the eight degrees of my surroundings.

I try again. With the same outcome. It feels like the water is rushing in with lacklustre power for a few seconds before powerfully pouring out in a torrent lasting many times as long. It is literally one step forward and three steps back. I flounder on the surface, exhausted, broken and frustrated. Surely the same amount of water goes in and comes out? More cannot always come out. It's physically impossible. After one last tired attempt, I am low on air and my strength has gone. The rope I used to descend has been pulled up, kept out of my way to avoid any risk of entanglement, but I know I no longer have the energy to safely climb back up in my dive kit and decide that the only option is to bail out and start the long swim home.

I swam around the headland amongst the huge sets of waves barrelling in from the Atlantic. I lay on my back and kicked continuously for about half an hour, getting slower and slower as my energy ebbed. It was becoming an endurance event. My air supply ran out and I inflated my surface marker buoy so my friends could better track my progress but the additional advantage was that I could drape the big orange, sausage-shaped balloon over my chest and help to keep my head out of the water. It also felt comforting to have something to hang on to, like a passing barrel to a shipwrecked mariner. I made it into the shallows and tried to stand. The final insult was another untimely large wave that knocked me on my face in the knee-deep water and ripped off one of my fins, never to be seen again. I was too weary to care. Stumbling to the beach, Dan had the camera ready.

'How was that, buddy?' asked Raz.

I ripped off my helmet, hood and mask. Face red, eyes bloodshot and looking a bit dazed, I peered down the lens.

'It didn't quite go according to plan . . .'

I had been giving a talk on this blowhole attempt at the Scottish Diving Conference and explained that I could not work out how or why the water movements were as I experienced them. Handily enough, a fellow came up to me afterwards and introduced himself as a hydrological engineer. He explained that the blowhole's horizontal tunnel was probably narrower at the seaward side than the end that penetrated into the cliff and that as the water rushed out it gained speed and power because it was forced through a narrower opening – a process called the Venturi effect. He then supposed that if enough water flowed into the vertical shaft, a head of pressure could build up as the water level inside the shaft became higher than that of the sea outside. This would further increase the power of the outflow compared to the inflow. In short, it looked unlikely I'd ever be able to swim into the blowhole's horizontal passage in anything like true, stormy blowhole conditions.

However, this conclusion did boot open the door to one other obvious course of action. I would abseil into the blowhole this time and then use the hydrological features of the formation to my advantage and be blasted out to sea. I'd dive a blowhole backwards. Genius. Or perhaps just the other side of the fine line.

*

It was a long time before I finally got to have another go. Once again, I needed the right conditions and, in the end, had to go midweek. With my erstwhile companions now gainfully employed on one project or another, I'd have to go solo. Somehow, this sat better with me. My friends often volunteer their time to help me and I can't always offer much in return. I feel pressure to look after them on one of my projects, to make sure they are enjoying themselves, that they are getting something out of it. Without them, I could focus on me.

Of course, some projects are impossible, as well as a lot less fun, alone. I am aware of the negative safety aspects of being on your own and, truly, the companionship of people – the right people – can make the difference between a mission being a success or a failure. The experience is more real and the effects will last much longer if good friends surround you. But in my current life, my missions are no longer of the necessity or seriousness of those undertaken in the Forces and most are of my own choosing. So the fulfilment and enjoyment of these projects is important, too. And I have come to realize that I am a man who enjoys the absolute freedom of being alone and how, for me, the experience becomes purer and more personal. Also, of course, you only have to bail yourself out and with fewer people to worry about and without an audience the possibility of ego spoiling the show is reduced. You can't show off if there's no one around. It becomes a personal experience, perhaps to prove something to yourself. But I see nothing wrong in that. You shouldn't compare yourself to others, either positively or negatively. Every day should be about being better than you were yesterday. It's about self-improvement over stagnation.

More than anything, me and the blowhole had a thing going on.

So I watched for the approaching storm and when it came I told no one. I packed my bags and drove west. I changed into my wetsuit and armour at the car and dressed in my diving kit. I climbed into my harnesses and clipped the rope-descending and -ascending equipment to me. I would swim across with only the ropes in a drybag, to make the kit encumbrance minimal. I hadn't altered my kit configuration much. I had taken two cylinders this time, only five litres each and back-mounted, with the valves pointing downwards where I could reach them and where they'd be protected from being bashed against the cave roof. Oh, and my wetsuit was now silver. This made no difference to the outcome but it did look cool.

Once across, I threw my kit up on to the grassy bank above the sheltered side of the island and clambered up after it. Another twenty minutes saw me ferry the kit and set the ropes up at the top. This time, I'd attempt to climb back up the cliff face rather than be forced to make the long swim around the headland through currents that, I hadn't realized last time, could sweep me off down the coast if I swam too far out from the wave-beaten rocks. I had thought to weight the end of the rope I would be ascending so that it would be more stable, easier to locate and grab. However, I now recognized that any amount of lead I tied to it would provide little competition against the force of the swell; it would only serve to create a more effective weapon out of the flailing rope and introduce something else to hit me on the head. So I didn't bother.

I stood on the lip of the blowhole and looked around once again. I was no longer met by the faces of my friends. It felt more daunting without them, more lonely and exposed. I have accomplished a number of solo projects, especially under-water, and I am used to this feeling. There is none of the camaraderie, none of the jokes to make light of the situation and lift some of the anxiety. I can usually take comfort and confidence from my own abilities but this time, without the certainty of having a true understanding of the risk, I was more susceptible to doubt. But I'd come this far. And I had my ascending kit clipped to my harness, so if I hit the water inside the blowhole and decided it was all too much I could always attempt to climb back out. Always have a Plan B.

I let the first few inches of rope slip through my hands and through the abseil device and begin the descent. I place my feet against the wet rock, moving slowly and picking the placements carefully to avoid slipping and clattering into the wall. At one point, the water within the shaft rises up to meet me, lapping my feet, before dropping away and revealing the seabed more than 30 feet below. The thought of Moses and the Red Sea momen-tarily enters my head, followed by the thought of Pharaoh's charioteers, and I shake that thought loose. I hit the water as an incoming surge beats me against the back wall. I quickly unclip from the rope but keep a solid hold of it in my right hand. As I descend, the rope flails around, goes slack and taut and has no real merit as a reference or guide but I still take comfort in its solidity in my grip. It doesn't matter where I am. I am not lost if I have it in my hand, as I can always follow it back to the surface and relative safety, regardless of the ever-coiling, serpentine path it may take.

I have paid out enough rope that I think I can drag the end with me as I enter the horizontal passage. It is thick, heavy climbing rope and I am content that it doesn't provide too much of an entanglement hazard. At one point, a large set of waves hits the blowhole and I can feel myself being thrust upwards inside the water column. The next moment, I am lying on my left side, head down on the angled seabed, high and dry and wriggling for balance like a fish out of water before the next surge rolls me against the back wall and envelops me in salt water. As the water starts to drain away again, I take the opportunity to swim quickly into deeper water. My main concern about such beachings is that my diving kit will take a hammering and fail. A few bruisings I can bounce back from. Being stuck inside a natural washing machine with no air is a more serious state of affairs.

The next few moments are chaos. I lose the rope as I have to use both hands to grip and wedge myself against the rocks and into a shallow crevice . . . I stop. I think. I can see very little and my sense of touch is overwhelmed by the pressures swirling around me. I can feel myself biting down hard on my mouthpiece, trying to ensure it's not ripped out but more likely it's a result of the stress I'm under. I make a token attempt to look for any wildlife taking refuge in the rocks but it is a lost cause. The darkness is now absolute as I enter the horizontal passage proper and ticking off a few more occupants of my *I Spy Book of the Seashore* is no longer a priority. With the noise, the movement, the lack of visual reference, my brain is working overtime to make sense of my new world. I can feel myself moving forward, though, I think. I hope. I just want to be out of here now. I am not in control and have no way to regain it. It becomes one of those rare times when I hope.

The absolute darkness seems to trickle away and the gloom brightens. I can see the rocks on the seabed a few inches in front of me and I decide I must have made it out. However, I don't ascend. Not yet. I do not want to be anywhere near the roof of the cave. I want to be well clear and out to sea before I surface. I count my fin kicks, one, two, three all the way to twenty, and can feel that the movement is different, more rhythmical, less dramatic and chaotic. I start to ascend, holding my depth gauge mere inches from my face so that I can monitor my speed as I rise. I break surface far from the blowhole on the other side of the bay, where I found myself catapulted so many times on the previous attempt. I am relieved but check myself and stay focused. I still have to climb back to safety.

I search the corner where I threw down the rope. I can't see it amongst the surge and spray but then I probably shouldn't have used a black rope against black rock. The power of hind-sight. As I cautiously approach the corner, I can see the rope disappearing into the water. I search around for it but can't locate an end. I should have put a float on it. I would prefer to clip to the rope within the safety of the sea rather than try climbing on to a ledge first. I can ascend quickly but it's during the transition period from diver to climber that I'm at my most vulnerable.

Eventually, I have no choice and receive a few solid knocks as I clip on to the rope, but a few shifts with my ascenders and I'm clear of the peaks of even the biggest waves. Once I'm clear of the water, I stop and realize how heavily I'm breathing, how hard I've worked. I am desperate to throw off my mask and helmet and peel off my hood. I am sweating hard. I continue the climb and stumble over the edge, drop my kit, pull off my gloves and savour the moment as I rip off my mask and hood. Freedom, relief, success.

But the feeling was different to other successes. I did not feel as though my training, my planning, my research and my hard work had paid off. It was less fulfilling than that. I felt more as though I had taken a gamble, rolled the dice and got double six. There is no real feeling of accomplishment when success comes down to luck. Yes, there was a feeling of immediate elation, a bigger rush, but ultimately I felt it had not been my victory. The success had not come from me. I had merely been fortunate this time and, for all I'd known, it could just as easily have gone the other way.

A quote from Randy Pausch's inspirational 'Last Lecture' came to mind: 'Experience is what you get when you didn't get what you wanted.' Sometimes the things we've done, the knowledge, experience, insight, skills or lessons learned – even if they result from failure or hollow success – can be useful the next time things go wrong. An experience today, no matter how small or negative, may just save your life tomorrow.

CHAPTER 8

Kayaking to Kilda

The greatest crossing in British sea-kayaking has to be the one between North Uist, an island on the western edge of the Outer Hebrides, and St Kilda, the most wild and remote island in Britain. The idea was to paddle my craft over 70 kilometres across the North Atlantic, which even in benign conditions still throws up huge waves that start life in Newfoundland and build in size with every inch they progress. On this stretch of ocean, you are a long way from help in a very big bit of wild water. This is the story of how the idea and the reality turned out to be rather different things.

My first experience of kayaking was on white water. Quite advanced white water. It was during part of my basic training in the Forces and we were taken to North Wales to do some adventure training (non-military activities that still have application or value either because they develop crossover skills or because they involve physical and psychological aspects beneficial to soldiering). For the kayaking, they split us into two groups. The advanced group, who had all kayaked before, would go down the rapids, and the kayak virgins would paddle in a flat-water lake. There were six of us in the novice group and four in the experienced one.

'It'd be easier if it was five and five,' said the instructor.

'No problem,' said our commander. 'Torbet, you dive and climb and all that sort of shit, you can go with the other group.'

'Sir, I've never sat in a kayak in my life,' I informed him.

'Yeah, but it's outdoorsy stuff – all the same thing,' he reliably informed me.

'Right you are, sir!', which of course translated as, 'You're an idiot.'

So it was that, at the age of twenty, I spent most of the day on a loop, either dragging my kayak down the riverbank from where I'd spluttered ashore after capsizing to the next safe place to relaunch, or hurtling down the river with the bottom of the vessel on show to the world and my face dragging on the river bed. I also got stuck in a tree. Not a log, or branch or piece of tree debris, but an actual upright tree. Twice.

Fast forward fifteen years and I found myself on a kayaking course. I'd always wanted to go back and learn to kayak properly but now the final motivation was not kayaking itself but freediving and snorkelling. It was spring 2011 and I intended that summer to set off on my 'Britain by Snorkel' mission. I realized that I could access far more of the coastline from a kayak than I ever could by just swimming. So I decided sea-kayaking would expand the scope and potential of the project.

When I first sat back in a kayak, I did not feel comfortable, even though I was at a slight advantage in that I was confident in water and the idea of capsizing did not really bother me. I think fear can hold us back in a training environment. We are reticent to push up to and beyond our capabilities but it is in this zone that we progress the most. Of course, at other times fear is entirely useful if applied correctly. It stops us from injuring or killing ourselves in embarrassingly dumb or point-less ways. But I accept it is rare, for me at least, to start genuinely enjoying something until I have at least become rea-sonably proficient at it. I don't like the feeling of not really knowing what I'm doing, not being completely under control and not having the skills to overcome problems. I never really started to enjoy skydiving, for example, until I'd completed over one hundred and twenty jumps. However, even on that first weekend of training, I started to see the potential of sea-kayaking in its own right.

After the course, I bought myself a fairly basic and cheap plastic sea-kayak in order to consolidate my new skills. I explored the Devon and Dorset coastlines and even completed a day where, along a 14-kilometre stretch, I passed over seven shallow shipwrecks, freediving them all from my kayak, thereby proving the point of my efforts. As with a number of my 'Britain by Snorkel' sites, I used the project as a good excuse to visit places I'd always wanted to see. One was Fingal's Cave on the island of Staffa – a small, remote island of the Inner Hebrides. The island is an amazing geological site made up of huge hexagonal basalt pillars (the pillars are actu-ally between three and eight sides but six is the most common). Fingal's Cave is famous not only for its geological distinctive-ness but it also inspired Mendelssohn to write *The Hebrides Overture*.

The crossing to Staffa from the main island of Mull to the east is about 16 kilometres. Only the last seven or so is an open crossing, the rest being coastal as one makes one's way down the southern edge of the island of Ulva (a small island reached from Mull by a ferry journey that's barely 100 metres long). There was a slight wind blowing from the west, the direction of my destination, as I packed my wetsuit and free-diving kit into my kayak. I'd decided to wear my kayaking clothing (comfortable fleece tights and top with a set of water-proof trousers and cagoule over the top), as it's much more comfortable. I'd be beaching the kayak and would get changed before jumping in to snorkel and dive.

I began to paddle out of the shelter of the bay and along the grey rocky beaches. Short turf-topped cliffs, dappled with the yellow of lichen, rose up beside me. The water was beautifully flat and the bright sun glinted and sparkled off the crest of the tiny wavelets as I cut through the peaks. As I exited the shelter of the narrow isthmus between Mull and Ulva and turned west, I began to feel the wind blowing in my face. The difference to my kayaking experience was obvious, as I no longer glided with little effort through the water but had to work to keep up a decent pace of forward movement. It was like going from a downhill walk to a jog on the flat, so I was still a long way from battling into a storm. But as I got further and further from my start and from land, the sea state rapidly started to pick up. The waves grew in size and power, and the wind seemed stronger. I was now having to work hard to make any progress and I began to break into a sweat. I could feel a small blister beginning to form on the inside base of my thumb (a consequence of over-gripping my paddle) and as the waves splashed over me I was feeling exposed, unstable and unsure of exactly what I was doing.

Looking back, the conditions were not that bad and, given my current skill level, I'd probably not even register them. But at the time, with minimal skill and experience, I was keenly aware of every incoming wave and how increasingly far from land I was travelling. No more so than when a pilot whale broke the surface off to my right, only 20 metres away. I had enough brainpower not being given over to staying upright to appreciate how lucky I was to see this huge beast briefly rolling over the face of the water to breathe. But it also served to highlight how small and clumsy I was.

The reason for the change in conditions was twofold. Apparently, the piece of water I was passing through is known for becoming choppy at certain states of the tides. As the waters move in or out through a narrowing between the islands, and also because of underwater topographical changes (submerged peaks, ridges and valleys), the water rolls and bubbles on the surface like a fast-flowing river running over a chaotically rocky bottom. The waters I was now in were exposed to the full force and length of the wind. When I began, the waters had been sheltered and the wind had had little time to act upon the surface. Simply put, the longer the fetch the bigger the waves. Fetch is the distance the wind has to act upon the water surface. So, if the wind is coming from the west and you have a big island half a kilometre west of you, the wind only has that half a kilometre to blow over the water and build up the waves. It's why some long lochs in Scotland, orientated with the prevailing wind, can be flat calm on the upwind end but very choppy on the downwind end. This is an oversimplification but you get the idea. The point is that there was nothing west of me before the Labrador coast of Canada. And have I mentioned I wasn't that competent?

The sense of adventure, the appreciation of danger and stress or outright fear an action can cause is a very subjective thing. For example, cave diving is dangerous. There is no point in pretending otherwise. The room for error is close to zero. However, a very good cave diver doing a very advanced dive is still far safer than an incompetent diver doing a very basic dive. The inherent danger level of the activity doesn't necessarily dictate the present level of danger. Rather, it's dictated by the person undertaking the activity.

So there I was, out of my depth, figuratively and literally. I decided to turn back. And that's where things got a bit more tricky. My repertoire of useful strokes contained two. A forward stroke to propel me forward and a sweep stroke to turn the boat in a fairly wide, slow arc. I had not yet learned the best timing and method for turning on waves, so I just started to bang out sweep strokes furiously. In fact, the best time to turn is when you are at the crest of a wave. If you imagine the kayak is balancing on the peak of a wave, then very little of the boat is in the water creating drag, so it can spin like a propeller on the top of the wave. I didn't know this, so I just hacked it through the sea. With a great deal of inefficiently expended effort, I managed to point my boat towards home. Not before I almost capsized at least half a dozen times. As you move through 180 degrees to turn your boat from facing into-wave to being with-wave, you are at some point going to be side-on to the wave. This is called a beam sea and is the most unstable position. Think about it: you can't tip a kayak over forwards or backwards but rolling it side to side, to the point where it rolls over and the person inside is now upside down, is very easy.

However, I didn't go in, which is just as well since I couldn't yet roll a kayak back up and would have had to get out, right my kayak and try to climb back inside. I'm pretty good at this, having done it all the time while freediving from my boat, but in this sea state it would have been very, very difficult if not impossible to get back in. I'd then have been faced with abandoning my kayak and having to swim at least a kilometre to shore. Of course, I'm far too thrifty to have abandoned my boat. I'd have towed it back to shore . . . even if it had taken me twice as long. As it was, I was now heading home, spurred on by the desire to find flatter water. But I found that paddling with a wave was actually far more difficult than paddling into one.

As a wave hits your rear end, it picks you up. If you know how to use the wave, you can actually surf along, covering a lot of ground very quickly with minimal effort. But if you don't know what you're doing, the wave will pick you and start to twist you side-on. You don't surf a kayak sideways. You capsize sideways. It's actually fairly easy to control if you extend your paddle behind you on one side and use it like a rudder to keep the boat going in a straight line. I did not know that you could do this. I was barely in control and fighting hard. I was furiously sweep stroking, trying to keep the boat facing forward, less because that was the way I wanted to go and more because it was the most stable position. As I held my course, I tried to crab across to be closer to land so that the resultant swim from a capsize would be a shorter one. Eventually, I made it back to calmer waters, more by luck than judgement, feeling thoroughly spanked and chastised for my naivety about how difficult the crossing would be and how inadequate my current skill level was. On the upside, I did freedive Fingal's Cave the next day . . . I caught a tour boat from Mull.

*

Fast forward a year or so and I'd amassed much more experience. On returning home, I did some one-to-one training. I needed to learn to roll and to surf. My sea-kayaking coach, Rob McIntyre, had become a friend and we'd done a number of trips together either for clients, with me acting as his assistant, or personal ones with Darren Sherwood, another professional coach. Very handy. I often feel I'm getting more out of our trips than they are. We were all mad keen to try the St Kilda crossing. Any serious sea-kayaker in the UK has it on their hit list. In order to step things up a bit in terms of preparation, we decided to do a number of trips. These included a crossing of the Bristol Channel to hone my tidal-planning skills and a circumnavigation of the Isle of Wight to test my endurance.

The Bristol Channel, if you're not aware, lies between Wales to the north and Somerset and North Devon to the south (and, to be accurate, it has its beginnings along a small stretch in Gloucester). It may have the second largest tidal range in the world. I say 'may', because the official leader is over in Canada but the difference is measured in centimetres and measuring methods have varied. Regardless, the tide rushes in and powers out of the channel at up to 12 kilometres an hour. The average sea-kayaker probably covers about six kilometres an hour when there isn't any wind or tide. So you can see the problem. Our destination was two tiny islands that sit, fortress-like, in the ever-moving high-speed conveyor belt that is the Bristol Channel – Steep Holm and Flat Holm, to the west and north-west of Weston-super-Mare.

The islands get the latter part of their names from the old Norse *holmr* – a small and rounded islet. The former parts stem from the fact that one is a high, steep-cliffed island and the other a much flatter, rounded one. Telling them apart is not difficult. Although the islands sit together they are on either side of the boundary that runs through the centre of the channel and separates England and Wales. Flat Holm is Welsh, Steep Holm English and I'm quite sure neither island cares.

The best place to launch on the English side is near Weston-super-Mare. Our timings had to be perfect: the window for a crossing is short and very specific. When crossing a tide, a technique called ferry gliding is often employed. Imagine you are standing on a riverbank and wish to reach an island one kilometre out, which stands in a pretty wide river. The river flows right to left at ten kilometres an hour. And say, for the sake of simple maths, you paddle at ten kilometres an hour. You wish to travel in a straight line between your point of embarkation and your destination; it's the most effective line to take. However, if you simply point your vessel straight at the island and paddle, you will miss the island. As you paddle ahead, the river pushes you sideways, in this example at the same speed, so for every metre you go towards your destination in this case you also go a metre to the left. You may be facing forward but you are in fact moving to the left at a 45-degree angle. So you need to counteract this. You need to paddle at a 45-degree angle upstream, to the right. The stronger the 'river' the more you have to point upstream.

You can think of the Bristol Channel as a huge saline river. Only this one is more complicated, as it changes direction four times a day and its speed is constantly increasing or decreasing, depending on the state of the tide. What all this meant for our trip was that we constantly needed to check and adjust our angle, either making it more or less acute depending on whether the speed of the tide was increasing or decreasing. We spent the majority of the trip pointing our boats so far upstream to counteract the fierce current that Steep Holm was back over my left shoulder. It was bizarre to be furiously paddling away from the very place I was trying to get to and even more bizarre to see it getting closer every time I looked over my shoulder. It was like the towering, green-topped island was chasing me.

We'd aimed slightly upstream in order to give ourselves some wiggle room. If you're too far upstream, as we were, you simply spin your kayak until you're pointing towards the island and coast on down. If you're downstream, then you're either battling like a demon to get back up to port or you've missed the island and, in this instance, the next stop is the wild Atlantic. We cruised toward the only beach on Steep Holm, a small, pebbled affair not more than 25 metres long and five metres wide. The water spins around the island but there is a small eddy along the beach at certain times of the tide, creating an area of relatively still water that you can punch into. This was why our timings were so critical.

It was about 12 kilometres from our launch site at Weston-super-Mare to the beach on Steep Holm and it had only taken us just over an hour and a half. But because of the fierce tides we had had to keep paddling hard the whole time with no let-ups, as this would soon have seen us being pushed off course. We then had four hours to wait before the tides turned and we could start our track north towards Flat Holm. So by the time we'd beached our boats on this deserted island beneath pure-blue skies and sunshine we were ready to strip off, get a brew on the go, have some lunch and stretch out for an afternoon siesta.

Suitably refreshed and with the tides now running in almost the same direction that we wanted to go we had an easier run

up to Flat Holm – for a change. We camped for the night outside the warden's building, which acts as a rustic home for the
resident warden, basic dorm-style accommodation for the sea-
sonal volunteers who live out here, and an information centre
for visitors. The island is a nature reserve and is important for
birds as well as being the spot from where, in 1897, Marconi
sent the first radio signal transmitted over sea. The message
was in Morse code and said: 'Are you ready?'

The journey back from Flat Holm to the mainland required
as much of a sustained effort with well-planned micro-navigation and timings as the journey out but we made it back
without incident. Most of my experience before this had been
on trips in fairly manageable tidal areas where, even if caught
at the wrong time, one could improvise or power on. But this
trip, in the most tidal waters of Britain, was a clear reminder
that on certain parts of the coast much more careful and accurate planning is required before we leave dry land.

St Kilda is a long, long way from the nearest point of land. So
for the next phase of my build-up training we decided to take
a trip around the Isle of Wight. The Isle of Wight does not
sit a vast distance off land, being only about five kilometres
from the Hampshire coastline. In fact, it is only one and a half
kilometres from Hurst Castle, which sits on the edge of the
New Forest, on a spit of shingle out into the water. The island
is an approximate diamond shape and the piece of water that
lies along the two northern sides, closest to England, is called
the Solent. What makes kayaking around the Isle of Wight
potentially difficult is the amount of commercial and recreational boat traffic in the Solent and also the savage and
sub-normal tides. But, more than this, a full circumnavigation

of the island is 105 kilometres. We broke it into a 65-kilometre day followed by a half day of only 40. Even this latter distance was more than I had previously done in one day and it hadn't been preceded by another mammoth paddle. I had every expectation of finding it quite tiring.

As the tide comes in from the west it is split apart, breaking on the western point of the diamond, half going round the southern tip, which is the English Channel side, and the other being forced through the narrow section of water between the island and the mainland. This causes the water to speed up, since the same amount of water needs to pass through a smaller space in the same time period and the only way to achieve this is by becoming faster. This may sound like a major obstacle, and it certainly can be, but used correctly it can also be your friend.

Which is why we chose our day and time for setting off very carefully . . . or we would have done had we planned this particular journey in advance. As it was, we'd discussed making the second of the big UK crossings from the south-western tip of Cornwall to the Scilly Isles. This was Option A. Unfortunately, the wind and weather were against us. Our Option B was to make another big tick on many a sea-kayaker's list of crossings and make our way from North Devon out west to the island of Lundy. Again, the winds were all wrong. So one of our party came up with Option C – the idea of a circumnavigation of the Isle of Wight. He'd taken a look at conditions and, with fortune favouring us for once, the winds and tides were just right.

You must be flexible in the UK with regards to any outdoor pursuit. You have probably noticed that our weather can be a tad inclement at times and is often not particularly predictable. If time is short and you want to get out and get something done, it's probably worth having a few options in different parts of the UK and hope that you don't get 'weathered' off them all. So it was that we decided to spin around the Isle of Wight. As I had severe reservations about my paddling-endurance fitness when it came to the distances involved for St Kilda, this excursion would prove useful as a marker as to where I stood and how much work was needed.

We set off in glorious sunshine and made our way anticlockwise towards the Needles from the spit of land upon which Hurst Castle sits. I'd not been back here since we'd climbed the middle one and I made a special trip around it to inspect how intact the line of my as yet unrepeated route was. The sea was lumpy in places and it required us to time our attempts to 'thread the Needle' – kayak between the sea stacks – without getting smashed or grounded by a wave. By paddling anticlockwise around the island it meant the tide would assist us for six hours before turning and working against us for six hours. Our routine was to paddle for about two hours, pull in for a quick pee break and leg stretch, then relaunch. In addition, we would have a half-hour lunch stop in the middle of the day. We carried this on for about twelve hours.

As we made our way around, I was struck but how deserted it seemed. The south-east of England is the most heavily populated part of Britain and it can be hard to find places that feel wild. A glance at the Isle of Wight doesn't show many areas untouched by human hand but a lot of the roads and houses are hidden from the sea. The majority of the commercial and recreational activities on the water, including the busy harbours and ferry routes, are all up in the north. So the south appears relatively undeveloped. In fact, it wasn't until we'd rounded St Catherine's Point, its most southerly location, and made our way east to the seaside town of Ventnor that we really encountered people. We hauled our boats on to a busy beach and scouted out the nearest public toilet, then swung into one of the many ice-cream merchants along the esplanade to carb-load.

After about half an hour, I was anxious to be back out on the water. I felt uncomfortable on the crowded, noisy beach and wanted to be back out in the serenity of the open sea. I find the confines of a flooded cave or the heights of a remote cliff a far less stressful place to be than, say, London Zone 1 at lunchtime on a Friday.

It was about eight o'clock at night when we rounded effectively the easternmost point of the island. By now the tide had reached its highest point and there was a pause before it started running out towards low. This, coupled with any wind dying off, meant the water, in the fading light, had become a flat black mirror and my tired body was re-energized as we flowed over the still waters at speed. Paddling felt easier, almost as if the water had become less viscous, and each near-effortless stroke seemed to allow us to glide further, like running down-hill. We could see the lights of Portsmouth off to the north and the Solent Forts, those solid man-made islands built in the 1860s to protect the city and its important harbours from sea-borne attack. On a dry and warm night, we didn't bother with tents, we simply threw our roll mats on the pebbled beach we'd landed on and jumped in our sleeping bags. I was genu-inely surprised at how remarkably fresh I felt and at how easily I had coped with the day. I didn't feel stiff or sore and my only concern about the next day's relatively short kayak was the amount of boat traffic we'd encounter in the Solent.

For now, however, on a tiny stretch of shingle, with our kit hung out on nearby rocks to dry, I drifted off to sleep, the twinkling lights from the mainland outshining those above me. And I was right to feel confident, as the next day brought similarly fine weather and I performed better than expected. Suddenly the journey to St Kilda seemed entirely within my grasp.

To paddle to St Kilda, you need favourable weather conditions. Any wind from the west will blow in your face, making progress hard, and too much wind from the west will create huge waves and make travel impossible and extremely unsafe. Too much wind from the east will create a following sea that pushes you along but can become hard to handle. Even a light wind from the east can make landing on the only sheltered area of this, the most exposed piece of land in Britain, very dangerous if not impossible. You do not want to paddle almost 70 kilometres across the intimidating and lonely North Atlantic to find your only parking space is out of bounds. The ideal scenario is no wind at all, but this is the far north-western edge of Britain. You don't really get days with no wind out there. But a light westerly would be fine, ideally a Force 1 or 2. Historically, the best times to attempt a crossing are September or occasionally April. So I kept September, October and April free (or at least containing only projects I could shift or drop if necessary). I did this for two years. We never got a window.

Eventually, after spending what felt like half my life on XCWeather, watching the wind predictions, we decided to take a chance and just plan a trip. In April, Rob, Darren and I blanked out a week in the diary to drive north and see if we could get a couple of days in which we could reach St Kilda. If not, we had a back-up plan so the week wouldn't be wasted. We strapped three boats to the roof of the car, piled the back with kit and one unlucky camper and set off on a journey which, in the end, turned out to be well over 700 miles . . . and that was before we launched a single boat. If you're thinking of driving 700 miles with three very expensive expedition kayaks on your roof, I can thoroughly recommend a glass-roofed car. I have one and it alleviated much of the stress that Rob, whose kayaks they were, had as we belted up the M5, M6 and M74 before snaking our way along increasingly windy Highland roads. A quick glance up from the passenger seat gave reassurance that all was secure and safe.

We were checking the weather reports for North Uist, our intended launch point for St Kilda, and, not unexpectedly, the winds were still proving just a bit too strong. There was little hope of them dying down in the next few days, so the St Kilda cause was lost for now. So, then, to Plan B. The Small Isles are part of the Inner Hebrides, which, as its name suggests, is more sheltered than the Outer Hebrides. The Smalls themselves – and again the clue is in the name – are a group of smaller islands west of Mallaig, which is pretty much due west of Ben Nevis. And if you don't know where the highest point in Britain is I suggest you consult a map. The main islands of the group consist of Eigg (pronounced Egg), Rum, Canna and Muck. We like a good name in Scotland.

Our plan was to paddle from the mainland to Eigg via Muck then on to Rum and up to Canna. From there we'd paddle over to Hyskeir to overnight in a fairly rare spot. Hyskeir is a rocky little island, less than about 900 metres long and even less wide, and home to one of the last lighthouses in Britain to become unmanned (in 1997 to be exact). It offers enough grass to pitch a few tents but is seldom visited let alone overnighted on. This seemed like a good plan until the weather in that area picked up, making it even worse than that predicted for St Kilda.

So there we were – three men in a kayak-topped car on our way north. I could pretend that we pulled in, pored over a map and quickly improvised a new plan over a beer, grasping an exciting new opportunity from the jaws of defeat. I'm pretty good at making stuff up on the hoof when the world forces a sudden change on me. But I've always found that the better prepared you are, the better able you are to improvise. The old military adage says: 'No plan survives first contact with the enemy.' But if you don't have a plan in the first place, you'll never have anything to change . . . in fact, you're unlikely even to get yourself out of bed. So, in anticipation of bad weather, we had a Plan C. It was a circumnavigation of the stunning Isle of Skye.

It was a rubbish plan.

It was too stormy even for that.

Now, did we pull off, buy a beer and try to plan something new on a beer mat?

No. We had a Plan D. And this one was on.

The Summer Isles are an archipelago lying off the west coast in the far north of the Highlands. They are further north than the Smalls and even than St Kilda. But they gain some degree of shelter from the predominantly westerly winds from the large Isle of Lewis that sits atop the Outer Hebridean chain of islands. The Summer Isles comprise eighteen named islands with many other smaller islets that don't warrant nomenclature. They are also contained within a fairly sheltered position, having the mainland to their north-east, east and south, and Lewis to their west.

We set off from the mainland near the hamlet of Polbain just before darkness fell, so our first priority was to find somewhere to spend the night. It was only a short journey to the islands but the sea was choppy, hitting us side on, and it was hard to judge the indistinct waves in the gloom. Finally, we entered an area shielded by a ring of islands. The problem was that only a few of the larger islands, which were too far away now, looked to have anything approaching a beach to land on. We found a small islet, literally tens of metres in an area that had a flat shelf about sea level. One at a time we judged the swell as the sea crept up over the shelf and glided on to the beach, where we were left high and dry when the waters receded. We then had to hop out of our boats and carry them up a few steps on to the soft heather of the higher ground. That accomplished with no bones or boats broken, it was time to set up camp.

Over the next three days, we tried repeatedly to make it to Priest Island, the most remote of the chain, but the weather kept beating us back. But we did manage to take tours around the many other islands. I encountered some of the hardest conditions I have paddled in as we spent time on the windward sides of islands, being battered and thrown around in unstable seas, the powerful waves rebounding off the cliffs and hitting us from multiple sides. Then we'd sneak into the lee and calm waters for a break and breather, sheltered by the islands themselves. But for me, on this trip, it is the campsite that is most memorable. It was a perfect little spot. From a rock barely large enough to pitch three small tents, with a small driftwood campfire, we looked out west on to a calm night as the sun set behind the Priest. For me, this is what sea-kayaking is all about – taking a day trip out along the North Devon coast is great but camping from your kayak is the best. Especially on longer trips and especially in places only really accessible by kayak. The more unknown and unvisited the spot the better.

And the best thing about camping from a kayak? You can pretty much take anything you want. It is not like trekking while man-packing your gear (i.e. carrying it all yourself), where weight and bulk soon become a major constraint. Expeditionary sea-kayaks are long, up to 18 feet and more, so there is plenty of room to store kit. It's more like car camping. And because weight isn't really an issue either, you can afford to carry a tent each, spare clothing, a comfortable and bulky sleeping system, decent food (we sometimes take fresh raw ingredients and cook over the campfire) and lots of water. You can even afford to take luxuries like Kindles and plenty of solar chargers. In an island nation like Britain, ringed by hundreds of other islands of varying size, a sea-kayak really does offer a form of freedom like no other.

We eventually ended our tour a day early. With the weather deteriorating and only predicted to get worse, we needed to make the mainland before the sea became un-navigable. We had not made it to St Kilda and, to date, I still haven't made the crossing. It is still on my list. But the journey I undertook in my attempts to get there – to become skilled enough to make the attempt in the first place, to gain enough wisdom and know-how to become proficient – rewarded me with some incredible sights and experiences. Alexander the Great is supposed to have wept when he saw the breadth of his domain, for there were no more worlds to conquer. I pity the man who has ticked off all those things he once aspired to achieve and has no dreams left. And, sometimes, as I firmly believe is the case in this instance, the journey is of greater value and a lot more fun than reaching the destination.

Above: Setting up above the tempestuous seas at the blowhole in Pembrokeshire. The blowhole is just behind us and this shot creates a great sense of scale.

Below: Tired and battered at the end of the first blowhole attempt.

Not kayaking to St Kilda – yet – but honing my
skills in perfect conditions at the Needles.

Above: Getting into rougher waters as we head around the windward side of the Summer Isles in the far north of the Scottish Highlands.

Below: You find a lot of rubbish on the shoreline, even in remote uninhabited places. But sometimes making a camp amongst the flotsam and jetsam, as we did on the Summer Isles, can provide some useful items.

Left: Dressed up with only my bail-out cylinders and headgear to get on before exploring the submerged passageways of the lost mine.

Below left: My cave-diving kit. This is the basic configuration I use in most cave and mine exploration projects.

Below right: A screenshot from some footage showing me next to the names and tally marks made by the mine's foreman in 1938.

Above: A mature grey seal pup, about four weeks old, lounging on a beach by our bothy in the Monachs. The wildlife was a marine spectacle.

Below: Filming amongst the ruins of the Monachs' village, which was abandoned in 1942.

Above: Waiting for a brief respite in the swell to grab the two cylinders in the foreground, clip them on and make my descent to the mystery shipwreck.

Below: The markings on the plate salvaged from the wreck of the MV *Shoal Fisher*, which told us she had to have sunk after 1938 and helped us to identify her.

All the planning,
research, training
and equipment
counts for nothing
if you don't have
the right attitude.

CHAPTER 9

Diving the Lost Mine

Britain has a long history of occupation by man, dating back well into the Palaeolithic era. And since that time we've been beavering away, trying to build better lives by making use of the plethora of natural resources to be found here. One of the country's oldest industries, with one example dating back to about 4,000 years ago, and arguably the most important in the UK in recent centuries, is mining. These workings, found across Britain, supported the industrial revolution in the UK that affected the future of the entire globe and continues to support major communities across the country. My father's side of the family were all miners and, although I was very young at the time, I can still remember how much of an impact the closure of the mines in the 1980s had on every individual in the town and the wider community where he grew up.

Not all mines closed in living memory. Some closed many decades ago when whichever precious mineral was being excavated started to be removed in quantities too small to support the continuation of the industry in that area. Many of these mines were dug deep underground with tunnels and passage-ways delving well below the natural water table of the area. Systems of pumps were employed to suck the groundwater out of the deeper shafts and tunnels used by the miners as they laboriously chipped away at the bedrock. Their extracted prize was then loaded into handcarts to be pushed through these networks of passageways on narrow rails, hauled to the upper areas and eventually to the outside world. When these mines were closed down, the pumps were turned off and the world beneath was slowly reclaimed by the rising groundwater that percolated through the earth in this subterranean realm. This left these tunnels – these places of men's labour, these focal points of a community, the evidence of men's lives lived – sub-merged in darkness, untouched, preserved and frozen in time by the water.

Many of these deeper parts of the mines, submerged as they are, have not been visited since the mines first closed. After the last miner left, they haven't been seen by a living soul and remain completely unexplored. One such example is an old slate mine near Llangollen in North Wales. Here, the last shaft of the mine is believed to have closed in the early 1940s, as it was no longer financially viable. Martyn Farr, a legend in British cave diving, explored the first few hundred metres several years ago and mentioned it to me in a discussion we had about places in the UK that were ripe for further exploration. He had been diving it using traditional scuba equipment, where each breath is released into the water, increasing the amount of gas one uses and therefore reducing how long you can spend submerged. The other problem was that the under-water system, the horizontal passages, started at about 30 metres – 100 feet – down at the bottom of a near-vertical shaft.

This meant the pressure down there was four times that on the surface, so four times more gas was required to fill a diver's lungs, further reducing the time that could be spent inside the flooded mine on standard scuba kit.

Pressure increases so significantly deep underwater because water is much more dense than air. The pressure at sea level is 1 Atmosphere or 1 Bar (the unit of pressure used in diving). This is the weight of the column of air above you from sea level all the way to the top of the atmosphere, a distance of approximately 11 kilometres. At a depth of only ten metres, you are already at 2 Bar (twice the pressure at sea level) because a ten-metre column of water weighs the same as an 11-kilometre column of air. And for every ten metres deeper you go you add another Atmosphere, or Bar, of pressure. So at only 30 metres you are at 4 Bar, four times the pressure you experience normally.

In cave diving, we tend to stick to what is called the rule of thirds. This means you use one third of your gas on the way in and one third on the way out, leaving you one third in reserve. This would mean, even using large scuba cylinders, you would only get about thirty minutes in the mine before having to turn around and head for home. That said, being thirty minutes' swim from the nearest exit is still a dangerous proposition if you don't know what you're doing. In this relatively brief time, you would be lucky to lay a few hundred metres of line. Laying line is important, since a significant number of cave-diving deaths over the years have resulted from divers becoming lost. We lay this line, this Ariadne's thread, so we can find our way back through the labyrinth and home to safety.

Martyn also told me that he had seen far more than would normally be expected in some of these flooded mines. Other mines across the country had been completely or mostly stripped of equipment before the pumps were turned off, with only the odd scrap of metal, wood or bricks scattered across the tunnel floor. Not this example, however. This one had machinery, old tracks and carts, and Martyn even described tally marks scraped into the wall of the passageway. The foremen of the mining teams would have made these marks to count the number of carts, each laden with slate, that their teams were bringing out. The marks on this wall represented those last few cartloads that had been mined on the final day. This to me was an incredibly evocative piece of history, a modern example of something akin to the ancient rock art found in caves across Europe. These were the marks left by a human hand, a human whose existence would have been centred on the time he spent under the earth, whose family and community would have relied on the work he and his comrades carried out in this mine.

This mine, like many locations for cave diving in the UK, man-made or natural, was not located in a position that would be simple to access and it would take a great deal of physical effort and perseverance to hump the mountain of heavy diving equipment I'd need into it. Initially, I decided to reconnoitre the topside site and access to see what I'd need in order to get to the waterline properly attired for the underwater phase. I also threw two seven-litre diving cylinders and some basic lightweight diving kit into the car, just in case it worked out that I had the time, energy and inclination for a short underwater recce, too.

It took me a couple of passes to confirm I was in the right location. I eventually parked up in a muddy space just off the narrow single-lane road that meandered through the hills and farmland of this part of Wales. Clambering over a stile, I followed a rough track down a grassy slope, twice almost skidding on to my backside before I'd even spotted the mine. The path led through a thick forest, which levelled off and swung round to the left. I heard a waterfall off to my right and could just make out its boiling top through the trees. This area was lush and green but it was also a channel for water running off the surrounding hills, creating the high water table that had sunk the mine's deeper reaches.

There is a defined level where groundwater sits. If you burrow below this level, you will need to pump water out continually to keep the passages dry. Once those pumps are turned off, all the chambers beneath groundwater level will slowly refill.

I continued down the track another few hundred metres expecting to see an entrance or at least evidence of a major sub-surface operation. Nothing. After a few more minutes, I was sure I'd come too far and doubled back. Another few rounds of this manoeuvre finally allowed me to spot the remains of an overgrown track leading off into the woods. High-stepping along this, I tried not to rip my trousers and shins on the entangled brambles that obstructed progress. Within less than a minute, I stood at the top of a very abrupt incline, which turned out to be the top edge of a steeply sided bowl-shaped crater.

The sides were heavily overgrown but through the strangely angled trees and twisted vegetation I could make out what looked like an opening in the cliff face below me. I skidded down the steep bank, ducking and sledging under low branches that swung directly across my path only feet from the ground. At the bottom, I dusted myself down – pointless considering my hands were as muddy as the rest of me and it only served to spread the dirt around – pulled the odd thorn from palms and thighs and gazed up at a gaping maw. A huge semicircular mouth opened before me, an entrance to the underworld. As I stepped closer, the daylight illuminated the scene just inside. I could see that the ground once again fell away at a steep angle but, this time, as it entered the mine, it was strewn with large, sharply angled boulders of slate. Water dripped from the roof on to the slate dust scattered around, producing a greasy veneer. All this made the descent fairly treacherous and I often required the use of all four limbs to stabilize myself, as a slip, landing in the crooked holes between rocks or against the razor-sharp slate edges, could result in a serious injury with little hope of immediate help.

At the bottom of the slope, the ground levelled out and the initial chamber began to look more like a troglodyte settle-ment than an abandoned mine. There were compacted paths and walled areas, huts, cabins and shelters all built from bricks of slate. Old boiler tanks the size of cars, huge teethed cogs, strops, tracks and unidentifiable metalwork were strewn across the ground. If the underwater passages were as full of artefacts and constructions as this, I'd be in for an interesting dive.

It then occurred to me that I wasn't the first person apart from Martyn to enter this mine in the eighty-odd years since its abandonment. Locals and those interested in urban history had been visiting it regularly. No doubt many items had been discovered and recovered as mementos over the years. However, only one person I knew of had ever dived the preliminary underwater passages, and much of the flooded system lay completely unexplored. Even more fascinating material could be waiting, untouched, for someone to discover.

I scouted out the various tunnel directions and decided to push left; it seemed to best fit the way Martyn had described the route to the entrance pool of the submerged sections. After leaving some huge, cathedral-like chambers, I made my way through tunnels low enough to necessitate stumbling forward bent double. Eventually, the tunnel opened up into another large chamber, the size of which I could not fully appreciate with the meagre beam from my head-torch. But what I could spot was a pool of water. It was not the first I'd come across but this one was evidently deep and I noticed an old piece of line, tied to a scrap of thick piping, which led off into the dark, forbidding lake and disappeared beneath its black surface. This was the line Martyn had laid down years before, following it back to this point to get out. This is where I'd start.

Enthused and excited, I raced as best I could back up the field of slate debris and back into the light. A thigh-burning quick march up the side of the crater and a jog back along and up the path had me back at the car. Deciding I hadn't come all this way not to dip down under the surface – just to see what the conditions were like, you understand – I grabbed my dive kit and an old rope and headed back. It was slower going this time. The dive kit I was carrying weighed in excess of 40 kilograms. At the lip of the crater, I anchored the rope and descended using a hand line to stop me taking a tumble that might result in injury or, worse, damaged equipment. The debris field at the mine entrance was even more precarious under the extra weight and trying to walk bent double was not doing my poor spine much good.

Gratefully, I reached the dive site, dumped my dive kit on the least filthy patch I could find, took a quick breather, then returned to the car for the second load. This time I brought a large rucksack full of everything else I'd need to dive. I'd taken a wetsuit, as it weighs a lot less than a drysuit. Although I'd opted for less weight, if I'd known when I was packing that the water was going to be about five degrees Celsius, I might have reconsidered.

Mines, like caves, can be psychologically oppressive environments to work in. Although the darkness can hold the promise of new discoveries and adventures, that same darkness, coupled with a claustrophobic atmosphere in which you're cut off from the world above and bereft of the senses, can also compel you to return to the ground above. The thought of the calming presence of daylight and the familiarity of the elements, regardless of their ferocity, is always a lure. I can only liken the time between arriving at a dive site with all my kit and actually submerging to an early-morning visit to the gym. The hardest part is getting yourself out of bed on a cold, wet, dark morning, getting dressed and out of the door. Once you're over that initial hurdle, you'll go. Perhaps, on an even more basic level, the desire to stay above ground in the daylight is like overcoming the hurdle of coming out from under the covers and getting upright. Once this is done, you're off. I try to not ponder on the subject too much: alarm goes off – get up. Don't *think* about getting up, otherwise it won't happen. So, like those pre-gym early winter mornings, pre-dive I take a few bolstering, if resigned, breaths and begin to strip in haste. Once you're naked, you may as well get on with it.

DIVING THE LOST MINE

Heaving on a 7mm foam rubber suit soon has me a little on the hot and sweaty side. I pull on my diving cylinders, clip on my reels and check my gauges and regulators. All work perfectly. I don my gloves, hood, mask and finally my helmet, since a bang to the head that may leave you momentarily dazed and confused on the surface can lead you to drown underwater.

(And that is the major safety implication with diving. There are certain physical dangers specific to diving physiology, but many deaths are caused by things that would be minor if they happened on land. Getting tangled in line, getting lost, momentarily passing out, having a mild panic attack – all, if land based, would either be minor or at least not life threatening. Underwater, these can often result in a fatality. I do not want to dissuade people from diving. It is an incredibly safe sport, even the more extreme forms, if conducted properly with the correct training, equipment, plan and attitude. But I can think of no other environment on earth so alien, so inhospitable to human life, where your survival, without the support of an array of modern technology, is measured in seconds.)

With that at the forefront of my mind, I sit on the water's edge and follow a process any experienced technical or extreme diver would go through. I play out the entire dive in my head, miming actions like checking depth, time and the gas contents of my diving cylinders, clipping lines, checking navigation and dropping lights. This only takes a few minutes of quiet contemplation but it assures me my plan is sound, my kit is ready for the task and I'm confident in myself and content to carry on. I start this dive confident and calm, as I always do. If you're scared or seriously apprehensive, that's a big combat indicator that something isn't right, probably with you. You shouldn't dive.

I come out of my near-yogic state relaxed and focused and move out into the water. Descending down the near-vertical slope, I spot a set of narrow-gauge rail tracks appearing out of the fine silt that sits across the mine floor in a deep layer. I follow these deeper and deeper, checking my gas supplies and switching regulators to make sure they both work. I alternate which cylinder I breathe from, flicking on and off my three torches to make sure everything is working. Turning back now is still easy. But all is well as the bottom of the shaft emerges from the gloom at about 28 metres below the surface.

I can see Martyn's old blue polypropylene line tied to the top right corner of the entrance to the horizontal passageway before me and I follow it in. Within minutes it branches off left, right and straight on. The two side passages appear to stop in dead ends, so I clip a clothes peg to the line and continue straight on, deeper into the complex. (The clothes peg is a trick to help you find your way out on previously laid line. At a crossroad or T-junction of line, a diver will clip a marker, in my case a common or garden clothes peg, to the side where the exit lies. So if you arrive at the junction in a hurry and stressed, all you need do is follow the line with the peg on it and you'll be heading along the same path as the one you came in on. It may not always be the fastest way out, but a longer route that you know, 100 per cent, will get you topside is better than gambling on a shortcut that may never get you home.)

I push further into the mine and begin to see some of the things Martyn has described to me. I see an old cart and some machinery off to one side of the narrow tunnel but I am acutely aware I only have enough gas for about fifteen minutes of pene- tration before I have to make a U-turn and find my way back out. This trip is just to check conditions and get an idea of where I can start my exploration next time. I try to float through the centre of the tunnel to minimize the disturbance of the fine dust covering the rough walls and floor. The last thing I want to do is disturb the silt and bring the visibility down. That will only reduce my chances of finding the line and getting home. The passage itself is not too small, being no less than a metre wide and a metre and a half high in places. I check my gauges that show me how much gas I have left and note I must turn back soon.

I look back up at the line. I can't see it. It no longer stretches out before me. I steady myself in the water. I invert myself, bringing my feet above my head so I am almost hanging upside down. This allows me, with the minimum of fuss, to look back the way I've come. And there is the line only an arm's length behind me. I have swum over the end of it while checking my gauges. All is well.

I have reached the end of Martyn's line and the extent of current exploration. I hang in the water for a moment, gazing off down the tunnel that stretches out before me, continuing deeper into the mine and far beyond the reach of my torch beam. It is tantalizing; the unknown beckons me into the darkness. But I am out of time and reluctantly turn my back on the new ground and go back the way I came. As I exit the tunnel and begin my ascent, spending time decompressing in the shallows, my mind spins with the potential. Just the brief glimpse of the artefacts in the initial tunnels has inspired me and I am already running through plans to return. But what is evident is that scuba gear will limit my time too much and constrain me from pushing significantly further into the system.

It would be months before I had a chance to return but this time I was armed with a closed-circuit re-breather. This machine recycles a diver's exhaled gas, scrubbing out the carbon dioxide and injecting tiny amounts of oxygen to compensate for that metabolized by the body. What all this means in simple terms is that no bubbles are produced, no gas is wasted and a diver can carry out dives of up to four hours or more, regardless of depth. I was also armed with a drysuit this time. When I'd exited the water after the first investigative dive in my wetsuit, I had spent less than fifty minutes in the five-degree waters but was still shivering as I peeled it off with pale-blue, violently shaking hands. This time I hoped to spend over three hours deep inside the submerged mine complex and needed to stay warm and alert.

Of course, no diving was going to take place until I had sherpaed the mountain of diving gear from the lay-by to the dive site. As well as my re-breather, drysuit, mask, fins, gloves and hood, I also had four metal reels, two with about 250 metres of line, one with 50 metres as a back-up and a thick ten-metre line for use in emergencies. This last one was in case of losing the line if the visibility reduced because of a silt-out or all my torches stopped working. If I lost the line completely, I'd drop a small weight tied to the end of this short line in my current position. This would keep the start of the line in one place as I made excursions out from that known fixed point. I'd then reel the line out to its end, trying to feel for the tiny piece of string that would guide me out to the exit and the right side of the life-or-death equation. I then had three cameras to capture some underwater footage, four video lights and three torches. Exploration was not to be the only mission on this dive, as I was attempting to produce a short film.

But that was not all. In case my re-breather had a catastrophic failure and ceased to work, I needed a bail-out plan. In technical dives like these, especially solo operations, you must pay a great deal of attention to redundancy plans. That's why cave divers carry three torches – a main, a back-up and a back-up to the back-up. Going blind underwater inside a complex cave system is not conducive to a long life. So I would be carrying five standard scuba cylinders. As I explored the flooded mine, I would drop individual cylinders at predetermined points. Then, should my re-breather fail, I would have enough gas from the fifth, the last, of these scuba cylinders, still strapped to my side, to make it back to the previous one I'd just dropped. This one would have enough gas to get me to the next, and so on. I'd leapfrog, dropping used and picking up fresh cylinders, all the way back to the entrance and the first cylinder. Here, I'd have dropped one full of a mixed gas containing 50 per cent oxygen and 50 per cent nitrogen, which, as I ascended, would allow me to decompress faster and exit the water sooner – something I'd be keen to do after an intense exit swim that could last well over an hour.

I had two friends with me to film the topside activities. In the end, it took us four round trips each to hump all my gear into the mine and down to the water's edge – fast and light this project was not. Although we had more kit than I would have had had I been alone, the distribution of effort made it much easier on me and probably halved the amount of ferrying time. Having the lads there with me also eased the psychological burden. But the biggest difference to my mood was made by the light. Johnny, the cameraman, had huge panel lights. These miniature supernovas fountained light across the chamber and I could finally appreciate its true scale. I also felt more positive and relaxed kitting up in the comforting light compared to the weak beam of a head-torch that I am used to in these circumstances. Its narrow, feeble light only serves to increase the feeling of claustrophobia.

I had briefed Raz, the director, and Johnny that if they wanted to reshoot these terrestrial scenes we'd return tomorrow and I'd kit up and strip again for the camera. Today, I had to focus on the job in hand and I didn't need distractions. Besides, being asked to repeatedly lift heavy, awkward kit on and off would only wind me up and I'd end up starting the dive in a bad mood, chuntering to myself about how those two blokes were a bloody liability.

I finally managed to don all the equipment and floated face down across the surface of the water as a test, wriggling around and making sure everything was secure and comfortable. Satisfied, I pulled up my head, gave the OK signal and a brief salute to Raz and Johnny, and disappeared beneath the ink-glazed surface. As I descended, I actually grew in comfort and serenity. As useful as my friends had been in the logistics, and as calming as their presence was, I was on my own time now, no distractions or influences. I had no one to think about, to consider or care about, but me.

The Long Walk is the nickname given to the approach a bomb-disposal officer makes on his own towards an explosive device. When this was my job, I would leave the safety of the Incident Control Point, where everyone else would wait, and in those moments as I sauntered towards the explosive I would feel a sense of clarity and tranquillity. At times like these, life's normal, multiple, everyday stresses become irrelevant and your life becomes about one single thing, and in that clarity and focus – regardless of how stressful that single thing is – its sole status means it is simpler to deal with.

So, as I descended, I relaxed. I reached the bottom of the shaft and dropped my decompression cylinder, clipping it to the line so that even if the visibility reduced, or I was left in complete darkness, I could follow the line out by feel and would hit on this emergency bottle. I took time to look at my surroundings, to appreciate the remarkable state of preservation and to study the artefacts around me. I always find the first few minutes inside a cave the most awkward, as I adjust to my kit and environment, but today I was in a state of wonder as I floated through my personal underwater museum to a bygone era, a heyday of British industry.

As I approached the cart I had passed on the recce dive, I had a chance to study it. The wooden planking that formed the deck was still in an incredibly strong state and the wheels still sat on the tiny railway line, looking as if a good hammering would knock the rust off and the little vehicle would roll on once again. To the right was the machinery I had also glimpsed last time. It was built into a recess in the tunnel wall and looked to be some kind of winch mechanism, all boxed parts and huge teethed cogs, some as much as a metre across. This dive I took the time to branch off the main line, left and right. Most ended in rubble or steep slopes and were likely to be other shafts that led to the surface and offered alternative entry points to the system somewhere above me.

As I moved through the passages, I tried to minimize how much I disturbed the water. The rough walls were covered in the same fine silt as the floor, and the roof was spotted with some kind of material that had leached from the rock or metal and looked like yellow fungus. Even the weakest waft of a hand or fin sent a shockwave through the water, which gently kissed the tunnel walls and lifted the sediment into suspension.

Still carrying four cylinders strapped to my side as well as the re-breather on my back, I felt weighed down and cumbersome, especially as I was also carrying a tripod with lead weights taped to each leg, the extra lights and three cameras. I decided to start capturing some footage, as it was essential for the final film. I set my tripod up and tried to illuminate the area I'd be swimming through. The first thing to go wrong was the arm support for the light, which was supposed to stick out from a tripod leg but fell off. I then tried desperately to use ledges on the walls, carts and even an old fence that I found to rest torches on. There were many false starts caused by unworkable lighting and my movements were causing the water around me to stir. Disturbed silt began to build up, forming a light dusting across the tunnel, which developed into a full blizzard. I moved on to another section and tried again.

It became evident that I had made a basic error in my plan. I had attempted to cut corners and achieve two conflicting goals in one dive. I could now either ditch the camera and lighting gear, forget about trying to film and just persevere with the exploration. Or I could ditch the extra cylinders, hanging on to just two, and remain in the first few hundred metres of passageway, filming the shots we needed. I couldn't do both. The film was a more pressing priority and I felt that the commitment of time and effort made by my friends back on the surface would be poorly repaid if I abandoned it. I made the call to film.

By this time, I had wasted almost an hour. I began getting the shots I needed of me swimming into and out of frame, which was a laborious process of setting up the lights and camera, framing it, swimming away down the tunnel until I was certain I was out of sight, then swimming back. I then had to check the footage on the camera screen and when it – inevitably – didn't work, amend the positions, reset and repeat. Once I had had enough of this, I focused on the points of interest I had passed on the way in. As I drifted back towards the entrance, through the white-out of silt I had created, I decided a shot of the entrance frame would look interesting. As I approached the final few metres of passageway, I recalled

Martyn mentioning that it was here he had seen the tally marks. I cast my torchlight around the area to see if there was anything scratched into the rock face and I came across something that caused me to stop suddenly. Written on the slate wall were initials, names and dates, the clearest of which read: 'TED – 19 JAN 1938'. Ted, whoever he was, had stood here, presumably on the last day the mine was in operation, the last day before the flood water reclaimed this subterranean world seventy-five years ago. It was a poignant moment and I spent some time floating mid-water, staring at the marks made by men whose world had revolved around this dark place.

As I made my way out, I was satisfied with the footage but the exploration had been a failure, having gone little further than 100 metres beyond Martyn's old line. During the spell I spent in the shallows, waiting for the decompression time on my dive computer to clock down to zero and allow me to surface safely, I was already pondering how to improve the plan for my next trip, the one that would centre its full attention on exploring as deep into the mine as possible. This trip had whetted my appetite; the artefacts, structures, tools, machinery and especially the old markings on the wall had all left me wondering what other discoveries awaited me.

Once again, it was months before I returned. In the meantime, other divers had been exploring the mine, working as two-, three- or four-man dive teams and using very large scuba cylinders to maximize their time underwater. I met one of these fellow cave divers at a conference I was talking at and we discussed what his team had found, where they had and hadn't been and the potential extent of the underwater mine. They'd been busy making multiple shorter dives, due to the time restriction of scuba kit over a re-breather, and had, over many dives, managed to build up a good picture of the mine and what potential lay in the outer reaches. This information was very useful, as it seemed the mine was unlikely to be miles and miles of passageways and I could dispense with some of the extra gear and reduce the number of cylinders. It also meant I could plan and target those last areas others hadn't yet reached.

In caving and cave diving, there is an unwritten rule, an ethical code (not always followed), which says that if someone has discovered a new system they should be allowed to continue to explore that system until they have clearly reached the extent of what their abilities will allow them to achieve. When they give up, they then open it up to others. However, I was happy that another team had made progress in the mine. I had only discovered it because Martyn had pointed the way. And it was not even Martyn's discovery, since we were merely redis-covering a small part of something that the local community had created decades before and knew existed all along – they probably just had more constructive things to do with their time than swim around in it. I was happy to see that the spirit of adventure is alive and well in the British diving community and that some people will still make time away from work and family to push themselves and the limits of our current knowl-edge. And now, armed with some of that new knowledge, I made a plan for one last trip.

As before, I made multiple trips on my own to groan and sweat my equipment into the dive base inside the mine. Because I now knew more about the layout of the mine, I had reassessed its size and how far, at the furthest point, I'd be from the exit.

I knew I'd not need as many emergency cylinders of gas to see me safely out should my re-breather, my primary breathing source, fail. So I only carried three extra cylinders this time. The first, my emergency deco-bottle (short for decompression-bottle, as the mix in this bottle is only used as you return to the shallows to decompress), I'd drop off on the way in at a depth of 20 metres. It was still filled with nitrox, a gas mix of 50 per cent oxygen and 50 per cent nitrogen. I'd then collect this on the way out. I could only use this bottle from 21 metres and shallower, so there was no point carrying it around the lower passageways that were all below 30 metres deep. And because I had reassessed the furthest point of the mine to be closer than I'd first guessed, I only took two other cylinders as bail-out gas. It was enough to get me back out of the mine tunnels if the re-breather had any catastrophic issues.

As on my first visit, I suited up in the faint silvery-fogged light of my head-torch, my breath creating a mist in the beam as it rose past my face. I had added two extra one-and-a-half-litre cylinders to my re-breather. One would fill my drysuit and remove the need to steal gas from one of my bail-outs. (You need to pump air into a drysuit to counteract the squeezing that occurs as the depth and pressure increase as you descend – it's not only uncomfortable, it's also very hard to move when you're effectively vacuum packed into your own suit.) The other was an emergency oxygen bottle. As I've already said, as the re-breather recycles the diver's breath it injects a tiny amount of oxygen to make up for those equally tiny amounts that are metabolized by the human body. If this failed, I would normally have to bail out on to one of the two scuba cylinders I had and ascend. But in these conditions, ascending is not an immediate option and it is much more beneficial to stay on the re-breather. This little bottle could be switched over and I could continue to use my much more efficient re-breather to exit the mine with extra time in the bank. Survival is usually a matter of preparation.

Dressed up, I waded out into the black water until it was waist-deep and bent my knees so that only my head was above the oily surface. I descended the now familiar near-vertical slope, following the cart rails down and in. I paused at the entrance to once again wonder at the writing on the wall. Past the cart and pushing onwards, I began to glance at my wrist slate on which was written some directions and notes from my meeting and communications with the other divers.

On this, my final trip, I found multiple new dead ends, those not already pinpointed by the other teams. I also saw evidence of a small roof collapse – a timely reminder that these places are not as structurally sound as they may appear and rock is not the eternally unchanging substance that people often assume it to be. I also confirmed the presence of two unknown ramps that seemed to lead to the surface and later confirmed the dry sections of mine tunnels they connected to. I found an old workman's hobnailed boot, a small tin mug and, most evocatively for me, the metal end of a small pickaxe. I was surprised at its size – no more than a foot or so across. Perhaps in these cramped conditions it was impossible to swing a huge tool. I saw no more large artefacts like the train of carts or the cogged machinery system near the entrance, nor any other writing or marks on the walls. As I reached what I believed to be the furthest corner of the mine, I paused with my back against the wall, looking down the passageway I had just swum through, as it disappeared into the blackness past the extent of my torchlight. I hovered there, pausing for a moment.

I'd first heard of this site over four years earlier and it had been over three years between my first and last dives. It had occupied my mind throughout that period, even if only in the background, and now I was leaving for the last time. As I drifted back towards the exit, I had an even greater appreciation of my surroundings. I really looked at the walls, their shape, textures and colour and how beautiful the rock looked even in the decreased visibility caused by my movement on the way in. As I swam past the names on the wall at the entrance, pausing to look at them for the last time, I felt a little melancholy. But I was satisfied with my dive and felt privileged to have been one of the few people who had ever – and will ever – see this lost corner of Britain.

By the time I'd collected my emergency decompression cylinder and ascended to my last decompression stop at six metres below the surface, my mind had already moved on to the next project. Which other mines or underground man-made history could I explore, perhaps if not in the UK then abroad? For any exploratory diver, whether it's a trip into the unexplored bowels of some unknown shipwreck, the deep Stygian gloom of the furthest fathoms of the ocean or the submerged subterranean world of an undiscovered cave, one thing is always true . . . the darkness beckons.

CHAPTER 10

A Mini-Expedition to the Monachs

'Expedition' is an overused word these days. People talk about doing diving expeditions to the Isles of Scilly when, in my opinion, the word 'holiday' would be more appropriate. I was once asked, when giving a talk at an adventure show, how I defined the difference between an adventure holiday and a true expedition. I replied, 'Expeditions by their nature should have a goal or purpose: to summit a mountain, to document new species, history or culture and, preferably, should bring back some previously unknown information rather than just be for the personal accomplishment or status of the individual.

'They should also be hard work. If you don't spend the majority of your time on the expedition wishing you were not on the expedition, then it's probably not an expedition.'

However, I'm now going to contradict all that. But to make myself marginally less hypocritical I'm going to call this particular trip a mini-expedition. The point I'm making throughout this book is that you can experience the same sense of accomplishment and encounter the same problems that you get with a major expedition somewhere exotic, while on a mini-expedition right here in the UK. We too have wild, remote, uninhabited places where you can feel like you are in a far-flung corner of the earth and be many days from rescue should something go wrong. This particular example of a British mini-expedition takes us to the Monach Islands.

The Monachs, a small collection of unpopulated islands, lie in the cold North Atlantic about eight miles west of the closest point of civilization, which is the larger, populated (albeit sparsely) island of North Uist, itself a remote and wild island on the edges of the Outer Hebrides in the far north-west of Britain. The Monachs are scarcely more than spits of sand surrounded by rocky reefs and skerries. These sandbars cling to existence despite the fierce North Atlantic storms of gale-force ferocity that are visited upon them from across the sea for six months of the year, winds which bring toweringly destructive waves to batter their shores.

The islands get their name from the Gaelic Eilean nam Manach – Island of the Monks. A monastery existed here in the eleventh century and it is said that the holy men would light a pyre to warn ships of the island's hull-ravaging rocks and reefs. It is even said that the modern unmanned lighthouse commands the same spot as the original friars' pyres. It is believed that the islands were once joined to the 'mainland' of North Uist by a narrow stretch of sand that was beaten out of existence by a huge storm in the fifteenth century, and historical documents seem to support this. It is said that up to about fifty years ago fishermen could still see the outlines of walls – possibly of fields, pens or even buildings – beneath the sea when the waters were still and clear.

Today, the islands are bereft of people. Up until the 1930s, there was a handful of folk living on Ceann Ear – the largest of the Monach Islands at about two kilometres square. They eked out a living by crofting on the extremely thin, sandy soil. However, in 1931, with the community in decline, the islands were hit by a storm that ripped up huge tracts of the marram grass, a plant that was essential in holding the sand, soil and land together against the driving wind. The meagre soil was then washed away. With no means of supporting themselves, the people abandoned the island. The last to leave were the lighthouse keepers, and it became unmanned in 1942. Only the skeletons of a few old buildings are still evident.

However, there are still plenty of inhabitants. Ground-nesting birdlife flourishes on islands without terrestrial predators like rats or foxes. Insect life is prolific in the milder seasons and the island is surrounded by a marine community that is fed by the nutrient-rich, cold Atlantic and thrives away from the pressures of large-scale commercial operations. Throughout the year, these remote, secluded and wild sand-covered spits of land are home to small groups of grey seals. These are Britain's largest land-breeding animals, with males weighing up to 340 kilograms – 50 per cent larger than a red deer stag. Every autumn, the islands play host to one of the truly great spectacles in the British nature calendar when tens of thousands of grey seals come ashore to fight, breed, give birth and wean their pups. For six weeks each year, the Monachs become the largest grey-seal colony in Europe and the second largest in the world. Witnessing an aggregation of this scale by an animal of this size is awe-inspiring.

But, clearly, the Monachs are not on one of the usual tourist trails and require more than a car, youth-hostel membership and a sense of purpose to visit. Eight miles may not seem a great deal but the seas between North Uist and the Monachs can be ferocious and there is no means of getting across on public transport. The only way to reach the islands is in your own boat and by crossing the often tumultuous Monach Sound.

The idea to visit the Monachs came about when I was looking for an idea for a diving magazine article. I liked the idea of doing some kind of wild, camping–diving excursion to a place in the UK so remote I'd never see another soul. I then decided an uninhabited island was perfect and scoured the Internet and OS maps for inspiration. I initially looked at North Rona, a tiny island 45 miles north of Cape Wrath and not to be mistaken for the much larger South Rona, but the presence of six scientists on the island at the time I wanted to go discouraged me – for now.

I then discovered the Monachs. As a Scottish diver with a degree in zoology, the fact that I had no idea we had this scale of marine spectacle within the British Isles shocked me. I decided to go further than just the article and thought that, since I'd wanted to produce my own film for some time, I would make this the subject of my feature. My intention, then, was to spend a week observing the seals, to write an article, take some photos and try to capture some of it on film. And I intended to cover the amazing grey seals wildlife event from above and below the surface. For a location as remote as this with no infrastructure, I would have to plan this trip as carefully as I would any true expedition.

After a great deal of research – checking routes, ferries, permissions, submitting a plan to Scottish Natural Heritage for approval and calculating some kind of budget – I could begin the practicalities. I first gathered my team – a group of friends who volunteered to take a week off and join me in visiting one of the most inaccessible dive sites in the country. At the very least I'd need a cameraman and another diver. These came in the guise of cameraman Stuart Keasley and dive instructor Martin McGrath. I managed to scrounge a small compressor, so we could refill our diving equipment with compressed air, and a lightweight portable generator to recharge electrical equipment and cameras. We'd fill a couple of jerrycans in North Uist and hopefully have the power to work the whole week. All this plus fuel, camping kit, dive kit, filming kit and food saw the equipment list start to pile up. Although we could squeeze it in and strap it to Martin's Land Rover to get it as far as North Uist, I still had no way of getting any of the equipment from there to the tiny collection of sand-covered rocks in the middle of the North Atlantic. Fortunately, Andy Moll, a friend from a local dive club, said he could lend me a large RIB (Rigid Inflatable Boat) on a single condition – that he could come too. I was more than happy to have a fourth member of the team to share the load, especially if he was bringing a boat. So the four of us set off, RIB in tow, and struck out north.

Fourteen hours later, having crossed on to the Isle of Skye via the bridge of the same name, we found ourselves at the port of Uig. After a short wait, and a visit to the brewery that shares the harbourside with the ferry, we boarded and sailed the three hours to the shores of North Uist. Disembarkation was followed by a circumnavigation of the island to overnight in another friend's house. He was living on the island for six months while filming for the BBC. We took advantage of the fairly negotiable timings of last orders to unwind after a seventeen-hour trip before retiring to get a good night's sleep in preparation for the hard work that lay ahead.

It was an early start, as we had to clock up at least 42 sea miles that day (equivalent to 46.2 normal miles, as there are 1.1 miles to a nautical mile) – we needed at least two trips to transport the manpower and gear from North Uist to the Monachs. From the closest slipway where we could launch and load our boat, it was 14 miles to a small bay on the largest island of the Monachs that could provide the closest thing to a sheltered landing. We'd then have to carry all our equipment and supplies the 400 metres from the beach to our new home, return to the main island and do it all again.

When the islands were deserted in 1931, the handful of buildings began to crumble. However, in 2007, a group called Friends of Heisgeir (that being the islands' name in Gaelic, from the Norse for skerry) decided to rebuild the old schoolhouse as a bothy to act as a refuge for local fishermen who, caught in worsening weather and powerless to cross the Sound, were unable to get home to North Uist. The fishermen could wait out the storm, potentially lasting days, in relative comfort. Extra provisions were always left in case of emergencies and the room was furnished with basic bed frames and old mattresses, a table and chairs. For a small fee to assist with maintenance, visitors were allowed to use the facilities. Although pretty rustic, those facilities were significantly more luxurious than a week in a Scottish October living, diving and filming from a tent, which had been my initial, miserable plan.

Of course, the building had no electricity, hence the portable generator, and no means of communication, so our only contact with the outside world would be daily check-ins with the Stornoway Coastguard via VHF radio. We'd receive information on the next day's weather and let them know we were all still in one piece and that no rescue was required . . . yet.

Our launch point was a beach called Stinky Bay, so named because as the tide receded it exposed rafts of seaweed in various states of decomposition that created a striking aroma. It was also the site where, according to written accounts of the time, a mermaid was washed ashore in 1830 and buried nearby in an unmarked grave. We loaded an embarrassingly large amount of equipment for our mini-expedition on to what appeared to be a rapidly shrinking boat, a domed heap of drybags covering heavy diving and fragile filming equipment. We set off at a somewhat sluggish and tentative pace, eyeing the mound strapped around the boat like a tinker's caravan and preparing to leap heroically into the sea to rescue any essentials that shook loose. As it happened, the sea was relatively calm and it was blowing no more than a Force 2. We managed to make the first crossing without losing anything important . . . like the obligatory bottle of whisky, for example.

Our anchorage in the small bay of Port Ruadh (Red Port) on the south-east corner was the best of many evils and by no means ideal, with numerous shallow sections and countless rocks skulking just under the surface, waiting to ambush a passing boat's bottom. We snuck in slowly, with all eyes watching the water surrounding us to spot any potential 'hull-rippers'. But this constant and necessary observation became more difficult within moments of entering the bay.

I'd had concerns that perhaps we'd not see any seals during our week, that I would have invested so much in this little expedition to achieve nothing, letting down my friends who had volunteered to help me, the magazine to which I had promised an article and those expecting a film. It might seem ridiculous to worry about not seeing any seals when tens of thousands are expected each year but wildlife can never be relied on to cooperate and I have experienced projects in the past where 'guaranteed' sightings have not materialized. Even if it's a one in a million chance that the seals won't come, it's hard, after all the effort and personal expense, for one's mind not to dwell on the singular. However, my fears were instantly banished. As we drew closer, what looked like a dozen small, dark buoys bobbing in the water formed into the heads of grey seals. They came within feet of the boat and it was then that the huge size of some of the big males could truly be appreciated. As we neared the beach, what appeared to be boulders strewn across the sand morphed into the grey bodies of females weaning small white pups. Finding a seal was not going to be an issue.

One tiny problem we had as we entered the shallows was the state of the tide. It was low and meant that our 400-metre walk to the bothy was now closer to 600, the first 200 of which would require wading through water, decreasing from chest to ankle, carrying some incredibly awkward and heavy masses above our heads. Sweating in our sealed rubber drysuits, we finally got the last of the shipment to dry land and decided to leave it on the shore and return for a second load before the forecast deterioration in weather began. Another two crossings of the Sound, similar in tone to the first but with the wind and waves picking up, and we were finally able to peel off our drysuits and watch the steam rise off our bodies in the rapidly approaching twilight. Another hour of hard graft, humping kit from the shoreline to the bothy, and we had all our equipment and stores housed within the homely and robust walls of the old schoolhouse, with a reassuring kettle boiling in the background. I say complete, but we'd decided there was no point lugging four sets of heavy steel diving cylinders up and down to the bothy every day, so we left them under a tarpaulin well above the high-tide mark. These things weigh a ton, so they were hardly likely to blow away. There is simply no point making extra work for yourself.

The old schoolhouse was a more impressive affair than I had expected. A small tank had been installed to capture any rainwater running down off the roof. It had a gas cooker – run from a bottle, as the nearest mains supply was about 100 miles away. The renovation had been a sound job and the building was now weather-tight and extremely cosy despite the gale that was building outside. We'd brought a bag of peat across from the main island but its use on the fire was always a gamble. The fire warmed the room and gave a satisfying and comforting light on the dark evenings. However, the chimney was blocked and a sudden swirl of wind from outside would launch a thick fog of black smoke into the room, obscuring everything. The air would clear and the coughing would diminish just in time for the next cloud to erupt.

After a long day at sea, with all the humping of kit up to our new palace, the success of finally getting there and seeing all the grey seals, we were relieved, satisfied and dog-tired. We settled down for a good night's sleep. Or so I'd hoped. Unfortunately, I am an incredibly light sleeper. Useful sometimes in my service in the Army but less so in my current incarnation, which involves work trips with hairy-arsed commercial divers, old-in-the-tooth wildlife cameramen and drunken directors. The wind howling around our little fortress was comforting as I snuggled into my sleeping bag, but the meteoric roaring that was coming from my slumbering com-patriots made me so frustrated I found myself running through various methods of murder. I tried to comfort myself by coming up with descriptions of the noise for my article. I think 'attempting to tie an alpine butterfly knot into an elephant's trunk' was my favourite. We had a second small room in the bothy in which to store our equipment – I slept in there from the second night.

As dawn broke and we rose, some of us more bleary-eyed than others, the kettle was thrown on the stove and the tea was brewed – we are British, after all. In the mornings, we all donned our undersuits – thick, fleecy suits, not unlike a baby's romper, that divers wear under their drysuits. We pretty much lived in these for the week and simply slipped our drysuits on over the top if diving or our waterproofs if we were heading out for terrestrial activities. The first morning, we took the opportunity to explore our new home, wandering around with the confidence that we were the only souls on the land. It is an amazingly refreshing feeling to strike out of a morning and know you are the only people around. There is a tangible sense of freedom and calm that no threat can strike unseen and unprepared for. If you chose to, you could wander around naked with no chance of anyone complaining. However, the harsh westerlies blowing off the North Atlantic discourage such wanton displays of personal liberty.

The island has prolific birdlife, including large flocks of Canadian geese that Stu chased around for the whole week, trying desperately to get a close-up photo of them. They would lure him in, teasingly waiting until he had stalked them to within a few metres . . . then fly off and land 100 metres fur-ther away and the whole process would begin again. He never did get that photo. Mute swan, lapwing, dunlin, redshank and shag were all in attendance, along with the usual collection of oyster catchers, herring and black-backed gulls. Amongst the wildlife was rusted metal wreckage, twisted debris providing a palpable display of the ferocity of the storms that hit the island. There was a cardinal marker buoy lying in the middle of the island and not far away was half a boat – both huge pieces of wreckage that had been blown along and deposited hundreds of metres from the sea by the tempests that visit the islands. But of course the most evident feature, covering every beach, sheltering amongst the dunes and even far inland in the grassy ditches, were the seals.

I'd spoken to Scottish Nature Heritage about this trip and wanted to minimize the impact on the seals. Scientists had visited the island during this season over many years and I took advice from them on certain protocols to follow. We had to try to cross the island inland rather than walking along beaches, which would limit disturbance to the seals. We should also only dive around one specific beach. Up in the north-east was an area the lead scientist, Dr Sean Twiss, had marked as 'male only' on the annotated map he'd sent me. During the six-week period of the grey-seal aggregation, females will come ashore, give birth within a few days and wean their pups for about three weeks. Towards the end of this period, they will come into heat fairly quickly, mate with a male and then head off to sea. Males, however, will remain for the majority of the entire six-week stint, attempting to command an area of beach and a harem of females within their sector, mating with them whenever possible and constantly battling other males for control.

But getting into ding-dongs every other hour with a creature that weighs 350 kilograms and satisfying all of your ladies' desires – ladies who themselves clock in at about 250 kilo-grams – understandably takes a lot out of a chap. So these males take periods of rest on one specific beach where the normal rules of male–male interaction at this time of year, i.e. fighting, are laid to one side and a peaceful truce descends. These battle-weary seals are also joined by adolescent males who are still too young to take part in the sexual melee hap-pening elsewhere along the coast. The reason this beach is the best dive site is twofold. First, we would not be interfering with the natural behaviour of the nursing and breeding seals at this crucial time of year. Second, because of the lack of both offspring and direct competitors, the seals are more relaxed, less skittish and regain more of the curiosity that they are nor-mally known for. They lose some of their wariness and, in this way, we hoped for a close encounter.

It took us more than a few dives to get what we needed. The big waves rolling on to the beach churned up the sandy bottom, flinging granules into the water and reducing the visibility to only a few metres. On the first three dives, we could only spot the seals on the surface, because as we descended and they followed us down they remained just outside the limit of our visibility. These seals seemed wilder and much more cautious of us than I have previously experienced. The seals I've dived with in the past around Devon, Cornwall, Lundy and the Farne Islands have been exposed to people and divers and have become more comfortable in their presence. The grey seals in the Monachs may have seen the odd small fishing boat in their lifetimes but nothing like us, so they were understand-ably wary.

But it was not only the seals who cramped our filming and photo style. On the very first dive, I thought I had flooded my camera. No matter how many times I turned it off and back on again (the solution to all electronic problems), I was at a loss as to why I could see nothing through my viewfinder. Finally, the obvious answer hit me. I spun it around with confidence in my own stupidity. I was rewarded with confirmation of my suspicions as I looked through the fish-eye port at my camera, sealed in its waterproof underwater housing and completely inaccessible, with the lens cap still firmly attached.

We continued to carry out more dives from our boat, which sat just off the beach, but the underwater visibility was not improving and was not likely to in the near future. We still had no underwater footage or photos of the seals except for tantalizing shadows moving around us in the rolling clouds of sandy fog.

Back on dry land, Stu and I headed off around the island to capture footage for our film, leaving Andy and Martin to sneak around the beaches grabbing some amazing still images of the rapid metamorphosis that happens in the young seals. When the pups are born, they are animals adapted for a life on land: white to camouflage them against the ice and snow that was their original home and thick, fluffy coats to keep them warm in the cold air. But this terrestrial life only lasts about three weeks and in that time they change considerably. Females were giving birth every day and so on any one beach we could see the entire three-week process in a single glance as these young pups were weaned alongside their slightly older cousins. The pups grow and increase in weight by up to two kilograms a day, due to the fact that the milk they are fed is 60 per cent fat – more like mayonnaise in consistency than the cows' milk we're used to. Their fat, or blubber, is a much better insulator than a thick coat when out at sea and it also helps to smooth the outline of the animal, making it more streamlined and torpedo shaped. The coat becomes slicker as that blubber takes over as the main means of insulation and changes to a mottled grey colour, darker on top – a perfect camouflage in the dimmer, dappled light of the open ocean. By the time the females abandon their pups to mate once more and head back out to sea, the young are capable of making it on their own.

We managed not only to score some award-winning photos (and when I say 'we' I should, for accuracy's sake, not include myself) but also bucketloads of seal behaviour on film, including some pretty graphic close-up mating footage that Stu captured alone one evening and which will, in some camps, always be described as pinniped pornography.

However, as divers, we knew that for us the main aspiration was getting footage of the underwater action. Andy took us to the male-only beach in the RIB and we sat offshore hoping a little patience might swell the seals' curiosity and diminish their caution. We descended the few metres to the seabed, which stretched out like a desert into the silty gloom, with the odd tiny oasis of seaweed-strewn rocks. We could make out the silhouettes of things moving at the extremity of the underwater sandstorm and decided that, rather than swim around chasing an encounter like some ineffectual predator, we'd sink down and chill out on the bottom, waiting patiently to see if the seals would come to us. We waited, and for about twenty minutes we stared into the bluey-yellow haze. The odd flash teased us as a seal spun into full view then was gone again. Then, from out of the murk, a large male approached. He began swimming around us, closer and closer with each lap, in ever-decreasing circles. As I lay on the seabed, Stu filming on my left and Martin snapping photos on my right, we waited.

Sure enough, the big bull swam towards me and settled down, nose to nose, eye to eye, less than a metre in front of me. He lay there for well over two minutes, checking us out, flicking his huge head back and forth, casually assessing the three of us. We remained still, not wanting any sudden movement to scare him off.

Then, with a final glance left and right and one, held, back at me, he flicked a fore-flipper and elegantly tumbled away with a gymnastic agility and command of his environment that is so lacking on dry land. I try not to anthropomorphize but it was very difficult not to get the impression he was assessing us, checking us out to see if we posed any threat before letting the others approach. This idea was further established when within moments of his departure we had seals spinning and cartwheeling all around us. Juveniles came in closest, mostly approaching from the rear, gently biting and pulling our fins. I got the brunt of this well-intentioned fun as I wore bright-blue fins, unlike the black of Stu's and Martin's. In my experience, seals tend to be attracted to brighter colours. It is not always the case, nor does it guarantee a close encounter, just as a lack of bright colours doesn't prohibit one. But I have found it does help. My friend and freediving partner Dan Bolt, who has won prestigious awards for his many seal photographs, uses his patented 'Seal Attractor', which consists of a ladies' exfoliating glove, neon-pink on the back and bright-yellow on the palm.

We spent an hour or more in the company of the seals before they started to drift back into the beige vapour at the limits of our visibility, becoming nothing more than shadows in the haze again, bored of these unusual, flailing, awkward creatures that had plopped into their world.

That night, as the wind howled, rattling the windows in their frames, and the rain drummed a frantic tempo on the roof, we sat in the bothy, fire roaring out a gratifying glow and suffocating smoke in equal measure, mulling over the successes we'd had so far and our diving plans for the next few days. But it was not to be. Andy had been in communication with the Stornoway Coastguard for our nightly check-in. They informed him the current terrible weather was only the forerunner to a huge storm heading our way and inbound by lunchtime the following day. We could attempt to get off in the morning but after that our window of extraction could be three or four days away. Our trip had to be cut short.

If we'd stayed, I'm sure we would have been fine, if perhaps bored to insanity. But no boat, no helicopter could have reached us in an emergency; no help would have come even if we could have got a radio signal out. The storms can be violent and dangerous. For those three or four days we might as well have been on the moon. Don't think there are not parts of the UK where you can truly be alone, but in these places you have to take your isolation seriously. Do not be fooled into thinking that because you're in the UK someone can come and help you. Self-reliance is key. In this instance, since we'd be incapable of achieving anything even if we stayed, we decided to pack up and make a run for home and safety first thing.

It was a wet, rough and, at times, bone-jarring crossing . . . or three crossings, in fact, since apart from some food and a bag of peat our stores were not diminished. But we made it back to the safety of North Uist just as the main storm front hit. With our little trip complete, we put in a call of thanks to the coastguard, got a hot, and by now much-needed, shower and did the only logical thing – we hit the pub. It was amazing how quickly we had adapted and settled into our routines on 'our' island, how quickly in general one can normalize a situation. We had only spent a week on the Monachs but for the first few days back in civilization the presence of other people, roads, radio and TV all seemed a little intrusive compared to the simpler life on our (mini) expedition.

CHAPTER 11

A Deep-Wreck Mystery

Britain is an island nation cut off from the rest of the world by the Atlantic Ocean and North Sea. We are a nation made up of islands – we've almost one hundred and forty around our shores and, as such, we have relied heavily on boats to travel and communicate, for defence, conquest and trade with the rest of the world and also for use internally. Up until the last few centuries, it was significantly easier to get anywhere by river or sea than by land. We have been using boats here since the first ancient British man scraped out a fallen tree trunk and for this reason, combined with the less than favourable or pre-dictable weather we often suffer around the United Kingdom, hundreds of thousands of vessels have sunk within our waters. Today, there are (according to the Lloyds' Register of Shipping) over 113,000 registered shipwrecks. These are only the ones we've written down and the list doesn't date back that far. The actual figure is likely to be many, many more times higher. And only a fraction of these shipwrecks have been located and only a fraction of those have been dived and explored first hand.

As I explained earlier, the vast majority of easily accessible shipwrecks around Britain's shores are found in areas of high energy, where rough waters, big waves and rocks mean that little of the wrecks are left intact. A shipwreck can, however, be lucky (if we can extend that concept to a ship which has already sunk) and sink in an area where it will be preserved. Sinking into soft sediment like mud or sand can support the structure of a wreck and also protect it from many of the organisms that will consume the organic materials and keep it from the damaging effects of the oxygen in the waters that rust away the metal parts.

The drawback of this is that they are then buried and hard to find, and impossible to dive unless they become uncovered. Once uncovered, you have to find and dive them before the decomposition process starts on the now exposed areas. The exceptions are those in very cold water with little movement and where there are minimal physical or biological attacks. The Baltic Sea, the waters around Scandinavia or the cold water of the Great Lakes in the USA and Canada are all good examples of still, cold waters that have furnished us with centuries-old shipwrecks over 90 per cent intact. But the other place where the waters are cold and relatively still is deep below the surface – the deeper we go, the colder, darker and calmer the sea becomes. So the most intact shipwrecks in UK waters can often be found not near the shore but out to sea and therefore are only accessible by the most experienced divers using mixed gases and technical diving equipment. With the exception of some shallower wrecks found in remote places like the Outer Hebrides, the vast majority of the wrecks that have come to light in the UK recently have been way out to sea in water below 50 metres. And that is where my latest discovery lay.

A DEEP-WRECK MYSTERY

My friend and main dive buddy Rich Stevenson is a handy man to know. Not only is he an underwater cameraman but he's also an exceptional diver. Diving is by far and away what I do best and I don't often come across people who are better at it than me. The best way to learn, to continue to be motivated and inspired to improve, is to surround yourself with people who are better than you or as committed to self-improvement and pushing boundaries. The fact that Rich also has an underwater support company providing everything from cameras and divers to safety supervisors and boats, and, along with other things, has some boats that I can use for free is also quite useful. One of these boats was being used by the Maritime and Coastguard Agency (MCA) in 2013 to survey an area out in the English Channel between Falmouth and Fowey in south Cornwall when their multibeam echosounder showed something of interest. We both wanted to know more.

Multibeam echosounders produce a fan of sound waves beneath a vessel and measure them as they rebound from the sea floor, or any structures beneath the surface, to give a three-dimensional picture of what lies on the bottom. One particular sweep showed an object proud of the sea floor that looked suspiciously like a shipwreck. Rich got the coordinates from the guys on board and gave me a call. The MCA were not interested in diving the wreck, they only needed to know whether there was a potential hazard there and mark it on the chart. With the latitude and longitude coordinates in our hands, the next step was to look at the site and plan how the dive could be done.

There are a number of factors to think about when planning a dive like this. The first one we looked at was depth. The wreck looked to be in about 70 to 80 metres of water. This is relatively deep in diving terms but we'd both been doing a lot of much deeper diving recently so this did not concern us. We would have a decent period on the wreck without racking up too much decompression time if we got our gas mix right.

When you dive, your body is under an increased pressure because of the amount of water above you. This causes greater amounts of the gas we breathe to be forced into our tissues. Some gases, like nitrogen, which makes up most of the air we breathe, can cause us to lose mental faculties at high pressures. It can also come out of our bodies as bubbles in the blood and cause 'the bends', which can kill a diver who ascends too fast – it's like shaking a Coke bottle and then quickly taking the cap off, where the bottle is your body and the Coke is your blood. The other problem is that oxygen, essential for life as it is, becomes toxic at high concentrations and can cause us to fit and pass out. Bad enough if this happens topside but when you're underwater, drowning is a likely outcome.

If we reduce the percentage of these two gases, we need something to fill the space. Ideally, we want to use a gas that, unlike oxygen, isn't poisonous at depth and, unlike nitrogen, doesn't cause drunk-like symptoms. For this we use helium. Adding helium reduces the toxic effects of oxygen and the mentally debilitating effects of nitrogen. But helium also requires a slow ascent to the surface, as it, like nitrogen, can cause the bends unless we make decompression stops at various depths for varying lengths of time on the way to the surface. The length of time spent decompressing on the way up is directly linked to how deep we go and how long we spend there, as these are the factors that dictate how much inert gas, in this case nitrogen and helium, is in our blood. We want to remove the cap from the bottle slowly, letting a little gas escape at a time, so that we don't froth up and lose all the Coke as it spurts out or, to put it more directly, so we don't die.

This dive was going to be 80 metres maximum, so we'd dive it on re-breathers using trimix – a mix of oxygen, helium and nitrogen gases. We decided that a mix of about 12 per cent oxygen, 52 per cent helium and 36 per cent nitrogen would do the trick and give us about forty-five minutes on the bottom to explore the wreck and try to find any identifying features. This bottom time would mean around an hour and a half in decompression, most of that being spent floating at only six metres depth, off-gassing. Decompression is very, very dull. You spend hours of your life hanging at a given depth getting bored and, especially in UK waters, cold. But it is the necessary price you pay for going deep.

We then looked at tides. Diving in the sea is not simply a case of moving up and down in a vertical world. It's not a static environment and the entire world around you, on all sides, in three dimensions, is moving. And the rate, direction and force of the water movement changes with time and often with depth. Off Africa, in 130 metres of water, a friend of mine called Dan Stevenson was filming coelacanths (a type of prehistoric fish that was thought to be extinct until the 1950s). As he descended, the current changed direction by about 180 degrees not once but four times. His team did well to reach the bottom at all, never mind hit the right spot.

In the UK, like most but not all places in the world, we get two tides – two low waters and two high waters – approximately every twenty-four hours. So the tide is either flooding, i.e. coming in to reach high water, or ebbing, i.e. flowing out towards low water. Different places experience different speeds and directions of these flows. The force and speed also changes with the phases of the moon. We get spring tides at new and full moon, when the tides are at their strongest, and neap tides during half-moons, when the tides are most subdued.

The final thing a diver wants to know is when is slack water and how long does it last. Slack water is that period at high or low water when the water has finished coming in or going out and pauses before starting the opposite journey. Throw a ball in the air and that split second of hanging time as it pauses at the top of its upward trajectory before it starts back down is like slack water. Sometimes, in some places, slack water lasts mere seconds, while at other times in other places it can last up to an hour.

Therefore, to create the best conditions for diving we wanted to hit neap tides and slack water. A bit of research suggested when our slack time would be and that it would last at least half an hour. So the plan was to launch the RIB – the best boat for small-team, single-dive operations – from the Cornish harbour of Fowey and motor the 15 nautical miles (17.3 normal miles) out to our mark.

On the day, we were blessed with good weather. I say blessed; in fact, we'd been waiting for weeks for a weather window that overlapped with our tidal window. We loaded the RIB with the kit it takes to get four divers from blue to black and back (blue being the shallow water where there is light and black being the deeper, darker water); we were diving as two buddy pairs, from the surface to the seabed and home again. So we struck out from Fowey and, with a relatively calm sea, covered the distance in less than half an hour. It's significantly easier to find spots at sea accurately and quickly with GPS coordinates and the set we had from the MCA took us straight to the site. However, you cannot afford to be even five metres off when you drop in. Five metres horizontally is a lot underwater and in poor visibility you can miss a large shipwreck. So it's important that you don't waste the dive or even part of it trying to find the bloody thing you've come all this way for.

We swept the area with the echosounder, a two-dimensional simplified version of the multibeam, in order to pinpoint the wreck. Having passed over an obvious regular-shaped protrusion on the seabed, we passed over it twice more to be certain before a fourth pass allowed us to deploy a shot line. This is nothing more than a small grappling hook attached to a long rope with a large buoy on top but it allows us to mark the wreck and divers can descend the line right on to the target. This can take dozens of tries but our team were pretty experienced and there was some quiet smugness spinning around our little vessel when we hooked it first time. You pull hard on the line to make sure it's attached to the wreck and not dragging on the seabed. If the latter occurs, it will simply be moved by the waters as you kit up, and when you descend you'll find yourself an unknown distance from the wreck with no idea where it is . . . which all makes for a very expensive and pointless salt bath. But with the shot line confidently in and secure, we began to kit up.

Each diver, on top of his drysuit and warm, fleecy undersuit, had his re-breather with trimix gas on board. There was a single scuba cylinder slung by his side full of more trimix to bail-out on to should his re-breather fail at depth, then a second individual cylinder with nitrox, a blend of nitrogen and oxygen, like air but enriched with a higher percentage of oxygen. The nitrox was to use in the shallower water in the event of a re-breather malfunction and, although toxic if used at depth, if used shallow it reduces the amount of decompression time the victim of any mishap has to spend in the water. We then carried reels of thin line that could be fixed to the outside of a wreck and reeled out as we swam inside. In the case of visibility reducing to nothing inside the disintegrating metal coffin, we could follow the line out to open water just as one would whilst cave diving.

The reels also doubled as lines for our DSMBs (Delayed Surface Marker Buoys). These are long cylindrical balloons that you inflate and send to the surface to mark your position. They can also let the dive supervisor or boat skipper on the surface know something has happened. We each carried an orange one and a yellow. The orange ones would be deployed when we had left the wreck to let those on the surface know all was well and we were on our way up. As the tide began to pick up, it meant we could drift with it as a group rather than fight the flow for hours trying to hang on to the original shot line connected to the boat. The boat would simply chug alongside at a safe distance, following our markers, until we surfaced. The yellow ones were for use in an emergency. If the guys on the surface spotted one of these, they would immediately grab drop-bottles – extra cylinders of spare gas with a clip attached. These would be clipped on to our DSMB line and dropped down to us. A great many problems underwater can be solved if the diver has enough time, and time underwater often translates as gas. The more of the latter, the more of the former, and the greater chance you have of going home.

We also had torches; it's dark down there. Some of the guys had cameras to film the wreck. Watching the footage back you often pick up on diagnostically important identification features you missed with the mark one eyeball. Finally, amongst an assortment of other tools, we carried knives or some other cutting instrument. These are not just for fighting off krakens, leviathans and giant octopuses (definitely not octopi) in the best traditions of 1950s B-movies or books by Jules Verne. They are in fact a safety device. The problem of fishing lines and nets becoming caught and entangled on ship-wrecks is a common one and a diver trapped in one of these could be facing a serious problem if he, or his buddy, can't extricate him quickly and without damaging his kit.

Once you are loaded with all this kit, especially on a hot day when the sea is a little bumpy, all you want to do is get in. Compared to the sweating restriction of a large rubber dry-suit, 80 kilograms of kit, a mask covering your face and blocking your nose and a heavy re-breather loop clamped between your teeth, the lure of the cool, sweet ocean, where you will become instantly weightless, seems like salvation. We started our drop run, where the skipper will judge the tide and drop the divers in at a set time above the shot-line buoy so that they will drift on to it. But it took two goes, by which time we were all dying to roll off the RIB and submerge.

People often get anxious when they think about throwing themselves backwards off a boat into a black abyss, particu-larly when out of sight of land. It is much the same when discussing parachuting. People always wonder how I, or any skydiver or parachutist, manage to motivate myself to jump out of a perfectly functioning aircraft at a height of anything from 500 to 28,000 feet. It's actually fairly easy. In the mili-tary, we jumped from low levels like 500 up to 800 feet. There would be eighty-eight men, forty-four down either side of a Hercules plane, sat on long benches running its entire length against the wall. You'd be cramped in with a bulky parachute, reserve parachute and a huge and very heavy bergen strapped to your legs with your weapon attached to one side. Sometimes you'd do low-level flying for hours, the planes sweeping in and around valleys and everyone generally getting very hot, sweaty and bothered and the floor of the Hercules becoming increasingly awash with vomit.

When the jump run began and you could finally unfold yourself and feel the air when the doors were opened, it felt great. The tantalizing freshness would waft to the back and then you'd hear: 'Red On . . . Green Go', and you'd shuffle forward, nose pressed into the man in front's chute, until you made it to the door. By that point, a team of wild stallions could not have pulled your arse back into the plane and leaping from it seemed like an absolute gift. Civilian skydiving is a little more civilized but you still pack as many jumpers into the plane as possible, literally sitting in each other's laps. By the time you've reached 15,000 feet, you welcome the chance to swap the cramped, numbing conditions for the freedom and comfort of freefall. The exit is still my favourite part of jumping. The roll back is one of my favourite parts of diving.

In the boat, the skipper cried, 'On my mark . . . Go!'

And we rolled backwards from the RIB, elbows tucked in, holding the cylinders at our sides in place, and a hand over our masks and mouthpieces to prevent them from slipping off. As I came up from the roll, I quickly scanned to locate the marker buoy and steered myself towards it. The water was not completely slack, despite our calculations, but then it's often the way at sea. There are always localized variations and one must accept a certain level of unpredictability when dealing with something as vast and complex as an ocean. Rich and I gathered at the shot line and, with a quick wave to the boat and a nod to each other, we descended.

This was my first chance to look down, to see the rope disappearing into the dark-turquoise gloom that stretched beneath me. I love descending on dives. Not only is it the most comfortable part of the dive – you have a feeling of flying or slow-motion freefall and can spin and play all the way to the bottom – but more than that it is at this point I feel the greatest sense of anticipation, of potential, of excitement as to what may lie beyond the darkness beneath me, beckoning me down.

So down we went, down and down. As I fell past 30 metres, I switched up the oxygen set point of my breathing mix – increasing the relative amount of oxygen being pumped into the system. I looked up and around. I was in green space, only a slight shade lighter above than to the sides and darker still beneath. The modicum of difference in shade was the only clue as to which way was up. As we dropped further into the darkness, we flicked on our torches. Cruising past 60 metres, the end of the line began to become apparent. As my eyes adjusted to this new perspective, the ghostly shadows of a structure began to solidify into something real.

This first tantalizing outline banished our unspoken concerns. Anyone who has spent some time wreck hunting will have had their fair share of disappointments. Even with a multibeam sonar picture you can never be 100 per cent certain that what you have is a wreck. There are plenty of weird geological shapes and boulders cast around the seabed that approximate the shape of a ship. Even old shipping containers, damaged and empty, have proved a disheartening result. As with any trip into the unknown, any attempt at exploration, the potential for disappointment – finding nothing – is all too real and often highly likely. But one must persevere.

We had dropped the shot line on the starboard (right-hand side) bow and as soon as the debris came into focus it was obvious we'd found a shipwreck. The ship sat upright, in the same position as it would have sailed upon the seas. The damage to the starboard bow was severe but as we drifted towards the stern of the vessel she became more and more intact. The underwater visibility was far from spectacular. Particles of brown sediment from the seabed kept the waters dark, suspended like a snowfall of dirty flakes frozen in time, hanging in the air. We were scouring the ship for any recognizable identification marks, notable features or, better yet, a nameplate or ship's bell (which always carries the vessel's name). As we moved aft, we saw that the more upright intact features of the superstructure had caught a variety of nets and fishing lines over the years. Much of the old, thick hemp rope had clearly been down here some time. Avoiding them, we made it to the stern itself, which was completely intact.

As we moved rearward, I heard Rich shouting through his re-breather mouthpiece. I looked around and he was pointing at something inside the rusting hull. I could see the ivory-white half-moon of an enamel plate sticking up out of the mud. This could be a key piece of the puzzle, I thought, and I stretched my arm into the gap, turning my head to the side to try to avoid cutting myself or my hoses on the rusted, sharp edges. I carefully prised the plate from the grip of the thick, gelatinous mud. I shook it as I pulled it clear and the mud dropped away in small clouds of grey-brown, revealing a perfect circle of white. I quickly checked it for markings, hoping the vessel's name would be on it. No luck. But there was a hallmark, a manufacturer's stamp on the back, which might help to date the wreck. I placed it carefully in a mesh bag and clipped it to my belt.

We dropped over the back deck and were met by the most impressive sight so far. The large, curved rudder, shaped like a short-handled, large-bladed hockey stick, sat on its hinges in perfect form. Then, beneath it, tucked into the hull and still preserved beautifully, was a sight synonymous with metal shipwrecks – the propeller. This one had three blades and was the most distinct and clear I had seen on a UK wreck. The ship was covered in marine growth, too. Even at this depth, far below where visible sunlight could penetrate, there was life. The hull was abundantly covered in plumose anemones – reds, oranges and whites – along with a variety of filter-feeding animals making use of the nutrients brought in by tidal currents to this man-made ecosystem.

We swam back up the port side of the ship, aware our bottom time was already approaching twenty minutes and our time to surface was creeping over the hour mark. When you are diving at depth, the amount of decompression you must perform rises. Ten minutes at 38 metres might get you two minutes of decompression, but the same time at 60 metres will not get you four – more like twenty. Time works in the same way. Ten minutes at 100 metres will require a great deal more than double the decompression penalty of five minutes at that depth. And I for one, having accrued days of my life in decompression, don't like to add more time to the process than I have to.

As we swam along the edge of the port side, it became obvious that this side, even towards the bow, was far more intact. Whatever had sunk this ship, it had clearly been a catastrophic impact to the starboard bow.

The overwhelming emotion now was one of excitement – of discovery, of pioneering. The excitement of the potential is a different thing. That's the sensation that builds as you do the research, heightens as the dive day beckons and becomes even more acute as you descend the line. What will you find? Nothing? A Spanish galleon? A secret war wreck? Once we landed on this wreck, we all knew that we had probably found a merchant navy vessel and suspected it to be circa First World War. But that did not diminish the excitement. Here we were, discovering lost history in a place no human had ever been before. When you do find something, there is always a sense of relief, too, since you haven't wasted your and everyone else's time and money. And, frankly, there's surprise that you've actually succeeded in what you set out to do – to explore and discover. Today, a great many people throw around the words 'explore' or 'explorer' with little credibility. But I feel justified using the term as long as I precede it with 'underwater'. I have found lost wrecks, rediscovered lost mine systems, mapped unknown caves and surveyed reefs and tracts of river-, lake- and seabeds all over the world.

We returned to the shot line and the little strobe light we had left tied to it, which was emitting a powerful flash every few seconds to lead us home should we wander off the wreck. It was with mixed emotions that we ensured the grappling hook was clear and slowly began to ascend back to the surface. I dallied an extra few seconds just looking out over the wreck, or at least what I could see of it through the sediment blizzard, not wanting to return to the surface, knowing there was still so much we hadn't touched, recorded or discovered. But there was work to do.

As I've said before, I believe that if one is to truly explore then there should be a greater purpose than simply one's own enjoyment (although often, on expedition, enjoyment doesn't always form part of the equation). In this instance, I needed to research and identify the wreck, report the findings to the MCA and pass on the coordinates and information to the UK Hydrographic Office, who produce the charts where wrecks are marked. After we returned to the surface and stripped off our kit, we talked excitedly about the find. The consensus was that it was probably a First World War merchant ship potentially carrying coal to Falmouth to support the war industries, as we'd seen vast quantities of the stuff cast around the seabed. But more research was required.

The first thing we needed to do was contact the Receiver of Wreck, a government department of the MCA responsible for collating information on wrecks and salvage. If you remove anything man-made from a wreck or the seabed you must report it to the Receiver of Wreck. They then decide who owns the item and whether you can keep it, have to give it to the Crown or return it to its owner, and, if it's the latter, what salvage payment is due to you, if any. It is the same process whether you salvage a small cheap plate or a chest full of jewels, although the latter is more likely to illicit some interest.

Once this was done, we needed to have the plate analysed. The hallmark on the back read 'Bristol, Est 1683 Pountney and Co Ltd, England'. I knew my ship wasn't that old but could the plate prove important to the search for the name of the vessel? After a chat with a pottery expert from the Bristol & Region Archaeological Services, I discovered something surprising. The plate itself was nothing special, a fairly standard hard-wearing item that was common on commercial vessels. However, the hallmark on the back proved more informative. Although the company had been going for over 330 years, this particular style of mark had only been used between 1930 and 1960. A plate produced during that period could still be in use on a vessel after 1960 but it at least gave me a start date. There is no way the wreck could have sunk before 1930, making our earlier hypothesis that it was from the First World War completely wrong. But the dates worked for a Second World War wreck.

Things began to come together. The damage to the starboard bow was extensive and certainly could have been caused by an explosive such as a torpedo or mine. Alternatively, there might have been an accident, maybe a fire in a compartment containing ammunition. Years as a bomb-disposal officer and a demolitions and explosives instructor has left me with the ability to tell the difference between this type of damage and that caused by a vessel hitting a rock or another boat. Besides, we were in 70-odd metres of water in the middle of the Channel. The only rock that could have struck it is one that had fallen from the sky.

We looked at shipping losses in the area and reports from the war of vessels being lost there. We could narrow our search further, as it was obvious from the size and shape that it was not a military ship, neither Allied nor Axis powers. So if we worked on the basis that it was a war loss, we could assume it was a merchant ship. However, whilst working on this assumption we had to keep one eye on the fact that our original thinking, that it had sunk during the war, although likely, could be wrong. It may have been carrying explosives for construction use that accidentally detonated or even have hit a sea-mine left over long after the war ended. I instinctively thought torpedo damage – I was wrong.

There was only one ship reported to have sunk in the area of our wreck: the MV *Shoal Fisher*. The *Fisher* was a merchant vessel on its way to Plymouth with supplies including gun barrels for a Royal Navy Frigate, the HMS_*Jamaica*. She had reported hitting a sea-mine and sinking in 1941 just under two miles from where we found our wreck. The damage to the bow of the ship supported this, since if you're travelling forward it's the front that will strike the mine and take the damage. You may think two miles is a long way off but at sea, navigating by sight and with the equipment of the time, it is not. There was no GPS in those days. And ships seldom sink straight down, they can often knife through water like a paper aeroplane, moving along as they drop, although this type of movement would not account for a discrepancy of almost two miles. The entire crew was rescued and the ship would have drifted with the wind and tide before sinking completely. She had certainly not rolled, nor had she been moved along the seabed by currents and storms, and apart from that damage to the front end, damage we now knew came from a sea-mine, she was in excellent condition.

But in order to confirm our findings another dive was necessary. We needed to revisit the site armed with this new information and conduct a targeted dive to confirm some of the key identifying features. I'd managed to view photos of a replica model owned by James Fisher and Sons. The MV *Shoal Fisher* was their first motor coaster and it explains why a merchant ship, not a fishing vessel, was called *Fisher*. I'd also seen photos of the ship's construction and maiden voyage held by the Barrow-in-Furness Dock Museum, where the ship was built. It gives a much clearer picture of what the ship would have looked like before it sank. This research not only made it easier to identify key features of the ship as it was now, lying in its grave, but also made one appreciate that this was once a fully working machine, operated by men and moving across the seas. It was not always the still, silent wreck on the seabed. Fuelled by the fascination that comes with understanding a thing rather than simply curiously observing it, a second dive would be far more inspiring.

We wanted to look at various elements of the ship's locations:

- derricks: ship's derricks are hollow steel booms that act like horizontal cranes to swing and winch cargo on to the decks to be lowered into the holds or, if the items are too big, lashed to the decks. The *Fisher* had two of these.
- gunwale: the gunwale is the top part of the side of a ship. It's effectively the low wall that stops you falling overboard when standing outside on the deck. If you've ever been on a ferry, gone outside, stood on the edge and gazed out to sea, then the thing you're leaning your forearms on is the gunwale. On the *Fisher*, it had a specific shape. About a quarter of the way along the ship, the gunwale dipped down, almost to the deck floor, then rose again about the halfway mark. This was to allow the on- and offloading of goods and supplies using the derricks.
- propeller and rudder: the rudder and propeller are obvious in the construction photos and model. She had a small three-bladed propeller fixed low between the hull and the rudder. The rudder was also small, its top being in line with the centre of the hull and its bottom in line with the hull's bottom. So it was only half the height of the hull. This was not as I remembered it. I remembered it to be

larger and flaring up higher on the hull. This was cause for concern.

- engines: she was powered by two diesel engines and I could remember seeing one. I didn't remember a second but then I hadn't been looking and had swum up over the one I'd seen and the second would have been off to one side, out of visibility.
- damage: I was convinced the explosive damage to the bow of the ship matched the official report of her cause of sinking but I'd take a second look to double-check my thoughts.
- length: she measured 56 metres in length. The actual point of the bow was recognizable if you made your way along the undamaged port side. If we swam down this side to the preserved rudder at the rear, we could make a fairly accurate assessment of the length. We could have taken a tape measure for centimetre accuracy but it seemed unnecessary and would eat in to bottom time that could be better spent elsewhere.
- gun barrels: she had been carrying gun barrels as deck cargo. These may well have been ripped off during the explosion or sinking but their presence would be a significant find.

This dive would be like the first as far as logistics were concerned but there was one subtle difference. The BBC had also decided that this deep-sea mystery was a great little story and wanted to record it. We had filmed the first dive, too, in order to better record and review what we'd found – all the professional underwater cameramen I know find it impossible to get in the water without a camera, paid job or not. So, compared to the first dive, in terms of extra work in the water it amounted to no more than a few pieces to camera from me. For this task, I was using a new system we had recently had approved for legal use in the UK, which connected a special full-face mask to my re-breather and allowed me to speak underwater to other divers and to the surface, even at great depth. It had had to go through various rigorous and expensive tests in the previous six months to ensure it did not create a dangerous level of carbon dioxide within the breathing loop, nor increase the effort of breathing too much. We'd field-tested it ourselves, but on a paid professional job we needed the final official seal from the Health and Safety Executive.

Despite receiving this approval, the new masks are not without issue. I think they are designed to fit the gentleman with the, shall we say, fuller face. Rich and I are fairly slim of mug and the masks have a tendency to leak a little around the chin. The plan was we'd get to six metres, make sure everything was good and carry on. Both our masks were leaking a little at this point but nothing serious. Because you have an internal bite valve in your mouth, the mask part around your mouth can flood entirely with no ill effect, it just means you can't spit the mouthpiece out to speak without clearing the mask of water first.

Rich was to float above in the shallower water to capture me on camera as I disappeared into the darkness below. We started drifting down together then he slowed and stopped as I carried on my descent. I was eager to get back to the ship but at about 45 metres down I slowed my freefall and waited for Rich to catch up. A few minutes went by and I presumed he was filming; another few minutes and I began to ascend. It's not ideal, ascending only to redescend, but neither is leaving your mate to his fate. I barely got back to 30 metres when I saw the 7,000-lumen floodlights attached to his camera above me and getting brighter. As we met, he signalled that his mask was giving him problems but only in so far as it was leaking into the mouth-pod. So, although all was safe, he might not be able to speak easily. A couple of mutual 'OK' signals later and our downward spiral continued towards the seabed.

It was at this point that I noticed my reel had fallen from my belt. Fortunately, the end was still attached to my belt but, unfortunately, I had 50 metres of thin white line dropping beneath me with a small plastic bobbin on the end. It's worth reiterating that getting tangled in nets, ropes and lines can be fatal for divers. But drowning as a result of being wrapped up in your own bloody reel line is just plain embarrassing. Of course, reeling it in around the spool was not an option, as the reel had unspun and was attached to the end that hung way below me. So, as we drifted down, I furiously wound the line around my hand, ending up with a mangled, tangled ball that, now useless for its purpose, I was forced to stuff into the depth of my thigh pocket. With these minor problems taken care of, and finally down on the seabed, we could get on with the job in hand.

Our shot had landed in almost exactly the same place as before, on the gnarled steel wreckage of the mine damage. A quick scan of this confirmed that what I had pictured in my mind's eye after the last dive was correct. Definitely cata-strophic explosive damage to the starboard bow, exactly where you'd expect it from a sea-mine. As we moved down the ship, I started noting the tubes lying on the deck. I had not taken much notice of them on the first dive and must have dismissed them as general nondescript wreckage, as I didn't recall them.

Armed with the new information, they took on fresh significance. At first, I thought they were all gun barrels but their size was wrong, their walls too thin and aperture too large. Then I realized these were the fallen parts of the original derricks, crumpled and broken across the deck. As I peered inside, a large conger eel popped his head out, its smiling predatory face a good ten centimetres in width and its body about two metres in length. He seemed a little shy but took an interest in the reflective surface of the domed glass in the front of Rich's camera, bumping his nose against it before dismissing us and withdrawing into his recycled house.

Then I spotted a tube amongst the metal rubble that did not look like the others. Its walls were much thicker, the hole in the centre much smaller. This looked like a naval gun barrel. But what clinched its identification was the obvious block towards its rear, which would have acted as a mounting bracket. We had found one of the pieces of cargo destined for HMS *Jamaica* and the maritime front line. It was then I knew we'd found the MV *Shoal Fisher*. But we wanted as much diagnostic ammunition as possible and carried on with the dive. Making our way further astern, we passed the diesel engines, two in number, finally reaching the stern. It was all coming together. But what about the rudder? Upon inspection, the propellers were the right size and shape and, low and behold, so was the rudder. It matched exactly in dimension and structure to the model and photos I'd seen but not to what I remembered from the first dive. Memories and eyewitness accounts are notoriously unreliable. It's why we create film or photographic records of these types of investigative dives. Perhaps I was overwhelmed and overexcited on the first dive and had upscaled part of the wreck when I thought about it afterwards.

Our final sweep was up the port side, inspecting the gunwale. We traced its line forwards, watching it drop away to deck level near the halfway point and return to its original height further on, just as I'd seen in the photos. At the end of the dive, on the way around the bow back to the starboard side and the shot line, we unexpectedly came across the port anchor. It was in perfect condition, still attached by the anchor chain through the hole in the gunwale. I smiled. The creases the action created made channels in my mask seal and caused it to flood slightly. I hadn't thought to check the anchor pattern but the ship, as if overly enthusiastic to show her heritage, was offering me up an extra piece of positive material – it looked identical to the one I'd seen in the photos and model of the *Fisher*.

By the time I reached the shot line, having accrued 51 minutes on the bottom, which presented us with almost two hours of decompression to do, I was more than satisfied that this was the MV *Shoal Fisher*. It may not have been a particularly famous or historically significant shipwreck but it represented an unfinished story and a loss, which was still important. During the Second World War, 30,248 merchant seamen lost their lives. Proportionally, this is a higher death rate than any of the branches of the British Armed Forces. This shipwreck was not full of treasures or great secrets but it represented the filling in of one small blank on the map of history. It erased a question mark and replaced it with the last true resting place of the MV *Shoal Fisher*.

CHAPTER 12

Walking the Longest Line – Part II

On any new project where anything is different, where anything is beyond boundaries either internal or external, there will inevitably be setbacks. Some of these setbacks will be my fault, others are a factor of the time constraints that are imposed upon me, the choices I make, surprise opportunities or the disorganization of others. Some are down to the weather and, although this is an often-used excuse, for this book it was perhaps the biggest problem I faced. During the period over which the majority of the projects were slated to happen, Britain suffered some of the most appalling weather on record, with multiple bouts of large-scale flooding, ferocious storms and record snowfall . . . the latter happening in May 2013. But then you must remain philosophical about such obstacles, especially the weather, if you're going to live and work in the outdoors, and especially if the outdoors in question is the British Isles.

There are always many factors battling against the explorer or adventurer. These difficulties can't come as a surprise; you must accept this before you start, otherwise, when you hit your first hurdle, you will want to fold. If it were easy, if success was guaranteed, then there would be no challenge, no achievement and no point. Something is worth exactly what you spend on it. If you spend nothing, if you sacrifice nothing, it is worth nothing and everyone would have it. Some projects require us to return to them again and again before we find success. Sometimes we must choose to turn back, knowing that we can never return and that, for us, a project will forever remain uncompleted.

This is the case with my planned paddle to St Kilda. It's still on my list and I'm confident that at some point over the next few years a window will open in diaries that coincides with something other than biblical meteorology and we'll tick that little trip off. But what of the Longest Line? The simplest, least-skilled project in the book appeared too difficult. Well, I did say I wasn't finished.

The obvious thing to change from the first attempt was the weather. Unfortunately, my powers don't extend to affecting our climate but by pencilling it in for a pretty empty June diary I stood a good chance of getting decent, dry and warm weather. With this in mind, I could alter my tactics and kit. For a change, I would utilize the weather to my advantage. With less need for multiple warm and waterproof layers, I could afford to strip my kit down. I'd also be able to make best use of the long days and short nights of summer, aiming to complete the trip as close to 21 June as possible (the shortest night of the year). My plan was to revert to the same strategy as I used on the successful Cuillin Ridge traverse – go light, go fast and don't stop.

The very act of planning a non-stop journey would slash the

majority of items and weight from my kit list and, like Perseus, add wings to my feet. It would be a throwback to my time in the Forces when I completed long marches across areas like the Brecon Beacons, off roads and tracks. This time I'd be ten years older and less tabbing fit. But I'd also be carrying a fraction of the weight, so I hoped it would all balance out. This was not super-alpinism and I had no intention of covering the distance at a run. As long as I started and finished in the right spot and didn't stray too far from my line, then it'd be done.

For kit geeks, and I confess to being a card-carrying member of those ranks, I wore a very lightweight pair of waterproof boots, softshell trousers, T-shirt, thin fleece top and carried a lightweight waterproof jacket. On my back, I had the same three-litre water bag with drinking tube I'd used in the Cuillins. This time water would not be in short supply and the plan was to refill it frequently but only to half-full, so that I was carrying no more than one and a half kilograms of water at any one time. Into a small bum-bag, I stuffed my maps in their waterproof case, a hat and buff, a knife, compass, head-torch, three protein bars, six flapjacks and a small camera.

The general plan was similar to the earlier attempt; the Line itself had not changed positions. But this time my brother couldn't get back across from France and no one else seemed up for it, so it'd be a solo trip. I decided to leave my car at the start point in Carrbridge, sleep in it and set out early in the morning. I wanted to be leaving the last road I'd see by 0600. I had decided the trek would take about thirty hours or so. On certain military-selection courses, I was required to move at five kilometres an hour over rough ground and carrying up to 35 kilograms in my bergen. I'd be carrying less for this walk but I'd not be moving at that speed, as the terrain was harder and, frankly, I had no intention of beasting myself until my eyes bled. These military moves were also along known and practised routes across familiar ground, whereas this was through territory that was unknown to me. A map only tells you so much and can only give a clue as to certain very localized aspects, like actual ground conditions or height of vegetation. It's much faster moving across firm ground covered in short heather than rutted, boggy ground or chest-high bracken. These timings meant I should be finished about midday so would only have to endure one night out on the hills. The single night would also help to keep my time down, as navigating and walking at night is often a slower affair. Besides, the view is usually pretty poor at night. An approximate midday finish also meant that, should something go wrong or my progress be much slower than anticipated, I had plenty of daylight in the bag to finish or get myself to safety.

Like any good soldier, I was at my start point by 0555. I decided to hang around, performing little warm-up and joint-mobility movements until 0600. I am more than a little OCD about certain things and time is one of them. So by 0601 I had left the A9 Perth to Inverness dual carriageway behind me and picked my way through a loose collection of trees. The sky was a little overcast but it was warm and dry and the cloud cover was saving me from overheating or any need for breaking out the Factor 50. Within 100 metres, I came to my first obstacle: a stream. In the darkness of the last attempt, we'd used a track to handrail our walking but I had no such excuse this morning so had kept a truer line. The stream was small and I cut left to where the banks were closer. However, on inspection, it also looked deep, which makes sense, as the same amount of water passing through a narrower gap means that it's either going to be deeper or flowing faster. I did a quick footwear change.

In order to keep my boots as dry as possible, I had something I could don for the river crossings, something that would give the soles of my feet a degree of protection from abrasions but be light and compact. Now the obvious choice is sandals but there are a few problems with these. The very lightweight ones tend to be flip-flops you just slip on and are held in place by a V-shaped strap, the point of which is between your big and second toe. But they have a tendency to slip off in water. Those with heel and over-foot straps tend to be more robust and therefore heavy and bulky. What I used weighed less than my gloves and the pair rolled up to the size of my fist: little gymnasts' slippers. Very dainty but they worked. The ultra-thin rubber soles did a fine job of helping me grip the water-worn smooth river rocks and pebbles. Quickly across the other side, I shook my feet off and dried them with my hat before slipping my socks and boots back on. Given the weather, my feet took priority over my head and a slightly damp hat would dry quickly and be less of a burden. I also gave my feet a quick powder, having taken a small amount of talc in a tiny sandwich bag. Always look after your feet. Wet feet can be a disaster. The one thing any soldier who has served in a foot-borne role knows – light infantry, airborne, commando, etc. – is how to look after their feet.

I also know my weak points and had taped up the area around my Achilles with zinc-oxide tape and kept a small roll in my bum-bag in case I felt the initial hot spot of a blister later in the trip. Prevention, in all things, is better than cure, and if a cure is required, get it done as soon as things start going wrong. The less the problem has escalated, the easier it is to recover. I also wore a thin pair of socks under my walking socks, which I find eliminates some of the friction on my skin. Dampness softens the skin of the feet and makes them much more susceptible to blistering. If blisters don't sound too big an injury then you've obviously never suffered from them. I've seen guys with half the skin sloughed off their feet who had to keep on walking. By then, their gait was so badly affected they were also injuring their hips and knees and back.

So with foot admin taken care of, I was off again. After half an hour skirting around thick, closely planted regular lines of a commercial coniferous forest, I'd made my first big river. Today, the River Dulnain was dramatically more benign than in winter and there was barely any white water. I spotted sandbar islands across a wide section and decided that the river was probably relatively shallow at that point. I grabbed a stick, giving it a quick test to make sure it was solid, changed my shoes once more and struck out. Unlike last time, when I'd merely rolled up my trousers, I decided I'd use the pants-only technique to make sure I didn't soak myself. The water was still much colder than I had anticipated and as it rose up my calves I could feel the chill seeping into the muscle. However, once the initial shock had subsided, and after a few breathers on the little sandy mounds, I made the far bank without incident.

The next section was only about a kilometre through grassy scrub and trees and I made decent headway. I was crossing through a bend in the river that my GCSE geography informed me was the beginnings of an oxbow lake. This meant I now had to cross over the same river again. I could see a little wooden-slatted bridge about 100 metres upstream and recognized it as the one we'd used last time. However, this water crossing looked no more hazardous than the stream I'd just crossed, so I decided not to use it. The crossing point I chose turned out to be a little deeper this time and rushing and, perhaps overconfident from the last crossing, I didn't make use of the abundance of fallen branches to fashion myself another walking stick for balance. No major disasters occurred but a slight stumble into some deeper waters did cause me to soak my gusset – and no one wants that. So before I donned my trews, I cast off my pants, wrung them out and fixed them to the water bag on my back to dry. One of the advantages of being somewhere remote is the lack of people and the confidence to show to the sun those parts paler than all the rest. And so, with some casual nudity ticked off, I walked a little further.

The next few hours were fairly uneventful. I was crossing open moorland with the odd tree and the gradient was non-existent initially before rising only to a fairly gradual and uniform slope to a spot height of 512 metres above sea level. I had started at about 280 and had covered almost 11 kilometres in two and a half hours. This speed was much faster than I had anticipated but I knew that it wouldn't last as my energy levels and beginner's enthusiasm wore down and the ground became more severe.

The next couple of hours were fairly enjoyable. The sun was breaking through the occasional split in the clouds and the terrain was on my side. Underfoot was a short, tight weave of strong heather, which hugged the hillside to separate me from the relatively firm ground. I had a gentle, if constant, slope to walk up, passing the rounded top mound of Carn na Guaille and making for a point about half a kilometre north of Carn Coire na h-Easgainn and my highest altitude so far at approximately 770 metres. I had to cross two re-entrants – mountain features created by water – during this stretch of almost eight kilometres but neither was too formidable. As a stream flows down the side of a hill, it cuts into it, creating a V-shaped valley running down the side of the slope. This required me to drop down into the valley and cross over the stream – which, only at the beginning of its journey, was blissfully small and did not even require the services of my acrobat's pumps – and clamber up the steep slope on the other side. At least I thought it was steep at the time . . . but I was to gain a degree of perspective on relative angles as my walk progressed.

The next few hours took me across an undulating plateau with only a couple of quite unpleasant re-entrants but nothing worthy of note compared to what was to come. Large expanses of relatively flat ground may seem like a good thing, and generally they are, but in the humid environment of the Scottish uplands the copious rain tends to lie as groundwater in the form of small pools, larger lochans or simply as general marshy, wet, pitted ground. The last of these was an apt description of the area I was now crossing. And to make matters worse I could see some foreboding and unpromising thick, dark-grey shadows cast across the skies to the north and coming my way. But, for now, at the end of the sodden plateau, I had a more immediate obstacle to overcome.

I stood on the lip of an incredibly steep slope, a valley with near-vertical sides and a river running through the sharp notch at its bottom. On my map, a name was written in black: 'Leac na h-Uaigh'. As best as I can make out, not being a Gaelic speaker, this translates as Slab, Ledge or Rock of the Tomb, or – to put it another way – the Gravestone.

It was not a vertical slab of grey rock prophesying my impending doom like the Ghost of Christmas Future. In fact, it looked technically very easy: it was just two steep slopes. Two very, very steep slopes, covered in slick grass tufts and pock-marked rocky ground. I was going to lose and gain about 300 metres vertically whilst only covering about 800 horizontally. It was not impossible. But it was going to be a real ball-ache. And it had started to rain – a light smur, if you will. Like the old adage about Inuits and snow, in Scotland we have many different words for rain. Smur is lighter than drizzle but heavier than thick, wet mist. I decided it wouldn't make me any wetter than the sweat I'd already generated inside my lightweight waterproof jacket. (You should note that no matter how breathable a waterproof jacket is, if you sweat you'll get wet, especially if the outside is wet, too.) So I scanned for a likely route, let out a resigned sigh through puffed cheeks and muttered something I don't recall but which would have contained a lot of short nouns and followed the usual line of questioning my own levels of intelligence – in short, some well-deserved self-abuse from that little man who lives in our heads and just wants an easy life. Then, with that little tantrum out of the way, I walked a bit further.

By the time I'd crawled to the top of the other ridge line, my thighs were on fire from the inside as the lactic acid pulsed through my muscles. As I caught my breath and the beautiful burn began to subside, I could feel the ache in my old knees and knew that would remain for the rest of the trip, especially on the downhills, regardless of how much rest I took. So I might as well get all this over with and get moving.

It may seem as though I did not appreciate the spectacular nature of my immediate environment or how privileged I was to be in a position of such relative solitude and wilderness in our busy little island. I have the tendency to become quite focused on tasks and projects and will give the time and effort required to complete them. Give it 100 per cent. Partial effort or the production of faltering and poor excuses are for those who choose a different way of life. I am of the steadfast opinion that hard work is the single greatest key to success. And so on this trek I was on a mission, my mentality had slipped back into military mode (most of my friends will passionately tell you I have never slipped out of it) and the walk became a Military Test Exercise. The geography, spectacular though it was – and I did take the occasional moment to revel in it – was mostly observed for its navigational usefulness rather than its aesthetics. The swathes of greens and browns, the shimmering blue-black of water, the purple-hazed grey of the scree slopes and even the bright-white of snow pockets . . . all were breathtaking. The land dipped and swooped, disappearing from sight only to soar upwards beyond the gap. So I did see this. But I have spent more time appreciating the mountain view subsequently, looking back on it, than I did while walking.

At the time, I viewed a different scene. I saw spot heights and ring contours. I related the topography of the ground, its shape and altitude, to what I saw on the map. I had left any forest blocks or pylons behind, anything specific and definite. I read those contour lines, the little brown marks on the map that join points of height like the isobars on a weather map. I saw the landscape as an Ordnance Survey 1:50,000 scale map and could envisage myself as a little red dot on it. I did not have a GPS; I was doing this old school. And although this may create less headspace to wonder at the beauty of the landscape, it also focuses one's mind very keenly on every bend and fold of that landscape. So you could argue that in my clinical navigator's mind, I appreciated my surroundings even more. Happy, therefore, that I knew where I was – if occasionally questioning *why* I was there – I walked a little further.

I crossed another 18 kilometres of undulating landscape. No major ups or downs but once again I was faced with bog-logged stretches of pooling black stagnant water. It was not the nice warm, sunny day I had hoped for but the rain and gentle breeze, although chilly if I stopped moving, kept away the bane of any Scottish mountain day between May and September – the midges.

A significant landmark in my trip began to draw closer as I worked my way south-west – Gairbeinn. This translates into Scots Gaelic as Short Mountain, which is somewhat ironic as it stands 896 metres above sea level and its peak would be my highest point on this little outing. I assume some ancient hill-naming amateur geographer was laughing in his final resting place at the thought of some hapless fool wanting to climb his 'short mountain'.

By the time I'd made the top, visibility was down to less than a few hundred metres. I had planned to take a break there, eat something, take a picture of the Line behind me and of what lay ahead to chart my progress. However, a few snaps and the obligatory selfie would suffice, as I could see little and, at nearly 900 metres up, it was too cold to stand around. This latter point was driven home by the long line of snow clustered all along the ridge I had just ascended. Before I set off, I checked my map and bearing. I could see there was a jumble of escarpments off to the south, on my left, and I didn't want to stumble over them – both in the literal sense, which would result in a serious fall, or figuratively, thereby forcing a back-track. I was in no mood to add extra distance to my journey. Getting colder and knowing I'd be generating less heat on the descent, I donned my jacket and hat.

Another spell of steep down-up-down-up-down, during which I gained and lost over 1,000 metres of altitude in the space of about seven kilometres, saw me reach a psychological marker. It was after eleven o'clock at night and sunset had passed. Or at least I thought it had. I had had visions of a beautiful mountain summer sunset but this far north in June it never gets truly dark and the cloud above me made any sunset indistinct. It was still light enough to navigate without my head-torch, especially as I was aiming for a very obvious feature on the landscape. The forest block was a good couple of square kilometres of thickly packed coniferous trees and fenced all the way around. The leading edge of it was well over a kilometre across and it would have been impossible, even in the failing light, to miss something that big. Not only was it a handy navigational tool but it was also only about 20 kilometres from the finish. This was still a fair old hike but if I had made it this far, having covered 75 per cent of my journey, then I knew I could make it through to the end.

My legs and mind were tired by now. I find the first thing to go is my proprioception – my balance and ability to react to a sudden change in the ground. I stumble more as my tired muscles and brain become slower to react in an instinctive way to the uneven terrain. I'm happy navigating in darkness. One has to be comfortable with this in the Army, since the vast majority of any moves on exercise were done at night. I remember that on my civilian Mountain Leaders Award assessment we did a night navigation exercise for which I volunteered to go first, since no one else seemed up for it. The examiner gave us legs of only 400 or 500 metres, which seemed incredibly simple to me, so I duly sauntered off into the night. I was quickly recalled.

'Andy . . . you do realize you are allowed to use a torch?'

It hadn't occurred to me to turn it on, since the use of a torch during a night move is both untactical and defeats the purpose of moving under the cover of darkness. The reason the rest of the group were so reluctant to get on with some night-nav was because they'd only been out navigating in darkness a few times in order to prepare for this assessment. Which made sense once I thought about it. Normally, people go into the hills to enjoy themselves, have a day out, see the scenery. It's rare for hillwalkers to navigate in the dark unless something has gone wrong, so it was not something they were familiar with.

I hit the north end of the forest block and took a moment to rest on a fence post. The block itself was not as thickly packed as the map suggested, but it was there. When navigating, you have to bear in mind that often the features like tracks, forest blocks and even buildings may no longer be there. Streams dry up to become ditches and the landscape can change. That's why contour lines, those clues to the shape of the mountains, are so important. Mountains do change shape but since it takes hundreds of thousands of years we can probably get away with considering them static.

I skirted around the north side of the treeline, going off the Line by 100 metres or so in order to not have to clamber into a fenced-off area and also because the ground was a horrible mess of stumps and humps. Although I had managed to keep the water out of my boots, my feet were still damp. The sweat that inevitably builds up will always struggle to escape even from lightweight, breathable boots if the outside of the boot is soaking wet. There is no moisture gradient to draw the water to the outside. So, although I had avoided any blisters, my feet were feeling delicate and the soles, untrained of late for such long distances, were feeling a little hot, battered and bruised. But I kept moving. I climbed again and dropped down into the flattest section I'd seen since I left the A9. It was a small river valley where two waterways met at a Y junction, with an extended floodplain on either bank growing outwards in all directions. It was a good kilometre and a half across. 'Good' in that it was at least that distance. And 'good' in that it was flat ground. But there was one problem.

The Line followed the centre of the river for about 300 metres as the course twisted its way around the mountains. I'd been off the Line before, of course, and I'd only have to go off this time by 20 metres or so to avoid the floodplain but I'd spotted it during the initial planning phase and had already decided I would cross it rather than avoid it as long as the river wasn't flowing too fast. However, I was way ahead of schedule. I had thought I'd reach this point around dawn as opposed to a little after midnight. So with head-torch on, shoes changed and no stick in hand, because I couldn't find one and hadn't thought to pick one up from the forest, I stepped into the black water.

The river turned out to be shallower than I had expected. The cold water, which always seems to feel colder at night, was both a shock and a welcome relief to my poor hot and bothered feet. The river curved slightly around to my left, so I decided to cross it and handrail the left-hand bank, the inside of the curve, as this is where the water would flow slowest and was likely to be the shallowest. I crossed over without incident, although the medium-sized rounded rocks were unstable at times. I continued to make frustratingly slow progress until I passed a narrow forest block on my left, a marker to let me know I had only about 100 metres to go. I then crossed over back to the north bank to put an end to the foolishness.

The old mountaineering adage that 80 per cent of accidents happen on the way down is true. People are tired but, more than that, they slip up psychologically. They make the mistake of thinking they have summited the top and therefore the job is done, mission complete. Mentally, they switch off. I may well have been suffering from this. That and very cold feet. In my haste to get out of the water, I was less careful with my foot placement than I should have been. I fell.

I threw my right hand out to break my fall and twisted to the right, arching my back and trying to keep as much of myself out of the water as possible. I did not make that great a job of it and my right side was completely submerged. To make matters worse, it was in my right hand that I was holding my camera, as I had been trying to take another self-portrait of my eccentric night-time river walk, thinking how handy photos like these are for giving talks. Well, not so much now.

When I reached the bank, my camera no longer worked. I didn't waste any time trying to magic it back into operational order. There was no point. It was wet and had water running out of its battery- and memory-card compartments. The only thing worth doing was to dry my feet (difficult, as my hat was also soaking), change my shoes and crack on. Miraculously my boots, apart from a bit of a splash to the top of the right one, had come off relatively unscathed, hung as they were around my neck. My socks, packed into the toes of my boots, got off scot-free. And so, wet to my pants and now without a pictorial record, I walked a little further.

The climb to the next peak was at a shallow angle up and along the side of the slope, so, although I came up from about 200 metres to about 750 metres, I did so over five and a half kilometres. The slope was on my right, which meant leaning in and mainly climbing with my right leg, for almost two hours. After I slowly scrambled my way through the buttress of Coire nan Eun, I crested the rise and felt exhausted. My knees ached. My thighs had been through the wringer and my ankles and feet felt pummelled. I was pretty much done with this and only wished, not for the first time, that this was the finish. But in these situations, self-motivation is actually much easier than you'd think, given that your only other choice is to sit down where you are and slowly fade away. And so, working on the basis that suicide by inaction would be a long, painful and embarrassing path to choose, I walked a little further.

I was now on what I told myself was the home straight. I had about eight or nine kilometres to go and knew, apart from negotiating a couple of cheeky re-entrants and some forest, the density of which I was unsure, I had pulled it off. I complained to myself, as I had all the way around. I got annoyed. With myself, with the weather, with my kit, with the heather, the rocks, the mountains. But I have learned how to internalize a lot of emotions, and how to make use of emotions normally thought of as negative. Anger (wrath) and pride are counted as two of the seven deadly sins but used correctly they can fuel you on to greater things. I may have been doing this for years prior to becoming a soldier but I first became aware of it as a personality trait in the Forces. It's the ability to continue on when your body is broken, sleep-deprived, freezing or starving.

It's the ability to choose not to stop when others give up. The drive for this can often be an emotional power source, an anger not lashed outwards but pressed and concentrated internally, acting as fuel for the fire. It's a sense of pride, not only in one's self but in what one is trying to achieve, and it extends to involve the people you represent: your family, your mates, the man standing beside you in the firing line, your unit. You don't want to let them down or fall short in their eyes. Pride and a feeling of duty can be an inspiration to drive you on further.

I finally approached the last few kilometres. I could see a road winding its way beneath me to disappear under the green horizon of a ridge to the spot where I'd meet it. As I descended in height, my world became greener. Scattered ferns, silver birch and scrub began to spring up around me. A lapwing, its flight and wing pattern distinctive, flew away in front of me. But even now the Line had a sting in its tail. The final kilometre was down a very steep slope. I had not really noted it in my planning. By this stage, less than 1,000 metres from the end, I had figured the terrain wouldn't matter. I'd done it. But it mattered a great deal now I was standing on it. Worse, the lower reaches were thickly covered with chest-high bracken. The ground underfoot was firm, if steep, and I was forced to fight my way down through the dense vegetation.

When I broke out, the first thing I spotted was a car driving past less than 100 metres in front. I walked the last steps through a long-grassed, boggy, flat field, now careless of keeping my feet dry. Like an old man broken by the years, I delicately climbed over the fence. Head rolling on tired shoulders, I stepped on to the A82, the first road I'd seen in almost 80 kilometres.

There is a phone box within a few steps of the finish line. My plan is to use this to call the taxi company who, for £80, have agreed to take me to my car in Carrbridge. I assume my mobile has no signal. I walk towards the phone box and think. Not just about this project but about all the things I've done in this new life I have carved out for myself. It has been a twisted, shaky and sometimes questionable path since leaving the Army. I think about the choices, good and bad, that I have made and the hard times that have come from both. I realize that I am a soldier. I will always be a soldier and the weapons the Army equipped me with I still carry today. If I am successful in these projects I have chosen to take on – from the small and tactical expeditions like the Longest Line, to the long-term strategic goal of becoming a professional explorer and adventurer and building a life for my family – it is only because of the man I became, the people I met and the experience and training I received in my ten years in the Forces.

It occurs to me that another two kilometres south along this road is the Commando Memorial. It is a statue of three Second World War Commandos, standing side by side, and it commemorates those Army Commandos and Royal Marines who have fallen in service. It seems a more fitting end to the project than this simple piece of tarmac I'm standing on. I turn south and I walk a little further.

Picture Acknowledgements

All images courtesy of the author unless otherwise stated.

Section one

Page 1: Exmoor courtesy Dave Talbot; the Needles courtesy Paul Thompson.

Page 2: The Needles courtesy Dave Talbot.

Page 3: courtesy Lynwen Brown.

Pages 4–5: Kit shots courtesy Stu Keasley.

Page 7: The Linn of Dee and High Force Waterfall courtesy Ian Tannock; HMS *Scylla* courtesy Dan Bolt.

Section two

Page 1: courtesy Gill McDonald.

Pages 2–3: courtesy Rob McIntyre.

Pages 4–5: pre-dive shot courtesy Johnny Rogers; cave diving and screenshot courtesy Rich Stevenson.

Page 6: filming shot courtesy Martin McGrath.

Page 7: courtesy Rich Stevenson.

Page 8: courtesy Martin Hartley.

Index

INDEX

INDEX